Celebrating the Other

A Dialogic Account of Human Nature

Celebrating the Other

A Dialogic Account of Human Nature

———

Edward E. Sampson

Taos Institute Publications

CHAGRIN FALLS • OHIO

CELEBRATING THE OTHER:
A Dialogic Account of Human Nature

First published in 1993 by
Harvester Wheatsheaf
Hertfordshire
Great Britain

Library of Congress Catalog Card Number: 2008935883

Taos Institute Publications
A Division of the Taos Institute
Chagrin Falls, Ohio
USA

ISBN-10: 0-9819076-0-1
ISBN-13: 978-0-9819076-0-4

Printed in the USA and in the UK

Taos Institute Publications

The Taos Institute is a nonprofit organization dedicated to the development of social constructionist theory and practices for the purpose of world benefit. Constructionist theory and practice locates the source of meaning, value and action in communicative relations among people. Chief importance is placed on relational process and its outcomes for the welfare of all. Taos Institute Publications offers contributions to cutting-edge theory and practice in social construction. These books are designed for scholars, practitioners, students and the openly curious. The Taos Institute's newest series is the **Taos Tempo Series: Collaborative Practices for Changing Times**. The **Focus Book Series** provides brief introductions and overviews that illuminate theories, concepts and useful practices. The **Books for Professionals Series** provides in-depth works, focusing on recent developments in theory and practice. Books in all three series are particularly relevant to social scientists and to practitioners concerned with individual, family, organizational, community and societal change.

Kenneth J. Gergen
President, Board of Directors
The Taos Institute

For information about the Taos Institute and social constructionism
visit: www.taosinstitute.net

Taos Institute Publications

Taos Tempo Series:
Collaborative Practices for Changing Times

Mapping Dialogue: Essential Tools for Social Change, (2008) by Marianne 'Mille" Bojer, Heiko Roehl, Mariane Knuth-Hollesen, Colleen Magner

Positive Family Dynamics: Appreciative Inquiry Questions to Bring Out the Best in Families, (2008) by Dawn Cooperrider Dole, Jen Hetzel Silbert, Ada Jo Mann, Diana Whitney

Focus Book Series

The Appreciative Organization, Revised Edition (2008) by Harlene Anderson, David Cooperrider, Ken Gergen, Mary Gergen, Sheila McNamee, Jane Watkins and Diana Whitney

Appreciative Inquiry: A Positive Approach to Building Cooperative Capacity, (2005) By Frank Barrett and Ronald Fry

Dynamic Relationships: Unleashing the Power of Appreciative Inquiry in Daily Living, (2005) by Jacqueline Stavros and Cheri B. Torres

Appreciative Sharing of Knowledge: Leveraging Knowledge Management for Strategic Change, (2004) by Tojo Thatchekery

Social Construction: Entering the Dialogue, (2004) by Kenneth J. Gergen and Mary Gergen

Appreciative Leaders: In the Eye of the Beholder, (2001) Edited by Marge Schiller, Bea Mah Holland, and Deanna Riley

Experience AI: A Practitioner's Guide to Integrating Appreciative Inquiry and Experiential Learning, (2001) by Miriam Ricketts and Jim Willis

Books for Professionals Series

Celebrating the Other: A Dialogic Account of Human Nature, (reprint 2008) by Edward Sampson

Conversational Realities Revisited: Life, Language, Body and World , (2008) by John Shotter

Horizons in Buddhist Psychology: Practice, Research and Theory, (2006) edited by Maurits Kwee, Kenneth J. Gergen and Fusako Koshikawa

Therapeutic Realities: Collaboration, Oppression and Relational Flow, (2005) by Kenneth J. Gergen

SocioDynamic Counselling: A Practical Guide to Meaning Making, (2004) by R. Vance Peavy

Experiential Exercises in Social Construction – A Fieldbook for Creating Change, (2004) by Robert Cottor, Alan Asher, Judith Levin, Cindy Weiser

Dialogues about a New Psychology, (2004) by Jan Smedslund

For on-line ordering of books from Taos Institute Publications visit:
www.taosinstitutepublications.net

For further information call: 1-888-999-TAOS, 1-440-338-6733
Email: info@taosoinstitute.net

To Marya
my love and my guide.

Contents

Preface

The title, *Celebrating the Other*, is based on Clark and Holquist's (1984) reference to Mikhail Bakhtin's dialogic theory as a celebration of alterity. Like Bakhtin's work, mine is designed to provide a long overdue celebration of the other. For too long our major cultural and scientific views have been monologic and self-celebratory – focusing more on the leading protagonist and the supporting cast that *he* has assembled for his performances than on others as viable people in their own right. Time now to celebrate the other – not only to set the record of our understanding straight but, of equal importance, to give voice, and in their own register and form, to those who have been condemned to silence.

In order to accomplish this purpose, I have organized this book into four major parts.

Part I, the Prologue, consists of the first two chapters. The purpose of this Prologue is to set the stage and provide the context for what follows in the remainder of the book. Chapter 1 locates the issues we will consider in the context of power and domination – a context which, I believe, is essential to any understanding of both why the monologic world-view has dominated and prospered for so long, and why dialogism is now emerging on the world's stage. Chapter 2 is another aspect of stage-setting, and is designed to introduce certain conceptual dilemmas that haunt both monologic and dialogic formulations.

Part II, "Monologism: Celebrating the Self", consists of four chapters all of which examine my contention that self-celebratory monologues dominate the entire Western project and appear throughout both popular and scientific culture. It is my intention to demonstrate the depth to which this self-celebratory stance has run by revealing how both our common-sense understandings of self and other and our psychological approaches reflect a monologic world-view. Given my argument that this world-view is part and parcel of the domination by one group over others, this first section should not be read merely as a bland description of Western culture and psychological science, but rather as a narrative about power, control and exploitation – albeit disguised, but reasonably clear to see once you know where to look and how to understand.

Part III, "Dialogism: Celebrating the Other", consists of four chapters that introduce the dialogic alternative, developing both its rationale and its implications for a transformed appreciation of human experience and human diversity. I build my analysis around several postmodern critiques of the monologic view as well as the dialogic frameworks and discourse analyses developed by Bakhtin, Mead and several British, continental and American theorists. Most of these critics, however, have ignored issues of gender and race as well as the dimension of power and domination that are so central to my own understanding. This "oversight", too, must be addressed. And so I devote some time to unfolding the themes of domination first introduced in the Prologue, using feminist analyses as a central paradigmatic case.

Part IV, "Implications", briefly examines several implications of the dialogic alternative for issues of ethics on the one hand, and for reframing and democratizing our understanding of human nature, on the other. I first argue that our views concerning human freedom, responsibility and justice will necessarily change once we abandon the monologic perspective under whose auspices our current understandings of these concepts appear. I conclude by examining the issue of democratization as applied to human nature – an application which, I believe, emerges from a dialogic view in which the experts' dominating theses are replaced by a more dialogically achieved understanding.

When all has been said and done, I realize that our current Western civilization cannot readily accommodate itself to the truth of dialogism. Were a genuinely dialogic view, and lives built upon it, in force, business as usual could not be carried on.

There are many times in my life when I have secretly wished that I could have written a book that is more congruent with our world as it exists. How much more comforting this would have been. Yet something never has permitted me to write from privilege about privilege. And so I salute that something and write as I must do, against the grain.

PART I
Prologue

1

The Context of Power

S carcely a day passes without reminders that the end of the Cold War has not brought about the end of humanity's endless dance of death and destruction. The dominant groups in nation after nation continue to use physical force and military might to accomplish their particular ends. No part of the world is now or, it seems, has ever been free of this charge. And the claims of advanced civilization and the rule of reason count for little when it comes to employing force to dominate.[1]

However, there is a somewhat more silent "killer" on the loose in the world, one whose form of destruction leaves its own special mark on its living victims, the kind of "mind-forg'd manacles" of which Blake (1946/1968) has written. This too is an ancient "killer", with roots – in the West at least – extending back to well before the Judeo-Christian era. This "killer", too, tries to achieve its ends through domination. But rather than using brute physical force, this domination is accomplished through construction. Construction through word – through the very frameworks by which self and other are experienced, subjectivity and self-understandings made known. Construction through deed – through the life opportunities made available to self and to other.[2]

We need not bother to pull out our scales in order to determine which "killer" – force or construction – is more destructive. Each one readily slides over into the other and back again. The boundaries that separate them are highly permeable and require no special visa to cross freely. How much easier to employ force against an other who has already been constructed as worthy of receiving our contempt or as masochistically enjoying our advances. How much easier to deny subjectivity to those who have survived our abuse.

Self-celebratory Monologues

The techniques devised to dominate through force are undeniably tragic. My concerns in this book, however, lie elsewhere, with those forms of domination that center primarily around the construction of the other: forms that deny life by controlling its definition and its reality. The effect of these constructions, if not their conscious design, has been to rob the other of any genuine standing in the world, thereby permitting the dominant groups to operate more freely to achieve validation for themselves and ensure the maintenance of their privilege.

Although it somewhat oversimplifies the complexities involved and makes it seem more conspiratorial than it usually is, it is nevertheless useful to suggest that every construction has a dominant group – the constructors – and its others, those who are constructed. Throughout most of recorded Western history, whether we look at religion, philosophy, cultural activities, economics, or science, including the physical as well as the human sciences, the primary constructors have been male, white, educated, and of the dominating social classes, while the objects of their construction have been defined as all that the dominant group is not.[3]

And so the other has included women, nonWestern peoples, people of color, people of subordinated social classes, people with different sexual desires. The dominant groups have given priority to their own experiences and their places in the world and have constructed *serviceable* others: that is, others constructed so as to be of service to the dominant groups' own needs, values, interests and points of view.[4] Indeed, although its specific forms may have changed throughout Western history, the Western project has had an unnerving continuity: dominant groups constructing *serviceable* others.

It is the construction of a serviceable other, one constructed on behalf of the particular needs, interests and desires of the dominating group, that leads me to describe the Western project as self-celebratory and monologic, two terms I will use interchangeably.

When I construct a you designed to meet my needs and desires, a you that is serviceable for me, I am clearly engaging in a monologue as distinct from a dialogue. Although you and I may converse and interact together, in most respects the you with whom I am interacting has been constructed with me in mind. Your sole function has been to serve and service me.

All such monologues are self-celebratory. They are one-way streets that return to their point of origin. They lead from the self back again to the same self, having passed briefly through the mirror that has been constructed to ensure that what Cixous (see Cixous and Clément, 1975/1986) calls "the Empire of the Selfsame" will be enshrined.

In Hegelian fashion, enshrining the selfsame means the obliteration of the other: "The other is there only to be reappropriated, recaptured, and destroyed as other" (Cixous and Clément, p. 71). To know the other on its terms is too menacing. Discard after use:

> society trots along before my eyes reproducing to perfection the mechanisms of the death struggle: the reduction of a "person" to a "nobody" to the position of "other" – the inexorable plot of racism. There has to be some "other" – no master without a slave, no economico-political power without exploitation, no dominant class without cattle under the yoke, no "Frenchmen" without wogs, no Nazis without Jews, no property without exclusion. . . . If there were no other, one would invent it. (Cixous and Clément, 1975/1986, p. 71)

Other theorists have proposed much the same kind of analysis of the Western project.[5] Dichotomies are created out of otherwise continuous fields, defining the master term (e.g. self, male, reason) "as possessing x, y, z properties whereas its 'opposite' is negatively defined. Not-A becomes defined by the fact that it *lacks* the properties x, y, z, rather than being defined in its own right" (Gatens, 1991, p. 93).

And so, if the self is to be rational, it is defined as such by virtue of considering all that is not-self (not-me) as lacking rational qualities. The female becomes the not-male; the "primitive" native, the non-European. Through this process, the other is made serviceable to the self, a creature constituted by the dominant self to represent what it is not, to be used and then discarded until it is needed once again.

It is now time to illustrate my meaning by calling upon two paradigmatic examples: the first involving woman as other, the second people of color – in this case, African-Americans – as other. These are not the only groups who have become the others for the dominant white male constructors of the Western world. Those with different cultural and social class background and experience, those with different sexual orientations, all that is not human, including animals as well as nature itself, and all those aspects of the self that have been associated with any of these, have also been constructed to be serviceable to the dominating groups.

Woman as Other

Many feminist theorists have insisted not only that woman has been constructed as man's other, but in addition that this is the master construction on the basis of which all other self–other formulations have been built.[6] It is not germane to my own concerns either to argue along with them in this regard or to claim that other distinctions have been even more basic to the Western project. I find myself convinced that whether it is the primary foundation or not, man's construction of woman reveals full-blown the processes that appear in all other spheres of the Western world.

I will illustrate three related aspects of this construction so that we may better see the processes by which woman as other has been constructed so that she is serviceable to man: woman as the absent presence; the male gaze and standpoint as the implicit standard and universal point of view; the unheard voice of woman's own specificity. These aspects also illustrate the manner by which other others have been similarly constructed by dominant Western groups.

The Absent Presence

Margaret Miles opens her book *Carnal Knowing* by presenting two classic epics: one involving the story of King Gilgamesh, an early text of heroic struggle written about 2800 BCE; the other involving the *Odyssey*. The precise details of each epic need not concern us. What is of central importance, however, is the depiction of women in both. Miles notes that women play several key parts in the Gilgamesh story: as unnamed and anonymous brides raped by Gilgamesh; as prostitutes who tame another male, Enkidu, who will eventually become a person of deep concern to the King; as a named human woman, Siduri, an advisor who tries to help Gilgamesh deal with his grief over the loss of Enkidu.

Miles observes that while we know a great deal about Gilgamesh and even about Enkidu, we know virtually nothing about the women except in their role as props servicing the needs and desires of the men. As Miles comments, "Where is the epic of Siduri? Why was her wisdom presented only as a foil for Gilgamesh's aspirations? What physical experiences, what struggles, shaped *her* self-understanding and the philosophy of life she articulated so poignantly?" (Miles, 1989, p. 4). In other words, from the earliest recorded times, woman is present as an element in men's lives who must simultaneously remain absent as a full figure with her own being, experience and subjectivity.

Little changes when we consider the *Odyssey*, where we meet the man, Odysseus, and the woman, Calypso. Again, although Calypso is present, her subjectivity is not. We learn of her love for Odysseus and of her grieving over his departure, but these are quickly glossed over as we turn instead to Odysseus's story. Miles asks: "Where can we read the epic of Calypso?" (p. 4). It would seem that Calypso's only purpose is to be of service to Odysseus, who "has constructed her as an enemy in order to rationalize hurting her ... her literary role ... [is] nothing more than a moment in his journey" (p. 4).

The depiction of woman in the Judeo-Christian Bible offers a further early illustration of woman's absent presence in the hands of men. Several accounts (e.g. Coote and Coote, 1990; Fiorenza, 1989; Pagels, 1981) reveal the power struggles between different early cults, each of which sought to ensure its supreme standing in society by having its version of the early biblical stories and early Church practices dominate. In account after account, women and all those qualities associated with their femininity were viewed as threats to the emerging male-dominated religious hierarchy. And so women were present but simultaneously absent: silent, background figures required to be of service to the men, but never having their own subjectivities or specificity represented.

Commenting on more recent times, Teresa de Lauretis (1987) makes much this same point in describing the play *Despite Gramsci*, performed in a small town near Bologna, Italy, in the summer of 1975 "in the town square and courtyards of two medieval castles" (p. 84) . . . by a militant feminist collective" (p. 85). De Lauretis's point – and the point of the play – is to remind us that although we have a literature detailing the life, imprisonment and death of the political revolutionary Gramsci, while we know of his major published work and his letters from prison, the letters written by the two women in his life, Giulia, his wife, and Tatiana, Giulia's sister, are not considered important historical documents:

> They were women's letters, dealing "only with children and marmalade," banal, insignificant. Little information could be found about these mute women, whose complex relationships to Gramsci and to one another constituted the most intense private aspect of Gramsci's life as a revolutionary. (p. 86)

The play *Despite Gramsci* was an attempt to rewrite history, "inscribing in it the missing voices of women, and therefore to examine the relationships between the private and the public, love and revolution, personal/sexual/emotional needs and political militancy" (pp. 86–7).

Miles, de Lauretis, Fiorenza and Pagels call our attention to a point stated eloquently by Virgina Woolf in her pioneering work *A Room of One's Own*. Woolf aptly describes the *absent presence* of woman: serving a vital role, and thus present; yet never developed in her own right, and so simultaneously absent:

> A very queer, composite being thus emerges. Imaginatively she is of the highest importance; practically she is completely insignificant. She pervades poetry from cover to cover; she is all but absent from history. She dominates the lives of kings and conquerors in fiction; in fact she was the slave of any boy whose parents forced a ring upon her finger. Some of the most inspired words, some of the most profound thoughts in literature fall from her lips; in

real life she could hardly read, could scarcely spell, and was the property of her husband. (pp. 43–4)

The Universalizing Male Gaze

Although the term *male gaze* is not original to the work of Morawski and Steele (1991), the concept captures the sense of their argument and directs us to a second aspect of woman constructed as man's other. Morawski and Steele conduct a textual analysis of Freud's paper "Medusa's head", in which Freud analyzes the frightening quality of the severed head. The gaze that Freud adopts – and calls upon us, his readers, to adopt as well – is one that is rendered horrific by the decapitated figure. The horror itself, he tells us, is based on an underlying link between decapitation and castration, and reflects the great fear the little boy experiences on first viewing the female genitals.

"His interpretation requires that we see the event through his male eyes and identify not with the beheaded female in the scene but with the male" (p. 110). In short:

> With centuries of convention to aid him, the author so controls the field of vision that he passes off a typical artistic and cinematic illusion as reality; that is, we do not see that our entire view of the phenomena is through an idiosyncratic perspective – the male gaze. (p. 111)

Although the gaze is specifically male, it is presented as a universal, objective vision, thereby not only silencing and dominating other possibilities but doing so in a manner that we have all, both male and female, assumed to be "the way things really are".

Morawski and Steele's point, echoed by many others – e.g. de Lauretis's (1987) analysis of the male gaze in film; Miles's (1989) analysis of the male gaze in the painting of nudes; MacKinnon's (1989) examination of the male standpoint in law and in the liberal state – is that we have learned to adopt one particular standpoint or gaze in looking upon the world, and to treat this standpoint as though it represented the way things actually are. In this often subtle manner, other ways of experiencing are silenced. The male gaze is presented as though it were neutral and universal, a standard by which all seeing, knowing and experiencing are in fact constituted. The process has become so ingrained in most of us that we are no longer even aware of the particularity of the standpoint we are employing. It is not even experienced as a standpoint at all; it appears to us, men and women alike, as though it were what Putnam (1990) has so aptly described as a God's-eye view from Nowhere and MacKinnon describes as a point-of-viewlessness (p. 117).

Several feminist critics of science have proposed much this same argument, commenting, for example, on the degree to which both the selection of problems and the conception of methodological objectivity reflect the male gaze passing itself off as the universal human gaze (e.g. Code, 1991; Harding, 1986). Code, for example, in addressing herself to the epistemological model underlying most scientific understanding, asks whether or not characteristics of the knower are considered by that model to be relevant to the knowledge claims that are made. She observes that we believe that when proper procedures are employed, the knowledge we discover will be independent of the person making the knowledge claim: Ideally, such knowledge (that is, good knowledge as opposed to tainted knowledge) is abstract and disembodied, a story about the thing-known rather than the knower's own specificity.

In proposing that the sex of S, the knower (in addition to other factors) matters, Code suggests that the very idea of a disembodied form of knowing has been historically associated with the world of the male and things masculine:

> it has long been tacitly assumed that S . . . is male . . . an adult (but not *old*), white, reasonably affluent (latterly middle-class) educated man of status, property, and publicly acceptable accomplishments. In theory of knowledge he has been allowed to stand for all men. (p. 8)

And thus, rather than being a view that is "universal, neutral, and impartial . . . [this view is] deeply invested in furthering the self-interest of a small segment of the human population" (p. 19).

As an alternative standpoint, Code recommends viewing knowledge as both embodied – recognizing, therefore, that a person's sex is important – and built upon an interpersonal rather than an isolated and abstract point of view. She persuasively argues that rather than adopting physics as the model for all knowledge, we would do better – physics professors included here – to base our conception of knowledge on the processes involved in our coming to know another person – as a friend, for example. These conditions, she maintains, better reflect the social – or, as I argue, the dialogic – basis for all knowledge processes. Code's suggestion in this regard receives support from several other theorists (see Harding, 1986). I expand on some of Code's ideas in Chapter 7.

Harding also adds her own critical commentary to this emerging picture. She suggests that this masculinist gaze in science has governed the definition of problem areas to be investigated as well as the methodologies appropriate for conducting these investigations. In both cases, women's lives and experiences are rendered invisible. Jane Flax (1990) offers a helpful understanding of how this one gaze has come to dominate:

"Perhaps only to the extent that one person or group can dominate the whole can reality appear to be governed by one set of rules, be constituted by one privileged set of social relations or be told by one story" (p. 28). In other words, the dominating male gaze may not only reflect the standpoint of one group, but is itself based on the kind of arrogance that comes from that group's historically extraordinary domination.

A Voice Not of One's Own

A third aspect of this dominant male construction of woman as his serviceable other involves the requirement that the silenced can be heard, but only in so far as they use the approved forms of the dominant groups. In reviewing the various forms that feminist arguments have taken, both Braidotti (1991) and Gatens (1991) distinguish between the reformers, who seek equality for women in a man's world, and the radical theorists of difference, for whom a separate voice reflecting female specificity is called for.

Whereas the former agree that they live in a man's world and hope to achieve equal standing by functioning on its terms, the latter argue that women becoming men in order to be heard loses the very specificity that has become woman's. The latter fear that the female difference will be erased if women agree to accept the masculinist terms of their being:

> If the conditions of patriarchical society is the repression of the feminine, then that which writes/speaks of the feminine ... amounts to the return of the repressed. Writing of a full feminine form and of feminine desire involves the return to patriarchical consciousness of that which it has repressed. (Gatens, p. 113)

These complex issues have divided various feminists. Luce Irigaray is perhaps one of the most eloquent advocates for the difference position, with all its problems and difficulties. This, however, is how she states the matter:

> Women's desire would not be expected to speak the same language as man's; woman's desire has doubtless been submerged by the logic that has dominated the West since the time of the Greeks. (1977/1985, p. 25)

> the articulation of the reality of my sex is impossible in discourse. . . . My sex is removed, at least as the property of a subject, from the predicative mechanism that assures discursive coherence . . . I can thus speak intelligently as sexualized male . . . or as asexualized. . . . All the statements I make are thus either borrowed from a model that leaves my sex aside . . . or else my utterances are unintelligible according to the code in force. (p. 149)

We are reminded here that merely having a voice is not sufficient if that voice must speak in a register that is alien to its own specificity, and in so doing lose its own desires and interests. While indeed, having a voice is preferable to being held silent, in so far as that voice is truly not one's own, not reflecting one's own interests, desires and experiences, then one may speak, but only to further the already dominant groups' agenda.

These three aspects by which the dominant male groups have constructed woman as their serviceable other reveal themes that are common to all similar constructions, including the example to which we now turn: the white construction of the African-American as other.

The African-American as Other

Ralph Ellison, writing in 1952, entitled his book *Invisible Man*, suggesting a parallel absent presence as the way by which the dominant white Americans have rendered African-Americans invisible, represented only through white eyes, lacking their own positive identity. Toni Morrison, writing in 1992, echoes Ellison's argument while advancing our understanding of this white-American creation of the African-American other.

Morrison is intrigued with the ways in which the dominant white literary genre has acted as though it were color-blind and race-neutral, all the while building its narrative around an essential African-American presence. She argues that the very heart and soul of what it means to be an American is founded on constructing an accommodating black presence. In short, the African-American has become a serviceable object constructed on behalf of the dominant white group's own desired identity:

> Africanism is the vehicle by which the American self knows itself as not enslaved, but free; not repulsive, but desirable; not helpless, but licensed and powerful; not history-less, but historical; not damned, but innocent; not a blind accident of evolution, but a progressive fulfillment of destiny. (Morrison, 1992, p. 52)

According to Morrison, the American character has been constructed through the construction of an other, the African-American, whose very qualities, created by the conditions of slavery, servitude and racism, give it a character that permits the dominant white groups to know who they are as free and autonomous agents acting with power in their world. In her view, racism is an essential ingredient of the American character, even as imperialism was ingrained early into the character of conquering European nations, and as sexism is an element essential to the very shape of masculine identity:

> racism is as healthy today as it was during the Enlightenment. It seems that it has a utility far beyond economy, beyond the sequestering of classes from

one another, and has assumed a metaphorical life so completely embedded in daily discourse that it is perhaps more necessary and more on display than ever before. (p. 63)

Morrison illustrates her argument by calling upon various white-American authors, prominently including Twain, Hemingway and Poe. I found her discussion of Hemingway's novel *To Have and Have Not* especially informative about her message and mine. Again, I will forgo the details of the story, except to note that its protagonist, Harry Morgan, represents a classic type of American character: "a solitary man battling a government that would limit his freedom and his individuality . . . competent, street-wise . . . virile, risk-taking, risk-loving" (p. 70).

Morrison notes that no African-American presence is allowed in Hemingway's story. There is a "nameless nigger" whose only job, it seems, is to get bait for the white man's charter fishing boat. "This black character either does not speak (as 'nigger' he is silent) or speaks in very legislated and manipulated ways (as a 'Wesley' his speech serves Harry's needs)" (p. 71). There is one particular moment, however, crucial to the book, that highlights the essential but tortured position of the African-American character in the white man's own story.

Morgan's boat is moving into waters that show signs of providing fish for his complaining charter customer. Morgan, however, is busy attending to his customer, while another crew member, who is white, is in an alcoholic stupor and so of little use. Hemingway's dilemma, says Morrison, is how to have his otherwise limited and silent black character discover the presence of fish without transforming him from a mere prop for the white man into a person with his own subjectivity and independent being. Hemingway resolves this dilemma in what Morrison considers a truly tortuous fashion: the captain says that he has just seen the nigger seeing the fish:

"Saw he had seen" is improbable in syntax, sense, and tense but, like other choices available to Hemingway, it is risked to avoid a speaking black. (p. 72)

The power of looking is Harry's; the passive powerlessness is the black man's, though he himself does not speak of it. (p. 73)

In considering why Hemingway made this choice rather than providing the black man with a real character as a gendered human being at the outset, Morrison arrives again at her major thesis. If the black man had been given his own being, then the main character, Harry Morgan, would have been dramatically transformed:

Harry would be positioned – set off, defined – very differently. He would have to be compared to a helpless alcoholic, a contemptible customer, and an individualized crew member with . . . an independent life. Harry would lack the juxtaposition and association with a vague presence suggesting sexual excitement, a possible threat to his virility and competence, violence under wraps. He would, finally, lack the complementarity of a figure who can be assumed to be in some way bound, fixed, unfree, and serviceable. (p. 73)

We have seen the same themes emerging in both paradigmatic examples: woman as other, African-American as other. The other is a figure constructed to be serviceable to the historically dominant white male group. In order to provide this service, the other cannot be permitted to have a voice, a position, a being of its own, but must remain mute or speak only in the ways permitted by the dominant discourse.

The stance from which the world is approached, experience charted and understood, is likewise the position of the dominant group. In both examples, the other is an essential presence without whom the dominant protagonists could not be who they claim to be. Yet in both examples the other must remain part of and party to the self-celebratory monologues of the dominant groups. No real dialogue can be permitted to intervene, lest in permitting others actually to speak in their own terms, expressing their own point of view, the entire scheme of Western civilization would collapse.

It is my intention to help to participate in that collapse – or, as Irigaray (see Whitford, 1991) suggests, to participate in jamming the machinery and challenging the technologies of domination on which the Western project has been erected and remains in force. Braidotti (1991) has suggested that the sense of crisis that marks our times is a crisis only for the dominant groups whose once secure hegemony is being challenged. For those who for so long have been silenced, these are times of challenge and hope.

Celebrating the Other: The Dialogic Challenge

Ever since Thomas Kuhn's groundbreaking writings, we have become accustomed to thinking about the paradigms that govern scientific and even broad cultural understanding, and of changes in those paradigms as having a revolutionary quality. I do not believe, however, that the kind of revolution that Kuhn had in mind even approaches the implications of revolutionary change that are involved in any movement from a monologic to a dialogic account. Monologism props up a many-centuried system of power and privilege for some few over the many, and is unlikely to yield graciously to an alternative framework. Yet the writing for just such a change does seem to be clearly on the wall – hence the sense of crisis for those currently in power.

The postmodern era has witnessed many challenges to the Western, liberal and Enlightenment-derived framework for understanding, with the repercussions of these challenges rocking philosophy, literary criticism and the human sciences, including psychology.[7] Our understandings of self, identity and subjectivity have been especially undermined by postmodern critics. In addition – and, I believe, of even greater significance – the postmodern era has witnessed the vigorous emergence of numerous social movements on behalf of the silenced seeking to gain a voice in the affairs of the day, and to name the terms of that voice.

The women's movement is one of the major forces leading this transformation, joined as well by movements on behalf of people of color, people with different sexual orientations, people with different lifestyles and experiences (e.g. the aged, the handicapped, etc.), people concerned about ecology and environmental issues, and a whole range of emerging nationalistic movements. Although there has been a significant backlash against several of these movements, and although I do not believe that there is any inevitability to the course of history, I continue to believe that the forces that these movements have set in motion will not easily be quelled.[8] Sides are drawn, however, with battles for power and privilege raging on various fronts – even including, unfortunately, the time-honored military battlefield itself.

In characterizing the issue in terms of monologic versus dialogic formulations, I am admittedly collapsing into one central and abstract idea the many complex and even divergent themes that are involved in each of these social as well as more academic movements. The women's movement, for example, is not of a single cloth but reflects numerous divisions within itself, separating reformers from radicals, women in the USA from their European counterparts, women of color from women of privilege, and so forth. In turn, the agenda of any one of these diverse elements within this one movement differs from the agenda that one finds, for example, among those advocating a voice for people with various sexual orientations. Yet in their common challenge to the domination of the monologic and self-celebratory formulations that have long reigned supreme in Western civilization, these diverse movements do share a concern with the nature of their otherness and, indeed, with celebrating that otherness through a dialogic alternative.

By now, the terms of the dialogic challenge should be taking shape, even if the specifics remain to be developed in later chapters. If the Western world's current story has been written in terms of self-celebratory monologues carried on by the dominant groups – especially educated, white and male – a genuine dialogue, with two separable speaking and acting parties involved, cannot occur unless and until that other emerges from under the yoke of domination and gains her and his own voice. It is unlikely that this will be a voice we are accustomed to hearing, nor one that is framed in terms governed by the dominant group's own version of a dialogue.

Moira Gatens (1991) sets forth the dialogic challenge – at least with respect to women – with a message, however, that is loud, clear and relevant for the other social and academic movements as well:

> Two present sexes – rather than one sex (the male) and its absence (the female) – introduces the possibility of genuine intercourse. Without two presences intercourse between the sexes could only result in rape. (p. 116)

Gatens's point parallels the point developed by Bakhtin, a theorist central to dialogism: a genuine dialogue requires that there be two separable presences, each coming from its own standpoint, expressing and enacting its own particular specificity. To speak of celebrating the other, therefore, is to call for just such a dialogue, not the self-celebratory monologues that have thus far dominated our understanding and our practice.

The dialogic challenge that appears in the various contemporary social movements is also reemerging as a strong counterforce within the human sciences. The ideas developed by G.H. Mead, later termed symbolic interactionism, the later work of Wittgenstein, as well as the pioneering work of Harold Garfinkel's ethnomethodology, mark several precursors to a more dialogic understanding of human experience. A group of social psychologists on both sides of the Atlantic, disenchanted with the directions of the discipline, have likewise begun to reorient their own theoretical work towards more dialogic-based theories. The writings of Billig, Edwards, Gergen, Harré, Potter and Wetherell, and Shotter immediately come to mind, as does the work of many others involved in developing a cogent theory of discourse and narrative analysis.[9] While I will call upon each of these and others in developing the dialogic focus, I will be especially interested in the contributions that emerged in Russia, led in particular by Bakhtin and his collaborators as well as several radical feminist theorists.

Almost all these academic authors, both American and European, reflect a dissatisfaction with monologic accounts and so have turned towards a more dialogic framework for understanding. Yet the dimension of power that drives the social movements of our time, and is central to my own thinking, is often sloughed off or appears not at all – at least in nonfeminist academic accounts, with some noteworthy exceptions.[10]

To celebrate the other is not merely to find a place for her or him within a theoretical model. Nor is it simply to analyze the role that conversations and talk play in all aspects of human endeavor. Rather, celebrating the other is also to recognize the degree to which the dialogic turn is a genuinely revolutionary transformation in the relationships of power and privilege that still mark Western civilization. This celebration has rather widespread implications, well beyond the academy.

Not surprisingly, perhaps, while we may speak abstractly about dialogism's other-celebratory stance, and even chart its course in the general terms of discourse analysis, none of us can really fathom just what these still unheard voices of the other will say when they speak, nor what all of this holds in store for a civilization founded on their remaining serviceable and without independent speaking/acting parts.

Notes

1. The questioning of reason, of course, follows the important and pioneering work of Horkheimer and Adorno's *Dialectic of Enlightenment* (1944/1969).
2. This distinction between force and construction has its parallels in Foucault's (1979, 1980) writings, but especially his analysis of the positivity of power.
3. The list of feminist authors who have emphasized this point is extensive, ranging from some of Virginia Woolf's (1929/1989, 1938) and Simone de Beauvoir's (1949/1989) early classics to some more current analyses as summarized, for example, in the writings of Braidotti (1991), Flax (1990) and Gatens (1991).
4. The term *serviceable* with reference to "the other" comes from Toni Morrison's (1992) work detailing how white Americans created serviceable African-Americans: i.e. African-Americans whose constructed characteristics were essential, says Morrison, to the definition of the white-American character.
5. See, for example, Hegel's Master–Slave dialectic (e.g. *Phenomenology of Mind*, 1807/1910; see also Findlay, 1958). See also Braidotti (1991); Cixous and Clément (1975/1986); Code (1991); Eisenstein (1988); Flax (1990); Gatens (1991); Harding (1986); Irigaray (1974/1985, 1977/1985); MacKinnon (1989); Whitford (1991).
6. See Braidotti (1991) and Gatens (1991) for a summary of various feminist theories, including several that emphasize the degree to which the male/female division is the basis for most, if not all, other cultural dichotomies. See also Flax (1990); MacKinnon (1989).
7. The postmodern movement and critique offers us an extensive array of authors. Any list, however, would necessarily include Derrida (1974, 1978, 1981), Foucault (1979, 1980) and Lyotard (1979/1984).
8. See Faludi (1991) for a recent treatise on the *backlash* against feminism.
9. In addition to those named, the list of both American and European discourse theorists is extensive and would also include Bruner (1986, 1987, 1990); Gergen and Gergen (1988) and Sarbin (1986).
10. In addition to most feminist analysts for whom power (male power) is central, several social psychologists have also seen power to be relevant: e.g. Billig (1982, 1990a,b); Billig *et al.* (1988); Gergen and Semin (1990); Lukes (1986); Stam (1987).

2

Conceptual Dilemmas

The dominant – and, as I argued in Chapter 1 – dominating – tradition of inquiry into human nature has increasingly sought the human essence in the characteristics of self, mind and personality said to be found *within* what I have termed the self-contained individual (Sampson, 1977) and what Carrithers (1985) – borrowing from Mauss's (1938/1985) classic analysis – refers to as the *moi*: the deep, sometimes mysterious but knowable psychophysical entity who forms "the living core around which society is built" (p. 242). We have come to "think of ourselves as people with frontiers, our personalities divided from each other as bodies visibly are" (Morris, 1972, p. 1).

Conventional wisdom tells us that each one of us is like a small container designed to prevent our "inner essence" from leaking out. We believe that in order to be a proper container, each individual must become a coherent, integrated, singular entity whose clear-cut boundaries define its limits and separate it from other similarly bounded entities.

Conventional wisdom tells us that this *moi* is what we must fathom in order to grasp the essentials of human nature.[1]

Conventional wisdom tells us that this self-contained individual is fundamentally monologic: "a hermetic and self-sufficient whole, one whose elements constitute a closed system presuming nothing beyond themselves, no other utterances" (Bakhtin, 1981, p. 273).

Conventional wisdom tells us that we can never understand people's real nature unless we first isolate them from their ongoing relationships with others and study them as though they were like objects in Whitehead's glass-enclosed museum case, exhibiting their own pure and essential form.[2] We are told that once we understand essential human nature in this monologic manner – that is, by removing people from their ongoing lives and connections with others – we can later reintroduce "the other" and see how social life unfolds on the basis of these essential individual properties we have just discovered.[3]

This account continues to drive Western culture and its understanding of persons, and is associated primarily with idealized conceptions of the male.

Monologic Dilemmas

Proponents of this dominant tradition have been so insistent on searching for the essential qualities housed within the individual that they have created *two* conceptual dilemmas for themselves – neither of which, however, they typically recognize as a problem. The first involves the investigators' failure to pay attention to their own activities; the second involves their failure to attend closely to their subjects' activities.

Doing Dialogues

While proponents of this essentialist argument recommend a monologic view of human nature, their own work involves them in interminable dialogues, thereby producing an incoherent conceptual situation: they require one theory to deal with their own nature and a different theory to deal with their subjects' nature.

Take the study of human rationality as an illustrative example.[4] The introduction to the typical research report begins by noting: "Whereas it is often believed that people are rational, the thesis to be examined here is that people are fundamentally nonrational in their judgment and decision-making processes." The report then proceeds to ignore this very feature of its understanding, seeking its answers within the self-contained individual rather than in this dialogic quality on which its own work is necessarily built. Is it not paradoxical to formulate an account of human nature that systematically deletes the very dialogic quality that enters into that formulation and its justification? While *doing* dialogues in collecting their data, reporting them, justifying and defending them, this dominant approach insists on a monologic framework for understanding![5]

Putnam (1990) has described this dilemma as it appears in the physical sciences, speaking of the *cut* made between the system and the observer. The cut refers to the failed attempt to separate the features of the system being studied from the observer doing the study. By making this cut or separation, the theory that explains the behavior of the observing scientist is excluded from the theory that is applied to the things studied. In Putnam's terms, the observing scientist seeks a God's-eye view from Nowhere, a pure seeing that somehow does not implicate the observer.

When dialogues drive the observers, but they ignore this feature of their lives in pursuing something intrinsic – that is to say, nondialogic – in the thing-being-studied, we encounter this same paradox and its now familiar failure in the sciences that study people as well. Both Shotter (1991) and Edwards (1991), for example, apply this argument to the cognitive sciences, noting how impossible it is for psychologists to study others' mental operations by developing theories that systematically exclude their own mental operations and the social world within which all this takes place.

Likewise, a growing number of psychologists and others interested in the practices of science – including, for example, the discourse analyses reported by Gilbert and Mulkay (1984) and by Potter *et al.* (1984) – reveal the intrinsically dialogic and social bases of scientific practice, adding further incoherence to the works of those who try to maintain the cut of which Putnam speaks. Fabian (1983) has developed a similar critique of anthropological work, proposing several ideas that I consider in later chapters.

In short, monologic approaches are vulnerable to the problem outlined by Putnam. They develop theories about human behavior that exclude their own human behavior from those very theories, thus producing incoherence at the very heart of their understanding.

Hidden Dialogic Partners

Not only have proponents of the monologic perspective ignored their own activities, but by failing to see the dialogic nature of their human subjects they have led us down the wrong pathway for understanding human nature. They direct us to look *within* the individual, when our attention needs to be focused *between* individuals. This failure of their conceptual vision also participates in covering up the dimension of power that is involved in the social construction of self and other. The monologic approach thereby helps to sustain existing relationships of power that require just such a failure of vision in order to be sustained.

For example, the processes by which a serviceable other is constructed by dominant protagonists is entirely ignored in most monologic accounts, which direct us not only to look within the protagonist and the other for the qualities each seems to possess, but also to ignore the very processes of construction by which those qualities appear. We ignore the manner by which dominant groups create serviceable others whose creation gives both self and other the very qualities that define their human nature.

Both paradigmatic cases we considered in Chapter 1, involving woman as other and African-American as other, clearly reveal this dynamic. For example, investigators discover that their subjects exhibit a virile and assertive character, and attribute these qualities to something fundamental about their nature as males. What they have deleted from this analysis is the dialogic construction of those so-called fundamental male qualities.

Morrison reminds us (see Chapter 1) that the apparent virility of Harry Morgan, the charter boat captain, depended on his being constructed as such through the silencing of the African-American presence. Feminist authors likewise remind us that the virile and assertive male (or the passive female) has been constructed on the basis of centuries of creating a serviceable female as other. All this, however, escapes the proponents of the dominant, monologic model who search within the individual for the story of human nature.

Thus, monologic approaches are not only vulnerable to the kinds of conceptual incoherence that Putnam, Shotter, Edwards, Potter and others have suggested, but in addition they are highly vulnerable to any serious effort on the part of their "hidden dialogic partners" to gain their own voice and so bring the entire monologic performance to a grinding halt.

Dialogic Dilemmas

Unfortunately, however, dialogic approaches are not immune from their own kinds of conceptual dilemma. The heart of any dialogic argument is its emphasis on the idea that people's lives are characterized by the ongoing conversations and dialogues they carry out in the course of their everyday activities, and therefore that *the most important thing about people is not what is contained within them, but what transpires between them.*

Little children, for example, grow up in a world of conversations – some directed towards them, others about them. They learn a great deal about who and what they are by listening to the stories that parents and friends tell about them to others. As Bruner (1987, 1990) has commented, we soon learn that what we have done is sometimes of less importance than how we talk about it to others.[6]

Not only are we socialized in and through conversations directed towards us and held about us, but we learn those skills requisite to engaging in conversations. We especially learn how to use our talk to *account* for ourselves to others and to ourselves.[7] We learn that telling a lie, for example, has little meaning until we develop ways of talking that give it meaning: "I did it to protect Sybil from feeling so bad"; "I did it because I promised not to tell the secret to anyone and I treasure loyalty over foolish honesty." We learn that hitting Johnny is often of less importance than being able to explain it by the story we tell about it to others (e.g. "he hit me first").

In short, what is basic about human nature is its dialogic quality. This involves processes occurring between people rather than events that occur inside a single individual. Therefore, whatever is essential about human nature is to be found between people in a social dialogue, talk, conversation, debate, and so forth, and not in the inner recesses of an individual abstracted from these ongoing transactions. To focus on conversations is to reject the self-celebratory monologic view that has dominated most thinking about human nature, knowledge and understanding.

Dilemma No. 1: Differences without Essences

This dialogic argument introduces us to a rather basic conceptual dilemma. On the one hand, I have argued not only that what we call human nature is socially constructed in and through dialogues carried on with others, but also that a genuine dialogue, as opposed to a monologue, requires two separable people, each with her or his own specificity or standpoint intact. On the other hand, how can we have two separable people with their own specificities without positing the very kind of essentialist doctrine that we find in monologic accounts and that dialogism tries to undo?

In other words, how can we have a relational view of human nature and simultaneously refer to a person's specificity? This dilemma has been especially in evidence in those radical feminist accounts that want to continue to hold onto a specific nature for women as distinct from men, yet also want to sustain the view that all human nature is socially (that is, dialogically) constructed.

The socially constructed (i.e. relational/dialogic) view suggests that there is no intrinsic, self-contained essence to human nature, that all human experience is mediated by the language, culture and times in which we live. Let us once again turn to feminist arguments as our paradigmatic case. The *body* plays a central role in these arguments. But is this the body of nature and biological fact? Or is it the body of culture – that is, the body as mediated by cultural sign systems?

The specificity that each partner to a dialogic encounter brings is a body that has already been socially marked; it is not the unmediated or so-called natural body. Where the other has been constructed to be a serviceable object for the dominant groups in society, this means that we are dealing with a body that is already marked by domination. Is this, then, the body's specificity that we wish to see played out in a dialogic encounter? Or do we want a body that is known differently? And, if the latter, what can this mean in a dialogic account?

Most feminists would agree with Eisenstein's (1988) position:

My point is not that the body – as established in biological "fact" – determines its own meaning outside discourse or the relations of patriarchical

society. There is no "outside" or biological "fact" as such. . . . Both the body
as "fact" and the body as "interpretation" are real, even if we cannot clearly
demarcate where one begins and the other ends. (p. 80)

Gatens (1991) uses both Irigaray's and Cixous's insistent claims on behalf
of the embodied nature of female specificity to set forth her view of this
situation, comparing Freud's use of the phallic metaphor with Irigaray's use
of the metaphor of two-lips:

Freud's morphological description of the female sex as castrated, as lacking,
receives no more nor less confirmation from biology than does Irigaray's
position of the female sex as made up of . . . two lips. The difference is that
Freud's morphological description of the female sex amounts to the inverse
of male morphology which is taken to be full, phallic; whilst Irigaray's
description presents the female form as full, as lacking nothing. Both
descriptions are clearly "biased" or political but French feminists would deny
that any discourse can be neutral or free from political investments. (p. 115)

These two passages illustrate one dilemma of the dialogic formulation.
We are dealing with two socially constructed personages whose differences
are also socially constructed and have no meaning independent of the
cultural discourses which have engendered them in the first place. Freud's
focus on the phallus and Irigaray's on two-lips differ because they have
been socially constructed and highlighted as key differences. If both
versions were equally viable in Western discourse, we would have the
possibility of a genuine dialogue between two differently constituted
presences. As it currently stands, however, we have a monologue in which
the defining presence is all on one side, the other becoming a not-male
rather than an affirmative female.

Most radical feminists ask us to remain in a state of tension – or, in
Braidotti's (1991) terms, dissonance – on this issue. This tension or
dissonance is usually adopted as a self-conscious political strategy,
necessary at least in the short run and perhaps in the long run as well.

On the one hand, to deny woman's embodied specificity is to run the
risk of losing woman entirely to the dominant male discourses. On the
other, to emphasize woman's embodied specificity is to run the risk of
returning us to classic essentialist stereotypes about men's and women's
nature. Note that the tension and the dissonance are *not* based on a worry
about some abstract philosophical incoherence (e.g. claiming specificity yet
denying essentialism). Rather, these dissonances are based on practical-
political concerns with the fate of woman under the rule of either side.
Hence the call to maintain the dissonance and the tension.

For those who need their dilemmas resolved, their tensions reduced and
their dissonance transformed into harmonious consonance, this approach

will undoubtedly seem highly unsatisfactory. I remain convinced, however, that something of precisely this tension-full sort is necessary, even if it retains a dilemma troubling to those who require neat solutions, and need them right now.

Dilemma No. 2: The Relativistic Morass

A second dilemma is based on what would seem to be dialogism's relativism. This relativism is apparent in Gatens's (1991) passage in which she appears to have no basis for choosing between Freud and Irigaray because neither offers a neutral description of the truth of human sexuality; each presents only a politically biased view. Relativism is also apparent in the passage quoted from Eisenstein (1988), for whom there is no "outside" to discourse, leaving us trapped inside with no basis for choosing between better or worse discourses.

The usual problem with relativistic accounts is that in permitting anything to have equal standing, they appear not to have any standards for choosing among competing formulations. The usual escape from the pitfalls of such relativism has been to turn to some external foundation that permits us to choose between better or worse ideas, proclamations, visions about reality, and so forth. The standard that permits such choices to be rationally made invites us to consider reality itself.

For example, if the world (reality) operates by a set of principles that hold for all times, all places and all peoples, and are thereby independent of people's needs, desires and cultural preferences, a good or correct formulation is one that corresponds with this reality. In other words, it is reality itself that permits us to escape to a realm "outside" discourse and to choose between good and poor representations of that reality. The standard we would use, in this case, would involve comparing ideas with reality and choosing those ideas that best mirrored reality.

It is not germane to the direction of my own argument to recite the standard repertoire of critics of this foundational view, nor that of all those who continue to try to work out some way for it and us to survive.[8] What I would rather do, however, is to suggest that reality and the correctness of our representation of it, presented as though this were *the only* standard of judgment and choice available to us, is actually but one standard by which to judge the value of a given idea or concept. Not surprisingly, this one standard that has been presented as the only proper standard has primarily occupied the interest of dominant males in philosophy and the sciences; thus it would appear not to reflect anything more than a kind of relativistic standpoint itself.[9]

Trying to anchor ourselves by believing in a belief-independent reality in order to avoid the relativistic morass serves the purposes of gaining sufficient distance and separation to permit people to master, control and dominate nature, a traditional masculinist project. If our purposes, however, are less technological and lie more in the moral/spiritual domain, designed to achieve the best possible conditions of living for all persons, then matching concept with reality may be the least of our concerns.

In this light, the dialogic formulation does offer us a standard for choosing. In other words, anything does not go, nor is everything equally acceptable. Although this standard does not lie outside discourse, dialogue or conversation, it does nevertheless offer a way to evaluate the worth of any given discourse-generated formulation. This standard moves us away from a concern with matching concept or mind to reality, and towards a moral judgment: does the formulation allow the parties jointly to determine the terms of their existence, or does one side dominate this process? This standard involves evaluating the distortion in the construction of self and other, and is clearly the standard that permits Eisenstein, Gatens, Morrison and other similar theorists to reject patriarchical and white monologues in favor of a dialogic alternative.

Let me reiterate the argument so that we can see where we stand and why I have suggested that although it remains within the realm of discourse, dialogism need not inevitably sink into the relativistic morass. To this point, I have argued as follows:

1. Human nature is socially constructed in and through dialogues, conversations, and talk, and is therefore to be found in relations between and among people rather than issuing from within the individual.

2. The social construction of human nature is distorted whenever one party to the dialogue plays a primary role in determining the qualities and life chances of its dialogic partner, thereby transforming a dialogue into a monologue.

3. The social construction of human nature is nondistorted only in so far as the parties to the dialogue have equivalent power in the construction of self and other.

4. This dialogic construction of human nature will not reveal the essence of either party, but rather will unfold an emerging, shifting and open horizon of human possibilities, which cannot be readily known in advance or outside the dialogue but emerges as a property of the ongoing dialogue itself.

According to this preceding argument, the Freudian construction to which Gatens refers, for example, is not simply a neutral alternative to the feminist account; nor is the white-Euro-American construction merely a neutral alternative to the African account. In both cases, the former distorts by controlling the terms by which the latter is known and lives, and so offers a decidedly inferior understanding. More to the point: any monologic formulation, because it is self-celebratory and constructs a serviceable other, is necessarily inferior, not merely a neutral alternative.

By the same token, as most dialogic advocates would agree, neither is a feminist or an Africanist monologue a neutral alternative to a genuinely dialogic possibility. The purpose of feminist analyses, for example, is to create a space in which the long-silenced other can be heard on its own terms, and so participate in the dialogues that shape both self and other.

In other words, we can operate within a dialogic framework and simultaneously avoid the pitfalls usually associated with relativism, all of this accomplished without the usual turn to some kind of essentialist foundation.

Another example – taken this time from a rather different arena – should help to advance our appreciation of this line of argument. This example appeared in a *National Geographic* issue examining the year 1491, America before Columbus (Ortiz, 1991). The Native American author of the lead article, a member of the Tewa culture, compared the archaeological story of the origins of his people with his people's own story. "Archaeologists will tell you that we came at least 12,000 years ago from Asia" (p. 7), offering a considerable amount of data to substantiate this version:

> But a Tewa is not so interested in the work of archaeologists . . . a Tewa is interested in our own story of our origin, for it holds all that we need to know about our people, and how one should live as a human. The story defines our society. It tells me who I am, where I came from, the boundaries of my world, what kind of order exists within it; how suffering, evil, and death came into this world; and what is likely to happen to me when I die. (p. 7)

It is obvious that the scientific world-view is not able to accomplish the purposes served by the Tewa's own account.

In like manner, the purposes served by monologic accounts founded in the desire to match theory with reality are unable to address the profound moral issues that are at stake. Dialogism is better able to handle these issues, offering us a way to choose among various formulations without, however, calling upon either an essentialist foundation or some nonexistent discourse-independent sphere.

Dilemma No. 3: Construction and Reality

Because dialogism emphasizes the conversations in and through which self and other are constructed, some critics of its viewpoint have argued that we are dealing only with the world of words and ideas in people's heads, nothing of true substance in the real world. I am reminded of the children's rhyme: "Sticks and stones can break my bones, but words can never hurt me." In proclaiming this, the young child seems to be saying that you may think whatever you wish of me, even call me any name in the book – that cannot harm me. Those are only words, thoughts and ideas. I can be harmed only by actual material damage – and that requires sticks and stones and broken bones.

A somewhat more sophisticated version of this position appeared in a brief commentary by Steven Watts (1992), who takes to task those constructionists he refers to as discourse radicals and linguistic leftists:

> Convinced that power resides in texts and their enveloping structures of language, discourse radicals have bent to the task of unlocking the codes, exposing the linguistic repressions, and undermining the basic assumptions of modern Western society. . . . Grasping the linguistic dimension of injustice only scratches the surface of the social, economic, and political environments that influence language and culture and link them to the material world. (p. A40)

Watts argues that this detachment from the concrete realities of people's everyday lives renders these discourse radicals impotent to do more than speak endlessly to one another about illusory and otherworldly events. Although I take up this issue again in Chapter 10, especially through the position developed by Catharine MacKinnon (1989), it is important at the outset to put this kind of critique to rest.

The ideas in people's heads both shape the actual concrete life experiences that people have and are shaped by those experiences. Nothing very surprising here. Turning again to the paradigmatic case of man's construction of woman, the point of all this is not simply to argue that men construct images of women that are discrepant from the reality of women, but rather that men's power has made women, in fact and in reality, into the images that men have of them: "Knowledge is neither a copy nor a miscopy of reality, neither representation nor misrepresentation . . . but a response to living in it" (MacKinnon, p. 98).

In this passage, MacKinnon joins with most other radical feminists to challenge the separation between a purely materialist and a purely idealist position. She argues – convincingly, for me – that in time, the idea becomes the actual material reality for those constructed in its image. Women become men's image of them; African-Americans become the image the white majority has of them. They become the image because the power of the image-constructors lies also in their ability to construct a world that conforms to their images of it.

The distance between the idea and the reality is too short and too intimately connected to argue that the former is otherworldly while only the latter is real. To a woman who has been raped because pornographic magazines depict her as welcoming that response of male domination, the event is only too real, not simply a representation in print or in men's minds. To the African-American who lives in abject poverty with little hope for improvement, the ideas of his laziness and enjoyment of welfare are in fact the everyday reality in which he lives out his life or erupts into one blazing moment of affirming presence.

Seen in close-up, the idea–reality distinction proves useful primarily to those in positions of power, for whom indeed one may meaningfully separate what is in the head from what takes place on their bodies. The distinction holds much less meaning for those in subordinate positions subjected to the realities that the dominant groups' ideas are able to construct. Dominant groups have the material power to make reality fit their ideas; less dominant groups become the reality the ideas suggest. In other words, for the dominated groups, the idea is the reality. What is said and thought about them becomes the reality of their lives, because those who have the power to say and think also have the power to construct the world in that image.

After the 1992 uprisings in the inner city of Los Angeles, in angry response to a jury verdict of "Not Guilty" in a highly publicized case involving the police beatings of a black man, numerous articles appeared commenting on the profound fear the white population had of "angry black youth". Reading the articles would lead many to suppose that "anger" is a property of "black youth", and so to miss the very real social processes by which the "black male" is made angry and kept angry by social policies that create the very conditions of hopeless living that would make any person feel rage.

Construction and reality do not describe totally separate realms except to those in dominant positions for whom it is indeed still possible to think and not worry that the thoughts may indeed become true for them. For those in less dominant positions, what is said about them can become what is done to them, thus intimately connecting idea and reality in their everyday lives. Our questions, then, need to be directed at the social standing and power that exist for those who proclaim the construction–reality separation.

If sticks and stones can break my bones, but words can never hurt me, why do I get so upset when the sign says "Whites Only"? The words on the sign tell the story of my life. Why do I find it so offensive to be called a "cold bitch" when I refuse men's advances? The words proclaimed tell the story of my life. What is so disturbing in being told "Guilty as charged", and then sent to prison? The words of the jury create the story of my life.

Notes

1. Carrithers (1985) critically examines the classic paper on the individual written by Marcel Mauss (1938; reprinted in Carrithers *et al.*, 1985) and argues on behalf of distinguishing between two senses of the individual: the *personne*, describing the person as a citizen, a member of an ordered collectivity; and the *moi*, the sense of the self-contained individual that I develop and use to describe the monologic and self-celebratory view. Wetherell and Potter (1989) refer to this latter type as the "honest soul or trait model" and distinguish it from the multiplicity of the more fragmented role model. I contend that even the role model adopts a belief in a basic core identity that transcends all the roles we play and, in an important sense, becomes the self-contained ideal. See Chapter 3, Note 2.
2. Whitehead, 1938, p. 90.
3. Clearly, I am describing the liberal individualist theory of the person whose ability to be a sovereign agent requires a thoroughgoing detachment from anyone or anything that might define and so limit its ability to set the terms for its life and wellbeing: see, for example, Cahoone (1988); MacIntyre (1984, 1988); Sampson (1989); Sandel (1982). And just as clearly – at least according to Gatens (1991) – I am also describing an idealized male:

   The apparently sexually neutral human subject turns out to be implicitly a male subject . . . [who] is constructed as self-contained and as an owner of his person and his capacities, one who relates to other men as free competitors with whom he shares certain politico-economic rights. . . . The female subject is constructed as prone to disorder and passion, as economically and politically dependent on men. . . . She makes no sense by herself. (p. 5)

   See also the discussion in Chapter 9 below.
4. This is not merely a hypothetical example, but is based on a comparison between the "rationality" theories developed, for example, by Ross (1977), Tversky and Kahneman (1974) and Larrick *et al.* (1990) – who emphasize the failings of human judgment; Funder's (1987) view of people as good and rational judges; and Taylor's (1989) and Greenwald's (1980) view of people as not rational but filled with useful illusions.
5. See, for example, Gilbert and Mulkay (1984); Mulkay (1979); Woolgar (1988) for a study of the role of conversations in science. See also Gergen and Semin (1990) for additional, relevant work.
6. Other narrativists include Gergen and Gergen (1988); Harvey *et al.* (1990); Howard (1991); Sarbin (1986).
7. Discourse analyses of excuses reported by Wetherell and Potter (1989) offer a useful illustration of this point.
8. See, for example, Arbib and Hesse (1986); Bernstein (1983); Putnam (1990); Rorty (1979, 1989).
9. For example Code (1991); Harding (1986).

PART II

Monologism: Celebrating the Self

3

Possessive Individualism and the Self-contained Ideal

In order to celebrate the self or the *moi* (Mauss, 1938/1985; Carrithers, 1985), we first need to think of the self as a kind of bounded container, separate from other similarly bounded containers and in possession or ownership of its own capacities and abilities.[1] In order to ensure this container's integrity, we need to think of whatever lies outside its boundaries as potentially threatening and dangerous, and whatever lies inside as sufficiently worthy to protect. These beliefs establish a possessively individualistic view of the person and the assumption of a negative relation between self and other, both of which understandings permeate much of Western civilization.[2]

Regardless of how life was once experienced, or how life may still be experienced in other societies (see Chapter 5), or even how much we may complain and protest:

> There is an individualist mode of thought, distinctive of modern Western cultures, which, though we may criticize it in part or in whole, we cannot escape. It indelibly marks every interpretation we give of other modes of thought and every attempt we make to revise our own. (Lukes, 1985, p. 298)

This inescapable cultural vise has given us – or, at least, the dominant social groups in the West[3] – a sense of themselves as distinctive, independent agents who own themselves and have relatively clear boundaries to protect in order to ensure their integrity and permit them to function more effectively in the world. This describes the self-contained ideal. This ideal is supported by the twin pillars of a possessively individualistic understanding of the person (primarily, the male person) and the sense of the self as being like a container.

Possessive Individualism

The hallmark of a democratic system involves its citizens' right to vote. For this reason, among all the world's nations, the United States is usually considered to be one of the prime bastions of democracy. Some assume that voting is a natural right of US citizenship, forgetting the long history of political battles that eventually enfranchised increasingly more people. It was not until 1870 that enfranchisement was granted regardless of race, color or previous condition of servitude; not until 1920 that women were given these rights; not until 1971 that these rights were granted to all those aged 18 and over rather than the previous age of 21.[4] If we regard citizenship as an essential aspect of what it means to be a person within modern society, we can view each of these constitutional amendments as enlarging the definition of "persons" to be more inclusive than it was previously.

But what do citizenship, personhood and voting rights have to do with the self-contained ideal? An examination of several debates held in seventeenth-century England, pitting the Levellers on one side and Cromwell on the other, will lead us to this connection and, in so doing, enrich our understanding.[5] The central issue in the debates involved who should be entrusted with the right to vote. Should everyone living in England have this right, or only certain people? And, if the latter, then which people were entitled, and which were not?

According to Macpherson's (1962) examination of the various sides in these debates, the issue boiled down to a question of personhood, while personhood itself involved the capacity to operate in a self-determining, autonomous manner. Did the mere fact of birth grant the individual the status of personhood, with its attendant right to vote? The Levellers argued:

> The birthright, we may presume, was not only forfeitable for acts against society, but was also forfeited, or not even entered upon, by those whose age or whose status as servants or beggars was deemed inconsistent with the free exercise of rational will. (Macpherson, 1962, p. 124)

In the Levellers' view, all people whose "living was not directly dependent on the will of others, were entitled to the franchise" (p. 128). The key point in their argument centered around independence from the will of others, considering criminals, servants and beggars either to have forfeited this quality of their character or not even to have possessed it in the first place.

It would make no sense, for example, to give the vote to someone who was held in servitude to another, for the master would then have more votes than he deserved: that is, his own plus those of people in servitude to him. Similar arguments suggested that it would be inappropriate to include wage-earners (who might simply cast their vote to protect their employment), beggars and people on welfare: after all, these people were not autonomous – that is, free from the will of others.

Cromwell's cynical view of the Leveller position argued that "The Leveller franchise proposals 'must end in anarchy' ... because they refer to 'men that have no interest but the interest in breathing'" (p. 126). He favored restricting the vote to property-owners whose freedom from others' will was clear, and whose interest in protecting their property rights warranted their self-determination through voting.

These themes from America's English heritage were involved in the later debates concerning voting as well as other individual rights. The US Constitution, for example, was initially interpreted to mean that white, male property-owners should not only have the right to vote, but should in addition be free from governmental interference in their affairs. Only later were both voting rights and other individual rights extended to larger classes of people (see Winkler, 1991). In all cases, the decision to grant an individual the vote or other individual rights was sculpted by the cultural understanding of personhood. This understanding, in turn, was defined by what Macpherson terms *possessive individualism*: being the owner of one's own capacities and self.

Possessive individualism first tells us that in order to vote, one must be free; and second, that in order to be free – that is, independent from another's will – one must be the owner of oneself. Any conditions thought to impinge upon the individual's personal ownership over himself would infringe on freedom, and thus deny such a person the right to vote.

Those who were still too young to be free from dependence on another should not vote, nor should women (then subjected to their husband's will or, if unmarried, to their father's); nor persons in servitude who were required to submit to another to sustain themselves. All these people were not in possession of themselves; thus they were not free, and thereby did not deserve the vote. In so far as voting plays a vital role in setting forth the conditions under which a person lives, to be denied the right to vote is effectively to be considered not quite a person.

It is clear that the possessively individualistic formulation defines the self-contained ideal and simultaneously establishes the negative self–other relationship that is at the root of the self-celebratory world-view. In order to be one's own person, one cannot be beholden to anyone else. In other words, possessive individualism posits a negative relationship between self and other: the more the other is involved in the life of the person, the less the person is involved in his or her own life. To be capable of voting means to be capable of making one's own decisions without being subjected to the will of others. Others are posited as potential thieves of one's personhood. The more others take priority, the less priority exists for the individual.

The second pillar on which the self-contained ideal rests involves a view of the self as a kind of container.

The Self as a Container

Most of us in the West today would subscribe to three relatively simple and seemingly "natural" ideas: (1) the boundary of the individual is coincident with the boundary of the body; (2) the body is a container that houses the individual; (3) the individual is best understood as a self-contained entity. The self-celebratory quality of our cultural understanding of human nature is built upon this tripartite foundation, with its container view of the individual.

Point (1) clearly connects the notion of the individual with the idea of a skin-encased body. It tells us that individuals begin and end at the limits of their body.[6] Some might say, "of course this is so", noting that because we all have bodies, our understanding of individuals must be based on this simple fact of nature. Since people everywhere have always had bodies and always will have bodies, this natural fact sets the terms for all people's understanding of what an individual is, where they are located, and so forth. In short, point (1) has a natural ring about it – at least *to us*. I will argue later (in Chapter 5) that this idea is found today primarily in the Western world, and is by no means a universal understanding.

Point (2) observes that bodies are very much like containers which house everything that is vital about the person. Housed inside the body-as-container, then, are both the physiological qualities that comprise a person and the psychological characteristics they possess. If we want to know where the stomach, liver and heart are located, we look *inside* the body-as-container. If it is the mind we seek, once again, we know we must look inside the body-as-container. Where are feelings? Inside the body-as-container, of course. What about opinions, attitudes, beliefs, values? Once again, seek them inside the body-as-container. Where are the will, motivation, drive? Inside the body-as-container, of course.

Point (3) simply completes the picture, telling us that if the individual is a body and the body is a container, then it would seem to follow that the individual must be a self-contained entity.

Although they came at this matter from a somewhat different place and arrived at a conclusion somewhat at variance with my own, the analyses suggested by the linguist George Lakoff (1987) and the philosopher Mark Johnson (1987; also Lakoff and Johnson, 1980) offer us a helpful examination of what they refer to as *the container metaphor*. Listen first to Johnson (1987):

> Our encounter with containment and boundedness is one of the most pervasive features of our bodily experience. We are intimately aware of our bodies as three-dimensional containers into which we put certain things (food, water, air) and out of which other things emerge (food and water wastes, air, blood, etc.). From the beginning, we experience constant physical containment in our surroundings (those things that envelop us). We move in and out of rooms, clothes, vehicles, and numerous kinds of bounded spaces. We manipulate objects, placing them in containers (cups, boxes, cans, bags, etc.). In each of these cases there are repeated spatial and temporal organizations. (p. 21)

Johnson argues that our everyday, repeated experience is of our selves as bodies and our bodies as containers. A collection of cultural sayings convey this meaning: "I've had a *full* life. Life is *empty* for him. There's *not much left* for him *in* life. Her life is *crammed* with activities. *Get the most out of* life. His life *contained* a great deal of sorrow. Live your life *to the fullest*" (Lakoff and Johnson, 1980, p. 51). We speak of ourselves and others as *filled* with anger; as unable *to contain* our joy; as *brimming* with rage; as trying to get anger *out of our system* (Lakoff, 1987, p. 383; original emphasis).

Even our mind is said to reason in terms of this container metaphor. For example, Johnson argues that the logical meaning of *transitivity* and of set membership is based on generalizing our experiences based on our body as a container. If our liver is inside our body and our body is in the living-room, then our liver is in the living-room. Johnson suggests that several other logical principles likewise derive from this sense of the body as a container.

In other words, thinking of the person as a container is a rather commonplace feature of our everyday lives. Whereas both Johnson and Lakoff would have us believe that this experience originates in the *natural* fact that our body is actually a container, generalizing outwards from there to encompass more and more features of our everyday life experience, my contrasting position is to see our culture as having shaped even how we experience our bodies. That is, bodies are not intrinsically containers or whatever; the hand of culture shapes how we relate even to our bodies (see Chapter 1 above and Edwards, 1991, for a similar analysis). As I noted, in pursuing the container metaphor I am choosing our own cultural view in order to expose our own understanding of the self–other relationship. For us, the body–person–container connection is central to this understanding.

Although I disagree with the Lakoff–Johnson position regarding "origins", I have found their examination of the container metaphor very useful for understanding the way we have come to consider self and other. Once we think of the person-as-container, we can then apply some of the properties of containers to understanding the individual.[7] Two ideas are central: (a) Containers have an inside and an outside; what is not inside must clearly be outside, and vice versa. In other words, there is a rather clear-cut in–out distinction. (b) Containers have boundaries that separate their inside from the outside, and offer a kind of protective shield.

Let us now apply these features of containers to our understanding of the individual. First, we believe that an individual has an inside that contains all the important features that comprise the person – everything that the person owns – and that this inside is distinct, separate and cut off from all that is not part of the person, located outside the container. The person's essence, whatever we believe this to be, is housed within the individual and is distinguished from everything that is outside. Because we draw the in–out line at the edges of the body, we insist that the human core lies within those edges, period, end of sentence. And so, when I describe our current conception of the person as the *self-contained individual*, I am referring to this container whose boundaries lie at the edge of the skin within which is housed the essence possessed by the person.

Secondly, we see the boundaries of the person-as-container to be vital in the defense of the human core, and in sustaining the individual's integrity as a viable entity in the world. Boundary maintenance and boundary defense are key features of being a person and in maintaining individual sovereignty. We believe that a loss of boundaries – for example, when the individual is not certain where she ends and her children begin – threatens the individuality that requires boundary maintenance in order to be sustained.

I remember a moment in my own family in which our son, who was quite young at the time, came home from school carrying his report card. Seeing it, we asked him about his grades. Somewhat defiantly, he showed us an "F" in one of his subjects (comportment would be my guess). Suddenly, my wife broke down in tears. After quieting down, we all three talked about it, discovering that "his F" had become "her F". In other words, at that moment, her boundaries fused to include his: she experienced his F as though it were her F, as though she had received the failing grade, not he. We tend to view such fusions negatively and believe that she should learn how to separate herself from him.

In my own somewhat unconventional young adulthood I wore a full beard, shed with advancing years and, if not maturity, at least a greater need not to look quite so old and worn out. Seeing me for the first time with my beard, my mother proclaimed, "My face [and she meant *her* face] doesn't look good with a beard", all the while stroking her own face. Again, the boundaries between self and other broke down. We even have a professional term to describe families in which these boundary-busting events appear: *enmeshed*. This term is never used to connote anything healthful or good!

The idea that boundary maintenance also involves the construction of a serviceable other is clearly implied in Chapters 1 and 2. In other words, I do not simply protect my integrity by erecting a firm boundary to separate me from the other, I also work to construct an other whose qualities ensure that my own integrity will remain unscathed and intact.

Needless to say, those who occupy dominant positions in society have this avenue more available to them than those who become their serviceable others, who most often learn simply to live with the hands that they have been dealt. Whether we erect a firm line separating self from other or construct a safely serviceable other, the message about the self–other relationship remains much the same: the other is a potentially dangerous threat. We do not embrace or celebrate the other as she is, but approach her with caution or with abandon – but only when she has been placed under our control.

Some Everyday Illustrations

Consider some everyday experiences that illustrate this self-contained ideal.

Of the many words of encouragement that today's parents might utter to their (male?) children, those least likely to be heard are "Learn to be obedient", while those most likely to be heard are "Learn to be independent" (see Kagitcibasi, 1987). We value individual independence and autonomy, and – as we have just seen in the discussion of possessive individualism – consider these to be qualities that some individuals possess, others once had but lost, and still others never had or never will have. The ever-present danger of losing our autonomy to others keeps us vigilant against threats to our individual freedom and self-determination.

As will become apparent in Chapter 5, not all the world's cultures value independence, nor believe so vigorously in a negative self–other relationship. As is also apparent from Chapter 1, when the male ideal is implicitly taken as the standard, we have a folk psychology of independence that represents an ideal that is often impossible for nondominant groups in society to realize. I return to some of these ideas in Chapter 11.

Consider our popular conception of human development. We operate by a folk psychology, aided by scientific psychology's own proclamations (see Chapters 4 and 11), which teaches us that the normal course of human development moves from dependence to independence; that the mark of maturity is self-reliance and autonomy from others; and that certain parental behavior can help or hinder progress along this "natural" developmental pathway.

The very young child's normal dependence on the family lessens during adolescence, when the child tests the waters of autonomy, and becomes minimal with maturity, when individuals finally leave the nest to make it on their own. Our parental role is to facilitate movement along this route by encouraging independence and discouraging dependence. Listen as those wise parents tell their children: "You're old enough now, you can do it all on your own"; "If you don't look after yourself, then who will?"; "You've got to make up your own mind about what you want; don't come running home; you've got to be your own person".[8]

We believe that if we interfere too much in our children's lives, doing too much for them, we will somehow stifle their growth, freeze them at some early stage along this developmental pathway, and then be stuck with an older, dependent and immature person. We all experience difficulty when, after our children have left the comfort of the nest to strike out on their own, a change in their situation forces them to return home again. Have we failed? Have they failed? Something just does not ring true for us when our 35-year-old son comes home to live again, or when our 32-year-old daughter, infant in hand, returns home to live "for just a little while".

That same folk psychology has also taught us that anyone who has not yet achieved independence will certainly fail to establish lasting intimacy with another human being. The latter requires the former, or so our folk beliefs and psychological science tell us.[9] People with failed or cloudy and confused identities who have not yet established a clear-cut sense of who they are as autonomous and independent human beings are presumed to make troublesome marriage partners. Not knowing themselves as freely self-determining individuals means that they will not yet be ready to take on the work of forming and of sustaining an intimate bond with another person.

As I previously noted, an implicit white male standard runs throughout these ideas. It is the dominant male who is to achieve independence and establish clear-cut self–other boundaries before *he* is ready to take on the full range of adult tasks, including establishing an intimate relationship with another human being: safe for him only after he has achieved and shored up his personal boundaries. The ideal is considered less attainable by women because it may interfere with their "natural" role as mothers and homemakers, even if they also have ancillary roles as full-time workers.

Several analysts have pointed out, however, that the ideal itself (if it is truly "ideal") can be attained only by those who have constructed "others" to take care of the remainder of their lives.[10] A man can be "independent" and "self-reliant" only if there is a woman or someone else around to allow him that possibility, taking care of the children, the home, the laundry, and so forth. In short, to achieve the ideal of independence, dominant groups must construct serviceable others on whom they can depend!

We hear a great deal today about co-dependent and addictive relationships. Our view of both addiction and co-dependence conveys our cultural folk psychology of human development. An addiction has become any pattern of behavior in which a person might engage that is done beyond a certain level of independent self-control, including nearly everything that people do: sexual addiction, eating addiction, sleeping addiction, waking addiction, working addiction, walking addiction, jogging addiction, people addiction, and so on endlessly.

Clearly, mature and healthy people are in charge of themselves and in control of their own behavior, beholden to no one or to no thing. Addictive people, like seventeenth-century English beggars, have lost possession of their own wills. The great fear is of dependence on anything other than one's own independent self.

In this context, co-dependence refers to any other person who collusively helps the individual to stay dependent and avoid acting in a mature, self-reliant manner. Parents can collude with their children and so inadvertently create an eternally childlike and dependent adult. A husband can collude with his alcoholic wife, helping her to retain her dependence on the drug. People can collude to help their friends remain compulsively trapped by whatever particular addiction they may have. In each case, the well-meaning other, in colluding with individuals' addictive problems, helps them to remain trapped in the troubled pattern, undermining their efforts to become free and independent again. The model of the ideal person is etched rather clearly in these bits of cultural folk wisdom; and once again we see a negative self–other relationship.

Addictions and co-dependence are but further manifestations of individuals' being threatened by another person, object, or activity because they lack genuine independence. We act as though any form of investment in another person, object or activity threatens autonomy. Our culture teaches us that we must guard ourselves against losing ourselves to "the other", in whatever form that other may appear: that is, losing ourselves to another person (e.g. women and men who "love too much"), an object (e.g. food, drugs) or an activity (e.g. gambling, shopping). Our wellbeing requires that we be a self-determining entity.

Once again, a negative relationship is posited between self and other: my wellbeing cannot be achieved unless I can manage to maintain the upper hand. Sometimes this will require my avoiding you altogether; at other times, it will require my ensuring that you are kept down: fear of the other, rejection of the other, suppression of the other. We will have to wait until

Part III and a very differently framed understanding before we can shed this view and embrace the other without fearing a loss or reduction of our self in the process.

Notes

1. There has never been agreement, nor is any likely, on just what this Western notion of the self is – or, indeed, how much it is Western rather than more universal. Mauss's (1938) classic distinction between the more personal sense of *moi* and the more social sense of *personne*, echoed by Carrithers (1985), reveals one facet of this theme. And when Mauss tells us that the *moi* is universal and Carrithers finds parallels between the modern conception and both earlier and cross-cultural views, we find ourselves even more implicated in a complex story without end. I will generally refer to the *moi* sense of self that currently predominates in the West.

2. As the study by Wetherell and Potter (1989) suggests, however, even this point is open to question. They distinguish between a view in which there is a core self, "a solid, unfragmented, coherent character and . . . a disintegrated, divided or split subject" (p. 206). Clearly, if the self follows the former line, then a negative relationship is more a possibility than if the self follows the latter line. While I find this distinction useful, as I commented above (e.g. Chapter 2, Note 1), I continue to insist that in much of the West – the USA especially – there remains a rather strong belief in the notion of a core self that lies beneath all the various roles we play. See also Chapter 8 below.

3. This connection between the self-contained ideal and dominant social groups should not be taken lightly. Much of the discussion about "the self" proceeds rather thoroughly from the white male standpoint – which, of course, is never fully recognized as such. Rather, that standpoint is presumed to be natural, normal, universal, despite the fact that the firm boundaries to be protected really describe the sense of the self that has been idealized by dominant groups; it does not apply with the same vigor or interest to society's nondominant others: see, for example, Gatens (1991 and Chapter 2, Note 3 above), who argues that the self-contained, possessively individualistic view clearly fits only the male ideal.

4. These refer respectively to the 15th, 19th and 26th Amendments to the US Constitution.

5. This discussion is based on Macpherson's (1962) work.

6. We know that ancient myth, and several current religious and mystical views, argue that people are both body and spirit. They tell us that while the person-as-body is like a container, the person-as-spirit transcends the container and ranges freely. While I do not take exception to this view, my point is that a negative self–other relationship requires that we view the person-as-container; and given the extensive support for this understanding, it would seem that although many might believe in an uncontained spirit, this belief has not affected their views of self versus other that are germane to my argument.

7. This discussion has been adapted from Johnson (1987), p. 22.
8. Several of these statements come from Shweder's (1984) discussion.
9. Erikson's (1959) very well-known and respected theory is but one of several that insist that individuality must precede and form the basis for intimacy.
10. See Braidotti (1991); Flax (1990); Gatens (1991).

4
—
Psychology's Celebration of the Self

W ithout a society organized around the self-contained individual, there would be neither a field such as psychology nor a need for one. On the other hand, without a field like psychology it would be difficult to sustain the belief that the self-contained individual holds the key to unlocking the major secrets of human nature and is the *raison d'être* of society itself. The science that studies the individual and the society within which those studies are conducted have developed a very cozy relationship. Our society needs its science of the individual even as that science needs the society which helped to create this individual as the object of its serious investigation.[1]

Even a cursory examination of the major traditions of psychological inquiry will reveal the degree to which psychology has participated in affirming a self-celebratory cultural belief and, in several key instances, encouraging the belief in a negative relationship between self and other. It should come as no surprise to learn that some of the most apparently innovative "discoverers" and "discoveries" in psychology owe much of their success to the fact that they emerge from within a predecessor tradition, offering ideas that are congruent with major themes of the society in which the work is carried on and to which it applies. This is said not in order to detract from these contributions, but rather to alert us to the degree to which their influence is based primarily on their conformity with ongoing societal interests.

The first tradition I will examine involves Freud and classic psychoanalytic theory. Here we will see not only the self-celebratory themes writ large but, in addition, how much Freud's work was less the discovery of something entirely new about human nature than the bringing to fruition of a line of thinking that was already prominent in the Western world. Carrithers (1985), for example, quotes from Gladston, who argues that

"Had Freud never lived and never labored ... psychiatric knowledge, psychiatric theory, and psychiatric practice would in all vital essentials not have been any different from what they are currently" (p. 256).

In seeking the answers to the riddles of human nature within the self-contained individual rather than in society, for example, Freud aligned himself with a line of predecessors – including Hume, Locke and Schopenhauer, among others – for whom priority was given to the individual over society. Freud's work in this regard also placed him in a Calvinistic Christian tradition that, as Dumont (1985) tells us, changed from viewing humanity in a more outworldly manner (e.g. wisdom involves renouncing the world) to a more inworldly and individualistic view.

Freud's work also fits quite well into:

> the picture of the *moi* at the beginning of the nineteenth century: it is deep, and therefore mysterious; but it is investigable, and to an extent malleable; it is the microscope through which the cosmos is seen; it is the living core around which society is built ... and it is embodied, and therefore bound to the vast organic world. (Carrithers, 1985, p. 242)

As Carrithers comments, this description better fits the Germany into which Freud would soon appear than the more collectivistic tradition of France as found, for example, in the writings of a Durkheim or a Mauss, providing Freud with a cultural climate hospitable to his ideas.

The preceding argument produces a picture of Freud as well as the other "innovators" in psychology that portrays them less like the Columbus we have imagined – whom McGrane (1989) describes as one who creates an entirely new tradition and conceptual universe – than as someone whose inventions take hold in a culture precisely because they already fit preexisting cultural frameworks.

Psychoanalytic Theory: Celebrating the Self/Worrying about the Other

Psychoanalysis – initiated by Freud, advanced by his numerous disciples, transformed in the hands of a group of British and American object-relations and interpersonal theorists and rediscovered in France by Lacan – offers us an excellent example of how psychology is an expression of its society's major beliefs while advancing those very beliefs through its "findings" about human nature.[2] One of the key elements in Freud's understanding of human nature was his insistence on the *nature* part of being human – that is, on the unrelenting call of basic, biologically rooted instincts which lie at the core of all that we understand to be human. In what his British and American revisionists refer to as his drive theory – to distinguish it from their own relational views – Freud outlined how basic sexual and aggressive drives serve as the mainsprings of human action, twisted this way and that by the demands of society.

Society plays a role in Freud's view of human nature, but that role turns out to be primarily a negative one, inhibiting the direct expression of these instinctual drives in the name of civilization. The human story is written in terms of the conflict between instincts and civilization and the distortions and pathologies that often result.

What is the Oedipal drama if not a story of a sexual drive seeking expression, only to be thwarted by the mores of society? The outcome of this drama is an eventual defeat for the instincts: the little boy does not get to have his mother. Either benign or pathological inner structures emerge, however, from this defeat. For example, one child develops a very stern superego, the angry and threatening voice of parents saying "no" to every impulse that seeks its moment in the light of day, while another child experiences a less stressful outcome. And of course, what is this little drama about boys, their mothers and fathers, other than a further statement about the absence of an interest in woman's own sexuality? The society that would eventually accept Freud's story, with its male protagonist and male gaze, is surely inhospitable to woman's separate reality.

For our present purposes, what is essential about Freud's drive formulation is its turning inside the self-contained individual to discover the mainsprings of human thought and action. We learn that if we want to know why people behave as they do, we must seek our answers somewhere within the play between their inner drives and the external world. Psychological structures emerge as the individual fights to balance instinct against society, orchestrated by an ego seeking to adjudicate these competing claims between the biological and the social.

But it is not only the individual whose behavior is to be understood by probing deeply within the psyche. All social life is transformed into an arena within which intrapsychic battles are played out. Marx gives us conflicts between classes with competing economic interests. Freud transforms those external conflicts between groups into intrapsychic conflicts within individuals.

How well I remember a Freudian interpretation offered by a Berkeley professor during the 1960s, as he explained the student revolt in terms of students' unresolved Oedipal conflicts with their fathers! In his view, protestors were taking out their inner conflicts with parental authority by acting against the authority represented by the University. It was as though there were no legitimate problems with the University; it only symbolized protestors' unresolved Oedipal conflicts with the real source of their troubles, their fathers. No wonder Freud's ideas eventually found a home in those societies whose preferred mode of dealing with social problems involved transmuting the social and economic roots of dissatisfaction and protest into intrapsychic conflicts.

Freudian interpretations have become so much a part of our everyday cultural landscape that we employ his terms and his framework of analysis as though they were part of our second nature. We accuse our adversary of being *too defensive*. We tell our friends that they are *projecting*. We are caught by our own *rationalizations*. We treat *dreams* as a secret code, the breaking of which will reveal all that is really going on inside ourselves and others.

Moscovici's (1976, 1984) classic work provides ample confirmation for this widespread use of Freudianisms – in this case, in French society. He reports for example, the relatively large percentage of people who employed Freudian conceptions when they examined features of their everyday lives. In these and numerous other ways, we have adopted the psychoanalytic world-view as our own, treating people as though they were really composed of all these inner mechanisms and processes of which Freud so eloquently wrote.

If the first piece of Freud's classic model looks inward for the answers to his questions, thereby celebrating the self, the second piece involves his treatment of the self–other relationship. Freud's group psychology and his development of the concept of the "stimulus barrier" offer us an especially helpful insight into his view of this relationship.

Freud was somewhat ambivalent about the role that others played in the individual's life. On the one hand, he was aware of the importance of others for the life and wellbeing of the individual, suggesting that because of this key role, "from the very first individual psychology . . . is at the same time social psychology as well" (1921/1960, p. 3). On the other hand, Freud was also profoundly influenced by Le Bon's (1895/1960) less than praiseworthy account of the effects of crowds in transforming the individual from critical thinker to something primitive and childlike.

Freud's Group Psychology

How often have we become so caught up in some activity that we literally lose ourselves in the process? In quiet moments of later reflection, we wonder what happened to us: "It's not like me to have acted in that way; I'm not sure what got into me." Our sense is that there is a real me that normally behaves in a proper manner and a me that is somehow transformed by the process that caught us in its seductive snare. For example, after a football game when our team pulls out a miraculous victory in the final two seconds, we join with the crowd in surging onto the field, tearing down the goalposts and acting in an uncharacteristically rowdy

manner. "Who was that person?", we wonder, "That's not at all like me."
This is the view that Freud confronted in considering Le Bon's description:

> Whoever be the individuals that compose it, however like or unlike be their
> mode of life, their occupations, their character, or their intelligence, the fact
> that they have been transformed into a crowd puts them in possession of a
> sort of collective mind which makes them feel, think, and act in a manner
> quite different from that in which each individual of them would feel, think,
> and act were he in a state of isolation. (Le Bon, 1985/1960, p. 27)

Le Bon did not view this transformation in a positive light. Individuals in a
crowd lost all that defined their individuality. They took on:

> the special characteristics of crowds . . . such as impulsiveness, irritability,
> incapacity to reason, the absence of judgment and of the critical spirit, the
> exaggeration of the sentiments . . . [qualities] which are almost always
> observed in beings belonging to inferior forms of evolution – in women,
> savages, and children, for instance. (pp. 35–6)

Le Bon leaves little doubt about the relationship between the individual
and the collective. The more the collective rules, the less the self can exist.
Each self is diminished and loses some of its finest essence when it is
caught up in the crowd. Nor does Le Bon leave any doubt about his view of
women's normal state, which for him is equivalent to the lost individuality
that men experience only in a crowd. I will shortly have more to say about
Freud's views in this regard.

Later theorists of collective life and group behavior (e.g. Lewin, Tajfel,
Turner, Sherif) did not adopt the Le Bon view that so profoundly
influenced Freud. For these theorists, groups offered a more inclusive
basis for the individual's own identity and so did not provide the same
negative self–other relationship that appears in the Le Bon–Freud
formulation.[3]

In short, although we need not invariably view individual–group relations
in such threatening terms, nor render the group the individual's other, this
is the feature that seems to have most impressed Freud. In his analysis,
then, groups could all too readily become the threatening other. And so
Freud advanced a view in which groups sapped individuality and our task
was to figure out how to retain or restore this lost individuality:

> The problem consists in how to procure for the group precisely those
> features which were characteristic of the individual and which are exting-
> uished in him by the formation of the group . . . we thus recognize that the
> aim is to equip the group with attributes of the individual. (Freud,
> 1921/1960, p. 25)

Although Freud mentions this task and even lists several modern-sounding ideas about what those helpful characteristics should be (e.g. some continuity in the life of the group; intergroup processes of rivalry; the development of group traditions, and so forth), the preponderance of his ideas details just how it is that the individuality he so esteems is lost by the formation of this crowd–group–other.

Le Bon's description made it clear to Freud that something dramatic happened to individuals who became invested in the otherness of a group. The principle that lay at the heart of Le Bon's account struck Freud as consistent with his own hydraulic view of the energies driving all human thought and behavior.

According to Freud's hydraulic metaphor, each individual has a set amount of attachment, love or sexual energy, termed libido. This energy could be invested in various ways, but because its quantity was limited, if it were invested in others, there would be less available for the self, and vice versa. In other words, Freud's hydraulic metaphor describes a negative self–other relationship and the other's potential danger to the self: the more invested in the other, the less available for the self.

Freud saw the important role that libido played in the transformation of individuals who became bonded together in groups. The essence of group formation, according to Freud, involved the libidinal investment by each individual member of the group in a central figure, the leader. And on the basis of these commonly shared investments in the same figure, each member became invested in the other members. The Church offered Freud one illustration of this dual investment, as members became bonded together as brothers in Christ. That is, their shared investment in Christ formed the basis for their shared investment in one another.

The dramatic changes to the individual in a group occurred because of these two separate but related libidinal investments. The first was the investment of each individual's libido in the leader; the second, the investment of each individual's libido in others who had taken the same leader as their object of attachment. Naturally, with these two investments of libido in others, the supply available for investment in the self was significantly reduced. No wonder then, reasoned Freud, that individuals were so dramatically changed in groups: they had given some key parts of themselves up to others.

Not content to rest his case, Freud pondered further aspects of this transformation of the individual who invests in others, finding a parallel with hypnosis: "There is the same humble subjection, the same compliance, the same absence of criticism towards the hypnotist as towards the loved object. There is the same sapping of the subject's own initiative" (1921/1960, p. 58). Once again there is little doubt about the relation between self and other that Freud posits: the more of the other, the less of the self. The self is "sapped" by the other; the self loses its individuality and its fine powers of reason and rationality to the other. The more of the other, the less of the self.

A close reading of Freud's work – including his view of group psychology but extending into his other writings as well – reveals the extent to which he truly fits the self-celebratory model so dominant in his times and in ours. The threatening "otherness" is not always to be found in groups or crowds, however; sometimes it dwells right within the individual's own desires. Freud's well-known formula "Where id was, ego shall be" communicates this idea, expressing the conviction that otherness – in this case, the otherness of the id – is dangerous.

Otherness of all sorts was seen as a danger to the integrity of the ego, the heart and soul of true individuality and of reason itself. The otherness of the id, with its surging impulses, threatened to overwhelm an ego ill prepared to protect itself from this inner onslaught. But the otherness of the world, of reality, of other people and of groups, also threatened to overwhelm an unprotected and ill-prepared ego.

Although Freud's group psychology does not take up the issue of sex differences contained in Le Bon's description (quoted above), it seems clear in much of what Freud wrote that he considered the world primarily from the perspective of the male gaze introduced in Chapter 1. Nowhere is this more apparent than in his understanding of just whose ego integrity is to be protected from being lost to "otherness". This "who", of course, was the man; woman had already been lost to otherness and was undoubtedly the underlying model for otherness itself.

In *Moses and Monotheism*, for example, Freud distinguishes between two forms of knowing – one that is in "bondage to the senses" (Freud, 1939, p. 147); the other that involves "the so-called higher intellectual processes" (p. 150). He attributes the former to woman and the latter to man. He argues that whereas maternity is always readily known directly through the senses, paternity requires inference and deduction. Freud sees the historical movement from direct sensory perception to higher mental processes as an advance that describes the movement of world history – revealed, for example, in the shift from a mother-religion to a father-religion.

The complexities of Freud's reasoning need not concern us here. Rather, his message linking woman with inferior mental processes suggests that he might very well agree with Le Bon's description of men-in-crowds, and with the idea that it is men's individuality and fine mental functioning that are lost in groups. It is already too late for woman, for whom any hope of individuality has already been compromised by her bondage to more concrete and immediate sensory processes. I do not think it unreasonable, therefore, to suggest that in Freud's view, "otherness" is primarily a threat to men. Women are already sufficiently suffused by otherness to be beyond concern.

The Stimulus Barrier

In a valuable paper published in 1968, Robert Martin discussed Freud's concept of the "stimulus barrier". In Freud's view, if the organism were not provided with a protective shield against stimuli impinging on it from the surrounding world, it would literally be killed: "*Protection against* stimuli is an almost more important function for the living organism than *reception of stimuli*" (Freud, 1920/1959, p. 53; original emphasis).

I can think of few other statements that convey in such a striking manner the threat to the individual that otherness provides – in this case, the not-me otherness of the external world. But Freud had still more to say, commenting: "The main purpose of the *reception* of stimuli is to discover the direction and nature of the external stimuli; and for that it is enough to take small specimens of the external world, to sample it in small quantities" (p. 53). In other words, otherness in small doses is safe; too much, however, and we are in serious danger.

Martin suggests that this protective shield changes its form as the person develops from infancy to adult maturity, arguing that the person's "own active ego processes" (1968, p. 482) represent that essential shield for the mature adult. Martin intends us to see ego processes such as attention, memory and concept formation, for example, serving a protective role in a manner that, a decade later, Anthony Greenwald (1980) would describe in equally laudatory terms as the *totalitarian ego*: an ego designed to distort reality in order "to protect the integrity of ego's organization of knowledge" (Greenwald, 1980, p. 613).

For Freud, as with Martin and Greenwald, the world-as-other is clearly dangerous, threatening to break through the barriers and shields we erect to preserve our integrity against its onslaughts. We – or at least some of us – are designed, it would seem, to protect ourselves from otherness, for only in this manner can our individual autonomy and integrity be maintained.

These accounts clearly portray a principle in which the integrity of the individual requires protection from the other. The other's role is potentially dangerous and threatening, never quite the very source of our being that will appear later when we enter the world of dialogism. As both Martin's and Greenwald's versions attest, the self-celebratory, other-suppressing view is not unique to Freud, or to his time and place. As we noted in Chapter 3, it expresses a basic belief that many of us have learned and practice even today. We act on the belief that our own integrity and autonomy as individuals requires that we be vigilant lest we become overwhelmed by the ever-threatening otherness around us.

Object Relations: The Interpersonal Turn

If Freud's world was best characterized by a story of biological drives battling society's civilizing imperatives, a somewhat different story emerged in the late 1930s. Rather than biology fighting against society, the new story line told of interpersonal dilemmas, of one social being trying to live among other social beings.

In other words, human relations rather than biological relations moved to the forefront. While people might indeed still be doing battle with their inner biological impulses, what seemed increasingly significant about the human predicament lay elsewhere: other people, not our biology, were the source of our problems. First presented in Paris in May 1944, Jean-Paul Sartre's play *Huis clos* (*No Exit*) said it all: hell is other people!

None of what I have said about this change means that new and exciting discoveries about human nature awakened society to a suddenly transformed understanding. Rather, encounters with diverse cultures and a growing disenchantment with the pessimism of biological theories suggested that any approach that saw human problems as the outcome of battles between biology and society held less appeal than theories arguing that human problems resulted from deficient human relations. We might not be able to change our biology (not, at least, in the 1930s and 1940s), but surely we could learn how to change our interpersonal relations. Thus changing human relations rather than managing one's inner drives became the new focus of understanding and "treatment" – especially within the American analytic establishment.

Interpersonal theories in psychoanalysis entered in earnest in the late 1930s, telling us that if we are in trouble as adults, it is because of disturbed early relationships with significant others in our lives. The parental and care-taker burden had shifted. While the Freudian parent could help the child's biology learn to lose gracefully to societal imperatives, the interpersonal parent faced a far more demanding task. After all, the parents' relationship to one another and to their child can leave either lasting scars or symbols of good mental health. Dr Spock's advice about parenting was but one of numerous works designed to tell us that people mess one another up; therefore people must learn how to behave towards one another in less destructive ways.

Despite the fact that modern technology and medical science have given a new optimism to the biological-based theories of transformation – hinting at once unthought-of possibilities for reconstituting a person's so-called basic drives and impulses – the main message of the interpersonal thesis seems more attractive than ever. The number of self-help guidebooks has increased enormously, as has the number of mental health practitioners who are primarily involved in helping people learn how to get along better with the people in their lives rather than helping them to manage their unruly drives (see Cushman, 1991, for a historical overview).

But how has this turn to the interpersonal world fared in terms of the self-celebratory cultural theme? On first reading, it would appear that at long last the other has been restored to a central place in psychology's scheme of understanding. Alas, this is not the result. Interpersonal approaches to understanding human nature did indeed give an initial tilt towards the other, but primarily in order to view the other as an impediment to personal health rather than the kind of co-creator that appears in the dialogic formulation (see Part III).

Furthermore, most interpersonal theories treat the other as a part of the backdrop scenery against which the main performers' actions are played out. The actual other is less relevant than the other as constructed by the individual's own inner needs and wishes. The other becomes a figure created by the mind of the individual. Therefore, it is into that individual's mind we must probe if we wish to fathom human nature at its best and at its worst.

Greenberg and Mitchell's (1983) account clearly reveals this self-celebratory position. First, they observe that the one element that ties together all psychoanalytic theories, whether drive or relational, is their insistence on "enduring, characteristic patterns and functions that typify the individual personality" (p. 20). Obviously, therefore, in order to achieve our understanding, we must probe deeply within the individual's psychic structures.

Secondly, the majority of interpersonal theories, say Greenberg and Mitchell, continue to emphasize for their therapeutic practice the restructuring of events inside the individual which have gone sour. Surely, this continues the self-celebratory themes that dominate the entire Western project. And just as surely, given the interpersonal basis of that "sourness", the other always enters our lives as a potential danger. Ideal others are fine, but the typical other is the source of all our difficulties.

And so, in both the original Freudian drive theories and in the revisionist interpersonal theories of psychoanalysis, we find a continuation of the self-celebratory themes that have become the hallmark of Western understanding. Although drive and relational theories differ, even rather markedly, with respect to what is important to know about the individual's insides, they both continue to insist that knowing the insides of the self-contained individual is vital for anyone who wishes to figure out human nature. And in most respects, they both cast a mighty suspicious eye at the other and its role in our lives.

Lacan

It has never been my intention to unfold the entire, complex and varied story of the psychodynamic approaches, in order to find either yet one more version that confirms my thesis, or – in the case of Lacan (1973/1981) – an approach that on first reading appears to offer an important counter-example. It is relevant, however, for us to pause *briefly* at this point to consider Lacan's contributions, but especially some doubts raised about them. Pausing only briefly will undoubtedly rankle with those for whom Lacan is not only – in Sherry Turkle's (1978) terms – the French Freud, but someone who many consider to be the most significant figure in psychoanalytic circles since Freud.[4] In being brief about Lacan, however, I am being even briefer – to the point of extinction – about other French and European variants on Lacan and Freud, as well as some recent American approaches that lie very close to – and indeed, even on – my own family tree.[5]

Disregarding for the moment all the features of controversy immediately encountered once one turns to an examination of Lacan's contributions – as much a function of his personal style as of his ideas – it is clear that Lacan's rediscovery of the classic Freud and his firm rejection of the Americanization of Freud's original ideas, his turn to language and discourse, and his granting a central role to the other, would lead us to presume that he must be an exception to my self-celebratory critique of the psychoanalytic model. Lacan's challenge to the wholeness and integrity of the subject (the ego) and his insistence that there is no neat line between individual and other – because otherness inhabits and constitutes the individual – locate him within the postmodern movement, in which the other plays a significant role, while distancing him from those self-celebratory, primarily American, views in which the subject's integrity, wholeness and distinct separateness remain central.

What is less clear about Lacan, however, centers around the issues raised especially by one of the most radical of French feminists, Luce Irigaray (1974/1985, 1977/1985; also Whitford, 1991), and implied at least by the differential treatment that Lacan and Toni Morrison have given to the writings of Edgar Allan Poe. If we are truly dealing with a theorist of the other, as an initial reading of Lacan would suggest, then why the severe break with Irigaray over the failure to deal adequately with woman in Lacan's still-patriarchal theory? And why the choice of Poe to illustrate

Lacan's approach, when Poe is among those cited by Morrison as representing one of the most important writers on American-Africanism?[6] In other words, here is a theorist who seems to celebrate the self less than the other, yet who, when that other is truly other (i.e. truly other than white and male), appears, in fact, to be celebrating the self!

Irigaray not only broke from Lacan but was ushered out of the Lacanian circles and institutes, even as Lacan himself had been ushered out of the strict psychoanalytic circles of which he once held membership. In each case, the challenge was too much for the disciples to take. Irigaray developed a scathing critique of Lacan's insistence on the patriarchal order of language, while affirming the female specificity that Lacan's writings had ignored.

Irigaray's important paper "The poverty of psychoanalysis" (in Whitford, 1991), for example, sets forth her blistering critique of how Lacanianism continues a tradition of "phallonarcissism" (her term), with its nonrecognition of woman's specificity. Irigaray accuses Lacan of failing to deal with the cultural and historical tradition of patriarchy in which his own works fall, even while he claims to reflect a sociocultural psychoanalytic doctrine. And she accuses him of melting down woman's otherness into the sameness of the male world-view:

> we do have to question . . . the imposition of formations which correspond to the requirements or desires of one sex as the norms of discourse and, in more general terms, of language . . . your would-be universal only meets the requirements of *your* sex. And as they are *yours*, you fail to see their particularity. You reject any inside or outside which resists, and would rather accuse the other of all kinds of idiocies than undergo what you call . . . symbolic castration: the possibility of an order that is different to yours. (p. 96)

Even more pointedly:

> Whatever you may think, women do not need to go through the looking-glass to know that mother and daughter have a body of the same sex. All they have to do is touch one another, listen to one another, smell one another, see one another – without necessarily privileging the gaze . . . without submitting to a libidinal economy which means that the body has to be covered with a veil if it is to be desirable! But these two women cannot speak to each other of their affects in the existing verbal code, and they cannot even imagine them in the ruling systems of representations. . . . The girl's earliest pleasures will remain wordless. . . . When a girl begins to talk, she is already unable to speak of/to herself. (p. 101)

Lacan's view of psychoanalysis locates the defining moment in the "desire of the analyst" – in this case the desire of Freud, the founding analyst. I found myself wondering what part of that foundation is male because of the desire of Freud's own male sex. What would Lacan say, for example, if Freud had been a woman, and thus the founding moment were based on woman's rather than man's desires? Similarly, elsewhere in his writings, Lacan repeatedly employs a visual metaphor, referring to a *scopic drive*, the desire of seeing, scopic satisfaction, and so forth. Again, I wondered how much this metaphor reflected the male gaze, thereby deleting woman's possibly less visual relationships to the world.

My point is that if we grant a certain reasonableness to Irigaray's critique of Lacan (as I believe we must), how can we hold up Lacan's theory as a genuine celebration of the other? It seems to me that his is a celebration of the self returning to the selfsame.

Much the same problem emerges when we compare the Lacanian interpretation of Poe's "Purloined Letter" (see Kurzweil, 1980), which he employs to demonstrate his own theory at work, with Morrison's consideration of Poe's tendency to silence the African-American presence (points I considered in Chapter 1). It would appear that once again we have an instance of a Lacanian approach that, while paying lip service to the other, fails to deal with genuine otherness when that otherness is other than himself – that is, other than white and male. Therefore, this is hardly a body of material to be included high up in our list of psychoanalytic views that are beyond the self-celebratory stance which, I have suggested, is reflected in the other analytic approaches as well.

Behaviorism

It is generally recognized that there are four major traditions that describe psychology's attempts to make sense out of the complexities of human nature: behaviorism, psychoanalysis, humanistic psychology, and cognitivism. Of these four traditions, the behaviorist is the only one that eschews searching within the individual's interior in order to understand human nature. While behaviorism for the most part successfully resisted the inward focus that the other three traditions share, it joins with them in placing its bets squarely on the shoulders of the self-contained individual.

Behaviorism resisted looking inward primarily in order to avoid becoming a nonscientific, speculative enterprise. In the founding paper, for example, John Watson (1913) proclaimed:

> Psychology as the behaviorist views it is a purely objective experimental branch of natural science. Its theoretical goal is the prediction and control of behavior. Introspection forms no essential part of its methods, nor is the scientific value of its data dependent upon the readiness with which they lend themselves to interpretation in terms of consciousness. (p. 158)

Behaviorism did not reject the possibility that events hidden inside the black box of the individual's psyche might be important, but rather insisted that because we could not conduct our inward probe scientifically, such approaches must be abandoned in favor of "objective" research. No less a behaviorist than B.F. Skinner (1989), for example, argued:

> there are two unavoidable gaps in any behavioral account: one between the stimulating action of the environment and the response of the organism, and one between consequences and the resulting change in behavior. Only brain science can fill those gaps. (p. 18)

In this passage, Skinner clearly implies that we need some information about inner processes if our accounts are to be complete.

Although behaviorism itself declines to probe deeply inside the organism's interior, it continues to assume that whatever the process is that joins an observable stimulus with an equally observable response, it occurs *within* the self-contained, individual organism. Thus behaviorism, while it does not posit concepts within the individual, insists, like the other major traditions of psychological inquiry, on the individual as the focus of its study and the source of its major principles.

On the other hand, Skinner (1989) also tells us that "Human behavior will eventually be explained (as it can only be explained) by the cooperative action of ethology, brain science and behavior analysis" (p. 18). This passage seems to suggest that Skinner may be an exception to the self-celebratory claim; it would appear that his form of behaviorism recognizes the importance of factors beyond the stimulus–response connections made within the individual's brain. He refers to these as *ethological* and includes concerns with the patterns of reinforcement, for example, that characterize a given culture.

Furthermore, in his ongoing debate against cognitivism's inward turn, Skinner insisted that "No account of what is happening inside the human body, no matter how complete, will explain the origins of human behavior" (p. 18), using a clock to illustrate his point. He says that no matter how much we may look inside a clock to study its mechanisms, we will never understand why keeping time matters; this can be answered only by examining the culture and its concerns.

This cultural turn would seem to whittle away at the self-celebratory point of view by suggesting that we must look beyond the individual and towards cultural contingencies for any real understanding. Yet on two counts, and despite its potential for breaking the self-celebratory spell, Skinner's behaviorism fails to move us beyond the self-celebratory stance that dominates current psychological understanding.

In the first place, because Skinner takes an uncritical view of the cultural contingencies of reinforcement of which he speaks, he must of necessity

accept our culture's self-celebratory schedule of reinforcement as establishing those contingencies. And so, Skinner leads us beyond the individual
only to return us back again to that same social character.

In other words, if we accept our current culture's framework of
understanding and argue that this provides the reinforcement contingencies
central to Skinner's account; and if those contingencies are built upon the
assumption of the self-contained individual as the source of all understanding, then Skinner's behaviorism can say all it wants to say about things
beyond the individual that must be considered. Given the individualistic
cultural contingencies that drive his entire theory, those other things of
which he speaks must remain mute.

In the second place, Skinner's behaviorism eliminates the interplay
between person and other that is not only central to dialogism (as we will
see in Parts III and IV) but is also essential to any theory that hopes to get
beyond the self-celebratory position and celebrate the other as well.
Skinner's person has no transactions with the other beyond those involved
in receiving inputs from the other (e.g. from the environment) which are
then acted upon in a rather mechanical manner. The mutual modifications
of a self and other who join together in creating the social world in terms of
which they operate are not part of the Skinnerian account – nor, for that
matter, of most other behavioral accounts. Rather, we are treated to a
person who simply receives inputs and renders outputs. Once again,
however much we may talk about the important role of culture in shaping
an individual's behavior, we remain fully centered on the self-contained
individual, and our posture remains fully self-celebratory.[7]

The Humanistic Movement in Psychology

> Psychology today is torn and riven, and may in fact be said to be three (or
> more) separate ... sciences. ... First is the behavioristic, objectivistic,
> mechanistic, positivist group. Second is the whole cluster of psychologies that
> originated in Freud and in psychoanalysis. And third there are the
> humanistic psychologies, or the "Third Force". (Maslow, 1971, pp. 3–4)

With this statement, Abraham Maslow introduces us to psychology's third
force, humanism, and its distinctive new challenge to psychological inquiry.
What humanism did not challenge, however – and, indeed, often took to its
farthest extremes – was its celebration of the self.

Perls, Hefferline and Goodman's (1951) classic work on Gestalt therapy
offers us a helpful illustration of some humanistic psychologists' concerns.
First, they tell us that self-discovery is the central process of our lives as
well as of their therapeutic program: "It involves the adoption of a rather

special attitude toward your self and observation of your self in action"
(p. 3).

We are next informed that most of our problems stem from the fact that
we rejected troublesome parts of our selves at an early age, leaving us
somewhat like the animal whose leg has been caught in a trap and who
gnaws off his leg – which, like the rejected self, menaces his life – only to
"spend the rest of his life a cripple" (p. 4). Unlike that animal, however, we
can be salvaged by systematically exploring that rejected part of our selves
that once menaced our lives, and reconstructing it in terms of a more
healthful present situation.

Finally, we are told of the therapeutic goal:

> we state some instructions by means of which . . . you may launch yourself on
> a progressive personal adventure wherein, by your own active efforts, you
> may do something for your self – namely, discover it, organize it and put it to
> constructive use in the living of your life. (p. 4)

Few of us would find fault with this advice, or question its reasonableness.
After all, why shouldn't we try to discover our selves? What is wrong with
learning to reconstruct a damaged and distorted self? If I don't look out for
number one, then who will? And if I'm a mess, then how can I ever be
available to you?

If this is carried to extremes, however, as it was in many cases, we end
up with an interpersonal policy of *laissez-faire*. Each individual does her or
his own thing, caring little for others. "I do my thing and you do your
thing. I am not in this world to live up to your expectations, and you are not
in this world to live up to mine. You are you and I am I; if by chance we
find each other, it's beautiful. If not, it can't be helped."[8]

But even short of these extremes, it is apparent that the humanistic
program is oriented around the individual's own self. It is not clear how
others are relevant, except as early traps that caused all the grief in the first
place or as current therapeutic aides who will assist in the process of
self-discovery. Humanism did little to transform the cultural agenda with
its celebration of the self; indeed, that agenda became its own.

Many in the humanistic tradition argued that people were basically good.
They were not filled with dark and dirty biological drives that needed to be
controlled. Freud's moralistic warnings were replaced with a genuine
openness to people's innate goodness. If we just let them be, people will be
good. The trick, of course, is just letting people be so that their good can
emerge. And so humanistic psychologists encouraged people to break free
from the bonds of their past, look deeply within themselves and let their
healthy child out into the world: only good could come of this.

Self-actualization became a leading idea (e.g. Maslow, 1971). Human needs were said to be arranged hierarchically, in a kind of pyramid: physiological needs at the bottom and self-actualization at the top, with stops along the way to deal with matters of security, belonging and self-esteem. In the primarily Western, white and affluent world to which most of their work was implicitly addressed, adherents of the humanistic movement felt that the higher needs – but especially self-actualization – had been denied expression for much too long. To self-actualize meant to realize one's own potential as a human being: to continue to explore, develop and grow; to be creative and enlarge one's currently restricted range of opportunities.

Linking Eastern religion and philosophy with the Western way of self-contained individualism produced a formula in which the individual's ego seemed to stand in the way of achieving a fully actualized self. If Freud's formula for health urged us to tame the id with the rational forces of the ego, the humanistic movement called for something akin to reducing the ego's stranglehold so that the healthful id could find expression.

Locating this message in a collectivistic culture might not prove as disruptive to sustaining a concern with others as locating it in a society that was already heavily self-oriented and focused around its primary protagonist, the self-contained individual (see Bellah *et al.*, 1985). In this latter case, the excesses of humanism's self-celebratory program went wildly astray, edging into and well beyond anyone's most narcissistic fantasies.

The humanistic movement offered a way of living for people who had the luxury of time and money to explore their own personal world and to find their way through the complex and constraining mazes of modern life. It gave people permission to challenge authority, to ignore others and to discover their inner self unhampered by others or by society.

I can think of few other theories of human nature that have been so self-celebratory as those driven by the humanistic tradition in psychology. Not only does the self and its personal development take center stage, but the other becomes a mere prop designed for little more than the growth and pleasuring of the protagonist's self.

While the African-American population was listening to Martin Luther King Junior's call to be "free at last, free at last", the humanistic movement also led its cheers on behalf of becoming "free at last, free at last". The words may have been the same, but the aims could hardly be more different. One group was trying to rise up to full citizenship and respect after decades of oppression, and joined together in a genuinely cooperative movement of mutual caring and aid. The other group, already living at the top, still felt empty and so found appeal in a message that gave each one of them, on his or her own and without much consideration for anyone else, permission to probe their insides, discover their real selves and express everything that was truly theirs: a genuinely Dionysian feast for the self.

The Cognitive Revolution

However much the terms of psychoanalysis have infiltrated our everyday vocabulary to become part of our second nature, and however attractive and familiar humanism's appeal, the real story of scientific psychology today is told in terms of the cognitive revolution.[9] Our everyday experience is of a world that is organized, coherent and meaningful. Things appear to us not as meaningless bits and pieces of random motion, but as meaningful patterns of activity. We see items of furniture, not molecules in motion. We see words, not simply chains of letters. We process information, solve problems, act intelligently. But what is the source of this order, meaning and intelligent behavior? The cognitivist's answer: the individual's mind – often, the individual's brain. In Chapter 9, I revise my harsh judgment regarding cognitivism's narrowness by contrasting the conventional account presented in this chapter with the newer sociocultural bent of some other work in the cognitivist tradition.

Gardner's account of the early history of the cognitive revolution places great weight on a conference held in 1948 at the California Institute of Technology, and an especially "memorable" address by the psychologist Karl Lashley. Arguing against the still dominant tide of behaviorism, Lashley insisted that human behavior did not simply unfold in an orderly way because it was under the control of external stimuli; rather, these stimuli themselves were organized in terms of central brain processes: "to put it simply, Lashley concluded that the form precedes and determines specific behavior; rather than being imposed from without, organization emanates from within the organism" (Gardner, 1985, p. 13). Thus was launched the cognitive revolution and its search within the individual's mind for those organizing structures and principles.

Equally memorable, however, was the computer revolution and the new mental metaphor it made possible. The human mind was said to be like a computer, processing the information it received from the world according to its inner structures and principles of operation (e.g. its programs), cranking out the organized and meaningful world in which we live. Our task, then, is to probe the mind's interior to determine its structures and principles of operation.

Since its inception, the cognitive revolution has taken on many shapes and forms, almost defying us to find a common core:

> Rarely has a label so lacking in any clear referent as cognitive science risen so meteorically to the top level of visibility in psychology. . . . How can we characterize this broad field? . . . In one direction are formal investigations of the abstract properties of computational systems that are basic to all intelligent behavior. In another are experimental studies of human observers

detecting signals of millisecond duration. . . . In yet another . . . are analyses
of verbal communications to find the rules whereby people resolve ambi-
guities in language. . . . The common core of these diverse enterprises may
be taken to be the task of understanding intelligence and intelligent behavior
. . . [and] how the constituents of intelligent function have evolved in the
human mind, the limits they set on possible achievement, and the possibilities that are open to improvement. (Estes, 1991, p. 282)

The author of this passage, William K. Estes, goes on to chart further
details of the subject matter of the new cognitive science, including
research "on computer and cognitive architectures, sensory information
and natural language processing, learning, expert systems, and applications
to science and mathematics education" (p. 282). Even a cursory consideration reveals that the cognitive revolution marks a dominant focus within
psychological theory and research, spreading its influence so extensively
that it has become the model of choice for understanding most aspects of
human experience and behavior.

For my own purposes in claiming that the cognitive revolution has not
fundamentally challenged the Western project's self-celebratory stance but,
indeed, has sought only to refine and extend its reach, cognitivism's
common core involves its continuing search inside the individual for the
answers we seek about human nature. What will we find when we look
inside? Mental processes that "work on" and process the outside material.
How do these internal mental processes operate? Look at the computer and
find an information-processing device that will serve as a perfect model of
the human mind.[10]

It is no mere coincidence that the cognitive revolution and the computer
revolution have evolved together and formed a happy partnership. Science
is often guided by dominating metaphors. Here is a piece of machinery that
functions in a manner similar to the way the mind operates. It is too
tempting not first to see the computer as like the mind, and next to treat
the mind as though it were a complex computer. Newton's world was
likened to a giant mechanical clock. The cognitive revolution gave us a
human world likened to a giant computer.

Selecting the computer as the metaphor for the human mind has had
some rather striking consequences, not the least of which is its removal of
the knower's sex and other specificities from any relevance, thereby
virtually keeping in place the very kinds of domination to which I referred
in Chapter 1. The computer metaphor provides us with a disembodied
view of human intelligence and mental functioning (see Dreyfus and
Dreyfus, 1987). I will return to this point later in this chapter.

In its inception and for the most part even today – with some striking
exceptions which I will consider in later chapters – cognitive science has
operated in a somewhat purist manner. Even though people are obviously

not only mind but also body and feeling, and even though people are also obviously social beings living their lives with others in particular social worlds, none of this was said to be fundamental to cognitivism's real task: to discover how the mind-in-itself operated.[11] The emphasis was on the mind removed and abstracted from everything else, as though its essential operations could be studied only in this pure manner. In this, cognitivism simply followed the dictates of every experimental science in which the thing to be studied is first isolated in order to study it and only later restored to its place in the world.

For example, while noting that both social and historical factors undoubtedly do play an important role in human life, Gardner (1985) tells us that addressing these factors at this time would "unnecessarily complicate the cognitive-scientific enterprise" (p. 6). His "own view is that there is a heartland of cognition which can be accounted for on its own terms, without necessary reference to (or reliance upon) these other, undoubtedly important elements" (p. 388). This view is echoed by numerous other cognitive scientists (see Bowers, 1991, for a critical summary).

Cognitive scientists dispense with the social world in a variety of different ways. Listen as one cognitivist comments that "In the final analysis, cognition cannot be understood separately from perception and motor systems. Human cognition only makes sense in the context of a physical world, which shaped its evolution and shapes each phenotype" (Lindsay, 1991, p. 299). While I do not take exception to this statement's recognition that we live in a physical world, the equally important fact that people also live their lives in a social world is ignored; the story of human cognition is treated as though it could be understood merely by seeing how a computational mind operates in a physical universe.

While making no mention either of the physical or the social world, another cognitive scientist affirms my point about its purism. We are told that while critics have complained about the lack of ecological validity in much of the laboratory work in cognitive science, "it should be clear . . . that we are seeking laws to describe regularities in nature, not just ecologically valid experiments" (Massaro, 1991, p. 303). Massaro continues: "The fact that these laws might only be revealed in well controlled, artificial laboratory situations does not make them irrelevant to explanations of everyday life. The laws will help us describe, simulate, and understand complex natural phenomena."

These are all familiar-sounding assumptions: a thing-in-itself, such as a mind, has an essential character that can be determined only by studying it in its pure form, isolated from everything else that might cloud its true essence. A corollary assumption is that when this isolated essence is returned to its "normal" world, nothing fundamental will have been changed. That is, what we learn by examining the mind in isolation is in no way changed once that mind returns to a human body living in the social world.

As it turns out, however – and as we will see in Part III – these are very questionable assumptions. What is learned about the way the mind works when it has been removed from its everyday world may give us little information about the way the mind actually works when it is in its everyday world.[12] Undaunted, however, a great deal of cognitive psychology still continues to seek the fundamental structures that describe the human mind and its basic operations.

Although cognitive science does not have the same enchantment with the self and its actualization that characterizes humanism, nor share psychoanalysis's attachment to the mysteries of unconscious drives, nor follow behaviorism's rejection of any look inward, it shares the same self-celebratory framework that marks nearly every scientific as well as common-sense cultural endeavor. Cognitivism's hero is the self-contained individual within whose mind we will find secreted the main story line of human nature. Cognitivism's attention is drawn fully to the abstracted, disembodied, detached person-as-mind: our old standby, the self-contained individual, probing its insides and neglecting anything or anyone else.

This failure to take cognizance of "the other" appears very clearly in several key places. One example has been noted by Jerome Bruner (1990), who comments on "the computational mind" as seen by cognitive science: "The system that does all of these things is blind with respect to whether what is stored is words from Shakespeare's sonnets or numbers from a random number table" (p. 4). To put it simply: a computer word-processing program operates in the same manner whether we are using it to write a novel, a poem, an equation or a memo to our boss. If the mind operates like a computer, and if our task is to uncover the mind's programs, then it likewise matters little whether or not the structures and operations – the programs of our mind – are directing us to create a beautiful sonnet or a banal memo. In short, the particular characteristics of the other are of little or no interest to the monologic search within the self-contained individual that continues to dominate the cognitive tradition (see also Shweder, 1990, p. 19, point no. 1, on this).

But perhaps the most egregious problem appears in cognitive science's disembodied view of knowledge, a view that has only been intensified by its adoption of the computer metaphor. At least Freud saw the important role that the body played in shaping the human mind. And since bodies are sexed, one supposes that this might figure in the manner by which the embodied mind operates.

Cognitive science's reduction of the knower to a computer-like mind, however, deletes the body, sexed or otherwise, from the processes of knowing, thereby providing us with a bodyless and sexless picture of thinking and intelligent behavior. As I hope I made clear in Chapter 1, however, whenever we encounter an apparently sexless portrayal, we need to be on the lookout for its actually highly sex-specific nature: the world understood through the eyes of the male. In short, cognitive science's adoption of the computer metaphor does not make it blind to the content themes that Bruner addressed; nor, more significantly, in purporting to be sex-neutral (after all, what sex does a computer have?) is cognitive science truly gender-blind or neutral: it is implicitly male.

Although neither George Lakoff nor Mark Johnson focused on the sexual body in any way, their ideas – which we first encountered in Chapter 3 – are nevertheless central to the issue of embodiment versus disembodiment. In a manner consistent with my own view, both authors insist on an embodied view of all mental processes, with the title of Johnson's major work providing a telling illustration of just what is meant: *The Body in the Mind*. Both Johnson and Lakoff challenge the prevailing Cartesian understanding in cognitive science that still searches for contextless sources of knowledge: the God's-eye view from Nowhere about which Putnam has written; the point-of-viewlessness to which MacKinnon refers.

In challenging the Cartesian model of objectivism, Johnson comments:

> The body has been ignored by Objectivism because it has been thought to introduce subjective elements alleged to be irrelevant to the objective nature of meaning. The body has been ignored because reason has been thought to be abstract and transcendent, that is, not tied to any of the bodily aspects of human understanding. The body has been ignored because it seems to have no role in our reasoning about abstract subject matters. (Johnson, 1987, p. xiv)

Johnson argues, however – and Lakoff would agree – that "*any adequate account of meaning and rationality must give a central place to embodied and imaginative structures of understanding by which we grasp our world*" (Johnson, p. xiii; original emphasis). Both have set forth a rather compelling theoretical and empirical case to support their contentions and to demonstrate the incoherence of the disembodied view of intelligent human activity.

As I commented above, however, neither Johnson nor Lakoff deals with the sexed body; if they had, their argument, I believe, would only have become stronger and much more valuable. As it stands, however, by insisting that meaning does not involve the application of some algorithm or formula to material, but rather is an embodied act of interpretation and imagination, Johnson and Lakoff lead us far from the computer metaphor.

It is that metaphor which has proved so compelling to modern cognitive science, including some of the newest developments linking computers in parallel networks so as better to simulate the presumptively similar manner by which mental/neural networks operate. I am suggesting that such approaches lead cognitive science directly into the self-celebratory realm.

From the specific standpoint of the inherent sexism involved in adopting the computer metaphor, of course, we once again have an example of one form of human thinking typically associated with dominant white males – a form, however, that, as Johnson and Lakoff demonstrate, does not even make much sense for that group – being employed as though it were the normative form for all people. This silences women's specificity as well as the specificity of other forms of embodied, context-bound thinking. The self-celebration, then, appears not only in cognitive science's locating the primary source of our understanding of human nature somewhere within the abstract recesses and networks of the human mind–brain-as-computer, but also in its inability to come to terms with otherness itself: that is, with the role of the other, whether that other be one's own body or the actual body and experience of other human beings.

Where in cognitive science does the other enter, if at all? Either the other is part of the background, of little or no interest when the task is to discover things that are fundamental about the individual; or the reality of the other is thoroughly determined by the structures and operations of the individual's disembodied mind. Who or what the other actually is has become of little or no importance; the only role the other plays in cognitive science is to be a plastic medium shaped by the operations of the perceiver's mind. As one author has noted (Westen, 1991), this forms a special bond between cognitive science and the object-relations approaches in psychoanalysis: both are not actually interested in the other as such, but see the other to be relevant only as an object transformed by the mental operations of the individual who continues to be our most revered object of study.

Common-sense culture and scientific psychology join together in affirming a rather enduring and nearly unshakable Western tradition which teaches us that if we wish to understand human nature, we must understand the individual within whom human nature is housed. It should not be surprising, of course, to learn that psychology, the science that studies the individual, shares the culture's common-sense framing. A psychology that sought to cast our understanding differently would surely clash with common sense, and perhaps fade rapidly to extinction.

Fortunately, however, various changes in modern life have forced us to doubt our own way of framing human nature, creating a much more hospitable climate in which to challenge these time-honored beliefs. Alternatives to our individualistic, inwardly centered and self-celebratory ideas about where to find human nature are less likely to clash with today's views than they would have done even a decade or so ago. But before we unfold the details of this alternative view in Part III, we must take on an additional task: to lay bare the peculiarity of our own world-view.

Notes

1. I realize that I am close to embracing Foucault's (1979, 1980) perspective joining the human sciences, including psychology, with the societal agenda involving power and control. Although I find much merit in that view, I am not attempting to argue anything more elegant here than the simple recognition that a field such as psychology, with its focus on the self-contained individual, could not exist as we know it in a very differently organized society.
2. There are numerous primary and secondary sources dealing with Freud's original work, the writings of his disciples and the work of the revisionists, but I have found Greenberg and Mitchell's (1983) account an especially useful guide.
3. For example Lewin (1947a,b); Sherif and Sherif (1953); Tajfel (1978, 1982); Turner and Giles (1981).
4. See Lacan (1973/1981); Lemaire (1977); Turkle (1978).
5. The Sampson in Weiss and Sampson et al. (1986) is my brother! He and his associates have developed a control–mastery approach to psychoanalytic theory and practice which is currently receiving widespread recognition, especially among US analysts. I have also not dealt with Harry Stack Sullivan's (1953) interpersonal theory, which – again on the face of it – appears to be an exception to my allegations.
6. Although Lacan's paper dealt with Poe's story "The Purloined Letter" (see Kurzweil, 1980), a work that is not mentioned by Morrison (1992), Morrison does comment that "No early American writer is more important to the concept of American Africanism than Poe" (p. 32), suggesting a general support for my contentions about Lacan's treatment of the "real" other.
7. Although I will not develop the argument, it is unlikely that any non mediated account, such as behaviorism – at least in its more radical forms – can do more than affirm the prevailing forms of social organization.
8. This philosophy has been attributed to Perls, one of the central figures in early humanistic psychology. I resurrected the quoted passage from an unknown source deep within my Berkeley files from the 1960s.
9. See, for example, Gardner (1985); Osherson et al. (1990).
10. A major portion of the September 1991 issue of *Psychological Science* was devoted to reviewing the three-volume work on cognitive science edited by Osherson et al. (see Note 9 above). A consistent theme throughout that issue is the important role the computer has played in all these efforts to understand and to model the human mind.
11. Gardner (1985) was very insistent on this point, while others have been equally critical: Bowers (1991); Bruner (1990); Dunn (1984); Goodnow (1990); Johnson (1987); Lakoff (1987).
12. Several investigators have provided rather striking examples of this: see Lave (1988); Rogoff and Lave (1984); Wertsch (1991).

5

A Most Peculiar Self

Clifford Geertz (1979), a well-known anthropologist, helped to set the record straight. The self-contained individual that we in the West have come to know so well and assume to be the only real way to exist in this world, when examined on a worldwide basis, is, in Geertz's terms, *peculiar*. That is quite some indictment of our own civilization's sense of self. This is what Geertz had to say:

> The Western conception of the person as a bounded, unique, more or less integrated motivational and cognitive universe . . . organized into a distinctive whole and set contrastively both against other such wholes and against a social and natural background is, however incorrigible it may seem to us, a rather peculiar idea within the context of the world's cultures. (p. 229)

In other words, the self-contained individual, the West's current cultural protagonist and hero, is a *peculiar* figure, however familiar it may be to us.

Geertz does not stand alone in his view. Colin Morris (1972), a professor of medieval history, has referred to the current Western view as "an eccentricity among cultures" (p. 2). Morris's depiction of its eccentricity parallels Geertz's description of its peculiarity: "It is to us a matter of common sense that we stand apart from the natural order in which we are set, subjects over against its objectivity, and that we have our own distinct personality, beliefs, and attitude to life" (Morris, 1972, p. 1).

Morris's perspective as a historian has made him aware of the temporal distance that separates our contemporary view of the person, with its sharply drawn sense of individuality, from earlier understandings:

> The student of the Greek Fathers or of Hellenistic philosophy is likely to be made painfully aware of the difference between their starting-point and ours

... they had no equivalent to our concept "person", while their vocabulary was rich in words which express community of being. (p. 2)

Both the meaning of and basis for Geertz's and Morris's views will become clearer if we examine several illustrative examples. Although most of the initial illustrations are based on more exotic cultures such as those of India and the Pacific Islands, we will move from there into the heartland of the more industrialized world, including Europe, towards the end of this chapter.

Illustrative Examples

Research comparing the explanations that Hindus and Americans offer for various actions reveals a tendency for American explanations to adopt a more individualistic frame (J.G. Miller, 1984). For example, when one American was asked to describe a situation in which a deviant act had occurred, she talked about a neighbor who cheated on her income taxes. Asked to offer an explanation of why her neighbor cheated, she responded: "That's just the kind of person she is. She's very competitive" (Miller, p. 967). These explanations are individualistic, seeking something inside the self-contained individual that would account for the behavior in question – e.g. competitiveness.

A Hindu, by contrast, told of being cheated out of his money by an unscrupulous contractor and then explained that action by commenting on the man's social situation: "The man is unemployed. He is not in a position to give that money" (p. 968). Hindu responses were socially oriented, placing people in their social world and using social explanations – e.g. unemployment – for their behavior.

In interpreting these and other similar findings, Shweder and Bourne (1984) contrasted two cultural themes: *egocentrism* versus *sociocentrism*. In the egocentric world-view, the social world is subservient to the individual; society has been designed primarily to serve "the interests of some idealized autonomous, abstract individual existing free of society yet living in society" (p. 190). The contrasting sociocentric view "subordinates individual interests to the good of the collectivity" (p. 190).

Cross-cultural work comparing several Pacific Island cultures with middle-class American culture adds further to our understanding of the nature of the Western individualistic self and some of the conversational mechanisms by which it is constructed. Ochs (1988) compared Samoan care-takers' and American care-takers' efforts to socialize children. While American care-takers encouraged the development of an individualistic understanding of both self and other, the Samoans' efforts were directed towards helping the children learn how better to fit into their in-group.

Ochs examined what she termed, "clarification sequences" employed by care-takers when children uttered something unintelligible. American care-takers preferred a clarification style of *guessing* what the child must have meant: e.g. "Is it the cookie you want?". By contrast, Samoan care-takers who did not grasp the child's verbal utterances simply asked the child to say it again.

Ochs suggests that guessing supposes that there is some intention inside the child that it is the adult's responsibility to discover. Furthermore, guessing suggests that it is the role of care-takers to adjust their behavior to fit the needs of the child. In tending not to guess but to ask for a repeat of what was said, the Samoan care-takers communicate their cultural desire to see children learn to fit into the adult world rather than to adjust to fit children's needs. Here we see illustrated a conversational mechanism by which American and Samoan children are socialized into their culture's individualistic or collectivistic view. Americans learn that others are there to adjust to them and their needs; Samoans learn that it is their task to learn how to fit into their group.

Ochs's study revealed another interesting conversational mechanism by which the culture's individualistic or collectivistic ethos becomes inscribed in people. Apparently, Samoans engage in what is termed a *maaloo exchange*. In this, every commendable action that *we* might attribute to the individual who carries it out is met with a response by that individual suggesting how much the other has been responsible for it as well. For example, if I have done something well and you commend me for it, the maaloo exchange requires that I respond by recognizing your essential assistance in my successful performance. In other words, the *other-as-supporter* is central to Samoan understanding.

Ochs offers several examples. For instance, a driver does some especially skillful driving. The passenger, complimenting the driving, says: "Well done the steering", to which the driver responds: "Well done the support" (p. 199). Or, after a group of travelers return from a trip and are greeeted with a welcome home, the exchange might be: "Well done the trip", to which the returning travelers respond: "Well done the staying back" (p. 200). As Ochs suggests: "Any accomplishment can then be seen as a joint product of both the actors and the supporters. In the Samoan view, if a performance went well, it is the supporters' merit as much as the performers'" (p. 200).

But what happens when Samoan children are sent to a Western school? As most of us reared in such an environment know all too well, the concept of a supporter and the joint production of excellence is replaced with an emphasis on individual performance, individually achieved. Samoan children in the Western classroom learn to avoid the maaloo exchange and to individualize their understanding: "they learn to consider tasks as an individual's work and accomplishment" (Ochs, p. 208). They learn to dispense with their Samoan world-view and its notion of a supporter, joint accomplishment and the maaloo exchange, and to take on the attributes of a Western, self-contained individual. Ochs also notes, however, that some successfully learn two contrasting views – one they employ when in the Western world, the other at home.

Revisiting the Chambri culture originally made famous in Margaret Mead's pioneering work, Errington and Gewertz (1987) challenged some of Mead's conclusions, demonstrating that unlike our culture, the Chambri do not have a well-developed concept of individual personality. As one illustration of this point, Errington and Gewertz describe the outpourings of their 25-year-old research assistant trying to explain why a fear of sorcery made it impossible for him to continue working on their project. As his story unfolded, it became clear that:

> he revealed no subjectivity. He described none of the dispositions, capacities and perspectives which, for us, constitute the self; he did not view himself as having a unique character which had been formed by his particular experiences with both natives and Europeans. Instead, by his own account, he was the catalog of his transactions. (p. 139)

In other words, unlike our own conception of people as composed of a personality and a subjectivity, an inner realm that uniquely defines who and what they are, the Chambri's identity is defined in more relational terms: as a listing of social transactions with others, neither caused nor directed by something lying within them.

Focusing on yet another culture, the Baining of New Britain, Papua New Guinea, Jane Fajans (1985) further challenges our own conception of the person. If the Chambri's conception of the person deletes a coherent, integrated and subjectively based personality in favor of a more socially embedded view, the Baining delete most references to "things psychological":

> The Baining exhibit a pervasive avoidance of modes of discourse about psychology. If we understand the latter to be a domain of culture which includes a concern with affect and emotions, concepts of person and self, theories of deviance, interpretations of behavior, and ideas about cognition and personality development, the Baining manifest very little interest in these areas. They are reluctant to speculate about the personal motivations, actions, and feelings either of themselves or others. They do not offer interpretations of the meanings of the behavior and events around them in these terms. (p. 365)

The Baining find it sufficient to understand people as social actors living in a social network with its traditions and expectations that explain what goes on and why. Unlike the preferred Western approach that turns inward for explanations, probing the private recesses of the self-contained individual, the Baining – and, as Geertz suggests, the majority of other cultures of the world as well – do not as sharply separate the individual from the social world.

Early in her stay on the atoll of the Ifaluk, out in the middle of the Pacific Ocean some 500 miles from any other settlement, the anthropologist Catherine Lutz (1985, 1988) made her first *faux pas*. A group of young women were visiting her hut. She asked them: "Do you [all] want to come with me to get drinking water?" (1985, p. 44). The question was asked in all innocence, motivated by her desire to become part of the women's group. Lutz's request, however, was met with crestfallen looks and some embarrassment. But what had she done that was so wrong?

Lutz's error lay in her use of "I", a separating and individuating term that to the Ifaluk suggested an egocentric lack of concern for others. Although the Ifaluk have a concept of "I", they are very sparing in its use, preferring to say "We" for most occasions in which we are likely to use "I". If you want company for water-gathering, it is better to say: "We'll go get some water now, OK?" (p. 44).

Lutz discovered additional differences between our use of "I" and their use of "We". For example: "On observing something unusual, a person would be more likely to say, 'We (speaker and listener) don't know what's going on here' than 'I don't know what's going on here'" (1985, p. 44). The use of "We" is not simply polite, but conveys the Ifaluk's emphasis on the shared viewpoint of the group rather than the unique viewpoint of the individual separate from the group, as conveyed by our own frequent use of "I".

In other words, "I" connotes exactly what we value and they find so disturbing: independence, privacy, separation from others. "I" is an announcement that touts the self over others and neglects the necessarily embedded quality of living together with others that is so valued among the Ifaluk. We work hard to separate ourselves from others and to shout to the world that we stand out from the group as a unique cluster of self-contained qualities that we cherish. Recognizing self apart from others, however, does not find a receptive response among the Ifaluk or many other cultures, in which this very usage connotes rejection and excessive egoism.

A Japanese psychologist, Hideo Kojima (1984), commenting on the difference between the American and Japanese understanding of the self, noted how in Japan:

the concept of a self completely independent from the environment is very foreign ... the Japanese do not think of themselves as exerting control over an environment that is utterly divorced from the self, nor over a self that stands apart from the environment. (p. 973)

Geert Hofstede (1980) provided an additional focus to this "peculiarity" of which Geertz spoke, taking us from the exotica of India and the Pacific Islands into the heartland of the more industrialized world, supporting Kojima's conclusions. Hofstede reported the results of a large international survey examining several differences, including a dimension he referred to as collectivism versus individualism: an individualistic culture is one in which individual interests and goals take precedence over group interests; in a collectivistic culture, the in-group and loyalty to it are supreme social values.

Hofstede's analysis of over 100,000 questionnaires obtained from 40 different nations revealed just which of these 40 was, in Geertz's terms, the most peculiar of all – that is, which led the pack in its individualistic focus: the United States, followed closely by Australia and Great Britain. Less individualistic nations included several European countries (e.g. Yugoslavia, Spain, Austria, Finland), but predominantly Asian and Latin American nations.[1]

Two Peculiarities

While Geertz and Morris tell us of the peculiarity of the current Western view, and while these several examples illustrate what this means, we must still probe further if we are to unfold the precise nature of the peculiarity that is involved. It turns out that it is much more complex and intertwined with other features of the different cultures than we might initially have thought. Our probe will reveal two related but separable meanings of the peculiarity of the Western – but especially of the dominant US – framework. The first peculiarity entails the narrowness and exclusivity of the Western concept of the person; the second presses us to examine the role of power in sustaining what I will claim is a lie about human nature.

Peculiarity No. 1: An Exclusive versus Inclusive Self

Marcel Mauss's (1938/1985) pioneering theoretical paper insisted "that it is plain, particularly to us, that there has never existed a human being who has not been aware, not only of his body, but also at the same time of his individuality, both spiritual and physical" (p. 3). Heelas and Lock (1981), quoting Hallowell's famous statement insisting on the universality of some conception of the individual, offered their own analysis based on a major cross-cultural survey of conceptions of the person. They concluded that no culture lacked some conception of individuality, although conceptions varied extensively. The "peculiarity" of which Geertz writes, therefore, does not revolve around having or not having some conception of the person as an individual; rather, the peculiarity would seem to lie elsewhere.

A variety of sources join with the examples we considered above to suggest that the key involves the degree to which the individual is defined exclusively or inclusively.[2] An *exclusive* conception defines the individual as a rather thoroughly self-contained, separate entity whose essence can be meaningfully abstracted from the various relationships and in-group memberships that she or he has. An *inclusive* conception, by contrast, defines individuals in terms of the in-groups in which they have membership and to which they owe a continuing loyalty.

Both the egocentric-individualistic-exclusive and the sociocentric-collectivistic-inclusive views have a concept of the individual. They differ in the degree to which that individual is significantly seen in terms of in-group relationships. Extremely exclusive conceptions isolate the person from in-group relationships, abstracting some central essence that is contained within the person, regardless of the relationships and memberships they may have. Extremely inclusive conceptions locate the meaning of the person within one or a few central in-group relationships, and thereby tend not to abstract some essential individual essence that exists apart from these relationships.

In Chapters 3 and 4, I argued that the self-contained formulation is self-celebratory, turning to the individual's self as the key to unraveling the riddles of human nature. Given that both collectivistic and individualistic societies have conceptions of persons' individuality – albeit quite differently cast – what can be said about their self-celebratory quality?

Both conceptions are self-celebratory but, because of their different view of the self, celebrate in different ways. One of the key differences between individualistic self-celebration and collectivistic self-celebration involves the nature of the celebrated self: it is far more narrowly and exclusively defined in the former case than in the latter. Both, however, define a self and a not-self, construct a serviceable not-self (other), and celebrate the former over the latter.

Research findings reported from several studies comparing American with primarily Asian samples, for example, demonstrate a high valuation of others who belong to one's in-group in the collectivistic societies (e.g. Hong Kong Chinese) as compared to more individualistic Americans. Collectivistic samples, however, were *not* inclusive of out-groups and, in fact, were more inclined than the individualistic Americans to emphasize the in-group versus out-group distinction:[3]

Harmonious relationships with members of the in-group are essential, but the out-groups can be damned. Individualists, in contrast, do not make such a sharp distinction because who is "in" depends more on what is up. (Wheeler *et al.*, 1989, p. 84)

While this passage clearly tells us that collectivistic cultures have their damnable out-groups, it does not go far enough in helping us to see how individualistic cultures have also constructed damnable out-groups, albeit somewhat differently. I contend that an individualistic culture typically has a more disguised view of the esteemed in-group and damnable out-group than is apparent in more collectivistic cultures, in great measure because the former denies the very distinction which is central to the latter.

In other words, individualistic cultures' emphasis on abstract individuality as an essence of the person mutes the awareness of any in-group versus out-group distinction, even while that distinction operates behind the scenes in a highly significant manner. Wheeler *et al.* lead us to believe that the in-group/out-group distinction is of minimal relevance in individualistic cultures (but central to collectivistic cultures). In my contrasting view, this distinction is highly relevant but denied in individualistic cultures. This brings me to the second peculiarity of the Western understanding.

Peculiarity No. 2: Power and the Lie

The second peculiarity of the Western, individualistic view is this very denial of the in-group/out-group distinction on which its individualistic understanding is based. Abstracting the individual from her or his relationships in order to secure a self-contained essence overlooks two conditions that typically operate in highly individualistic cultures. First, the individualistic formulation is reserved primarily for the dominant groups in society. In other words, individualism is necessarily founded on an implicit in-group/out-group distinction – in this case, between the in-groups who are understood to be self-contained and the out-groups who are not.

Second, because the particular standards for defining the nature of proper personhood are determined by the dominant groups, their perspective becomes the presumptive normative standard for all, thereby concealing its own particularity. The in-group/out-group distinction on which their conception of individuality is built is thus concealed, leading everyone to assume that individuality is a property of persons rather than of in-group/dominant and out-group/submissive relationships. Thereby, the interests of the dominant groups are served and their position of dominance is sustained. In short, the self-understanding of the dominant groups is held to be the normative and natural understanding for all; this places us in a situation that involves a lie about human nature built on a necessary suppression of any self–other differences in order to be sustained and so serve the interests of the dominant groups.

Carol Gilligan's (1982) research offers us one entry point into this issue. She selected a group of women visiting a clinic seeking information about abortions. Extensive interviews revealed that their decisions were guided by what Gilligan termed a "different voice" of reasoning from the one observed among men making moral decisions. This different voice was much more socially embedded and interpersonally connected than the self-contained male voice. Gilligan argued that women may have a more connected, relational understanding of people than the abstract and individualistic world-view that characterizes men.[4]

In this, Gilligan aligned herself with many other scholars who have contrasted the sociocentric tendencies of women with the more individualistic tendencies of men in a wide variety of situations.[5] Geertz's indictment of "peculiar" and Morris's of an "eccentricity" seem to refer more to the way dominant groups in many Western societies – usually men – define and value persons as self-contained than to the way everyone in the Western world defines and values persons.[6] We are dealing here not with a cultural view that is merely self-celebratory, but rather – as I noted in Chapter 1 – with one that is so only by actively suppressing differences and otherness.

In Part III, I will argue that all people everywhere are necessarily interconnected with others in their social world. In other words, a relational or dialogic view is descriptive of the nature of human nature. The idea of self-containment as a way of being a person in the world is a belief without foundation in the actual terms by which *all* people must necessarily live. It is a lie.

Therefore, it is *not* true that we can divide the world's cultures into two categories and argue that because of their conditions of living, people in societies of Type A are interconnected with one another, while people in societies of Type B are self-contained. It is true that Type A and Type B societies may differ in their dominant beliefs about persons. It is not correct, however, to describe people in B as though they were in fact capable of living in a self-contained manner consistent with their cultural belief.

For example, as I commented above, for men to insist on the self-contained ideal and attempt to operate on its terms, they must construct a group of others (e.g. women) as serviceable foils for their own self-contained desires. In so far as those cultures of the West that have become dominant on a worldwide basis have defined their own ideal as self-contained while relegating the rest to a collectivistic category, this too reflects the manner by which dominant groups sustain their own ideals by constructing serviceable other cultures. As those others increasingly refuse to play their parts, however – whether women in the West or nonWestern cultures – the possibility of sustaining the self-contained ideal begins to crumble.

If we agree to accept this position provisionally until I develop its supporting arguments in later chapters, we can see this second peculiarity better: Type B societies appear not only to be suppressing a truth about human nature but also to have built that truth, which is a lie, on the essential exploitation of others.

If we examined the conditions of modern life in the West, we would see how much they affirm our mutual dependence and interconnectedness far more than the kind of self-sufficiency and autonomy that characterize the self-contained ideal. Furthermore, if we give close consideration to the devices and technologies of power by which the dominant groups sustain their self-sufficient, self-contained ideal, we would see just how many others have to be held down and in check for this act to continue without disruption. In other words, we would see not only the lie of self-sufficiency and self-containment, but the power that undergirds that lie.

And so we confront a contradiction between the realities of our own everyday existence and the belief in self-contained individualism that guides many of our self-understandings. We value the very kind of person that no human being could realistically ever be. We value the very kind of person that requires the suppression of the other to sustain. This is the real basis of the peculiarity of the Western understanding.

Notes

1. A complexity emerges in interpreting these survey results. For example, the 1980 data placed Yugoslavia among the more collectivistic European countries; in 1992 Yugoslavia is no longer one nation, but a hotly divided collection of nations at war with one another. The complexity is useful, however, in revealing the in-group harmony and out-group hostility that characterize collectivistic nations.
2. See, for example, Triandis *et al.* (1988); Wheeler *et al.* (1989).
3. See references in Note 2 above.
4. Not everyone has agreed with Gilligan's sex difference findings: see Mednick (1989) for one type of "feminist" critique; Colby and Damon (1983) comment more on the empirical base of her work.
5. There are many references to relational conceptions of the self, including, for example, Code (1991); Jordan (1989); J.B. Miller (1984, 1987); Noddings (1984).
6. Harding (1986) presents a rather lengthy discussion of the similarities between some African understandings of the person-in-relation and seemingly parallel feminist understandings. Because these Africanist views appear in otherwise patriarchal societies, she addresses how relationality-in-itself may not invariably

lead to the feminist perspective, building much of her argument around the extent to which both Africans and women have been constructed by the dominant white, male Westerners to serve the latter's needs, desires and interests.

6

The Enlightened Suppression of the Other

A fter completing several items of the day's news, one of our local television stations turned to its special features, introducing the newest trendy fad in the San Francisco Bay area, the computer café. Apparently, some enterprising computer wizard thought up the idea and put it into immediate use: while people were sipping their espressos, they could hold computer network conversations with anyone around the area who was a network subscriber. The wizard installed computer terminals in several cafés, lined up hundreds of subscribers, and went into business. The television special featured one of the cafés and interviewed several users.

A young woman, holding a cigarette in one hand, pecking away at the computer keyboard with the other, carried on a conversation with several anonymous persons. She commented on the pleasures of meeting people in this manner: "It's so great not having to deal with all these macho come-ons any more. This is *all mind*." An excited young man, apparently instrumental in creating the whole concept and clearly proud of its potential, noted the benefits of its *anonymity*: "People can communicate with one another in total anonymity, never knowing anything about race, age, sex, or even accent."

My distinct impression was that for these people, anonymity offered the real hope for intergroup harmony and equality. This impression was only furthered by listening to my students' reactions to the 1992 uprisings in inner-city Los Angeles, and to the variety of sexual harassment and discrimination issues that seem to be an everyday occurrence: "Perhaps someday we will simply treat one another as people, plain and simple; and not divide us into black and white, male and female. After all, we are just people beneath all of those surface differences."

Moscovici's (1985) examination of European social psychologists' preferences for minority influence models contrasted with the Americans' fascination with majority influence and conformity also came to mind. Whereas the Europeans, says Moscovici, build upon conflict and group differences, the Americans seem to be intent on melting down all differences into one anonymous and harmonious humanity – just as my students want, and just as the anonymity of computer contacts allows.

As I watched and listened with my current writing project in view, I thought how the processes begun in the Western world during the Enlightenment had come home to roost right here in a San Francisco café several centuries later. Two comments especially caught my attention. One: "It's all mind". Two: "Total anonymity, never knowing anything about race, age, sex, or even accent". Mind and anonymity were key qualities introduced in the Enlightenment.

Listen to Richard Shweder's (1984) description of the Enlightenment view:

> the mind of man is intendedly rational and scientific ... the dictates of reason are equally binding for all regardless of time, place, culture, race, personal desire, or individual endowment ... in reason can be found a universally applicable standard for judging validity and worth. (p. 27)

Here we have a story whose protagonist is a mind equipped with the ability to reason, thereby ensuring a common basis for judging all humanity: an anonymous being, a no one in particular from nowhere in particular who applies this universal measuring instrument.

Reason would overcome the superstitions that had previously dominated the civilized world, and bind people together as individuals whose common denominator was their shared ability to use the powers of reason. Reason had no particular standpoint: it was impartial, a God's-eye view from nowhere in particular, belonging to no one person in particular but shared universally by all. No longer would any particularistic perspective based on a person's group membership rule. Humanity was free at last to chart its own course, directed only by this anonymous individual's reasoning powers.

And now this, the computer café, where mind could meet mind without body attached. Where one anonymous individual could meet another anonymous individual without the presence of any of those potentially stigmatizing signs of each person's particularistic identity. Where stereotypes that once shaped destinies were null and void. Where life would henceforth be shaped only by the neutral qualities of reason's modern voice, the electronic messages on the computer screen.

The story of the Enlightenment is of a confrontation between two contrasting theses, the presumptive victor being the Enlightenment view itself. The Enlightenment affirmed the fundamental unity of all humanity, and sought to use that unity to vanquish the traditional view in which differences and otherness were central. Enlightenment understanding sought not merely to mute otherness but actively to suppress and eventually to extinguish it wherever it appeared and in whatever guise it happened to adopt.

Of course, as Moscovici reminds us, this enlightened understanding did not settle in equal amounts everywhere in the West. In his view, as we have seen, Europe remained sensitive to various differences that joined some people together and separated them from others; in the United States, however, the great myth of the melting-pot took hold. Despite the fact that the myth has been challenged and, presumably, finally put to rest, its hold on the greater American imagination remains strong even today, as the wistful desires of my students will testify.

We are generally familiar with the Enlightenment's message. Beneath all diversity and difference there exists a fundamental universality, a kind of deep structure that all share. Beneath the diversity in the world's languages we will find a deep generative structure shared by all human minds. Beneath the diversity in phenotypic behavior we will find a deep genotypic structure shared by all. Beneath the diversity of mental forms we will find the deep structure of reason itself shared by all. Beneath the diverse pathways possible for human development we will find a deep structure leading inexorably from the primitive and concrete to the advanced and abstract.[1]

The Enlightenment's systematic suppression of differences and otherness was encouraged by a desire to replace the chains of autocratic rule with a democratization of political life, made possible by rendering all people (all white male people?) equal because they were fundamentally the same. It was assumed that equality between people could exist only on the firm foundation of the unity and impartiality of reason itself. Only through reason's impartiality could competing claims be settled without tilting towards any one group's interests.

For people to be accorded equal treatment, their differences must be submitted to a single judgmental standard applied to all. The courtroom of everyday life must follow procedures that are impartial and blind. Any particularistic identities that would warrant special treatment must be ignored. We must be blind to people as women, men, black, white, Jew, Christian, Muslim, straight, gay, young, old, and so on, so that we may treat every one individually – that is, in terms of their individual merit alone.

Each individual is to be considered as an anonymous runner in a race. Since the runners lack either the advantages or the disadvantages that would accrue to them were they given their traditional identifiers, victory goes only to the swiftest. This liberal humanist, Enlightenment view does not ignore differences *per se* but, rather, only differences that are based on traditional categories of birth, family background, income, and so forth. Individual differences in merit warrant individual differences in outcome.

I will refer to this as the *equality-as-sameness* position – not because every individual is in fact the same as every other individual, but rather because the only differences that are allowed to count are specific to the particular individual now before the bench, based only on that individual's personally owned capabilities. Other characteristics are ruled out of order in this court.

The Enlightenment was not merely blind to traditional identifiers, but actively sought to undermine these bases of identification so that the self-contained individual could be cast as the only worthy player on the world's stage. The suppression of the other was required for this new character to emerge and remain dominant. People's otherness, their differences and diversity, were denied so that each could be placed under the same universal, transcendent standard.

The victory of the Enlightenment was not simply that reason conquered superstition or that the anonymous self-contained individual won out over the socially organized person, but that diversity lost to unity. People were equal because of their naked sameness. Each individual was said to be equal to any other individual by virtue of having the same capability to use reason in order to see in the same way as everyone else could see.

In positing the underlying unity of a singular perspective, the hope of the Enlightenment was to suppress socially organized differences that would provide conflicting views of the world. The perspective of reason, a God's-eye view of no one in particular standing nowhere in particular, would hold it all together. Traditional categories of human difference threatened a return to those times when people's lives were endangered by the clashes of diversity, and no court but brute force could settle competing claims.

The story of the Enlightenment is not simply one in which we find an unabashed celebration of the individual, but is better told in terms of the active suppression of the other – where the other is a particularistic standpoint available to people because of their group memberships and collectively shared experiences.

Iris Young (1990) comments critically on the Enlightenment ideal of impartiality: "By claiming to provide a standpoint which all subjects can adopt, it denies the difference between subjects" (p. 10). Her account parallels the accounts we met first in Chapter 1, and corresponds also to most critical, postmodern, and – as we will see – dialogic accounts. In one form or another, all these argue that by denying differences in standpoint, impartiality substitutes one standpoint – that of reason, the God's-eye view of no one in particular standing nowhere in particular – for each and every particular standpoint based on a people's specificity. By this one stroke, the Enlightenment sought to enthrone one standpoint over a diversity of views and to treat that one standpoint as though it were natural – that is, based on the purity and impartiality of reason itself.

As it turns out, however, far from being a standpoint without a point of view, this position of presumed impartiality is closely associated, both historically and currently, with the perspective of dominant societal groups, primarily white, Western and male. To operate in its terms, therefore, is to play not on a level playing-field but, rather, on one tilted to advantage some over others by denying the specificity of those others.

The voices of diversity and difference, however, have never been completely stilled. We hear them raised loudly today, staking their own claims and insisting that even reason has its heart that reason may not know.[2] These voices have never been completely silenced. Today they challenge the politics of equality-as-sameness that has been the Western heritage, calling for an equality based on differences.

These voices call not for a return to the old ways, but rather for a second transcendence. If the first transcendence – carried by the Enlightenment view – sought to go beyond all traditional distinctions by seeking the unitary point of view that impartial reason would provide, this second transcendence seeks to locate reason itself as a particular group's form of thinking which must itself be transcended so that *equality-through-diversity* can have its time.

The current voices of diversity have been raised both to challenge the idea that there is a place to stand on that is – as those white, Western, male claimants insist – neutral, and to insist on a hearing for their own otherness and their own specificity. They demand a genuine dialogue among equal voices reflecting different perspectives, rather than the hegemonic mono-logues that have for so long dominated our understanding and our practice.

Catherine Lutz (1985, 1988), whose work among the Ifaluk we first considered in Chapter 5, offers an instructive example. She argues that every understanding implicitly assumes some group's standard (in this case, the Western world's), even when we think we are merely describing another culture's practices:

> If, for example, the handling of children in one culture is described as "indulgent", that statement is equally one about the nonindulgence of Euro-American children. If the Japanese are said to be quick to "shame", that is also a description of how the ethnographer does *not* see her or himself. (1985, p. 37)

So, when the claim is made that we can actually describe something in neutral terms, the voices of diversity and difference rise up and join with Lutz to insist that neutrality conceals a definite partiality:

- Kohlberg (1969) thought he was merely describing the natural course of human reasoning when he posited abstract thinking as the foundation for principled moral judgments, until Gilligan (1982) demonstrated that abstract thinking was not a neutral description but rather the preferred manner by which dominant groups, especially males, framed their understanding. But as Code (1991) has commented, even Gilligan succumbs by talking about the *different* voice in which women speak – meaning different from the male standpoint – rather than about the different voices in which both men and women speak, making neither voice the standard!

- Mental health professionals thought they were merely describing the healthy, mature adult, until Broverman and her colleagues (1972) came along and demonstrated that their healthy adult fitted the stereotype of the male – not only relegating women to unhealthy status, but also revealing the partiality contained in their "neutral" descriptions.

- Subjects in an experiment thought they were providing an objective description of the typical American voter, until D.T. Miller *et al.* (1991) revealed that the typical voter they described was male – hardly a "neutral" point of view.

- Well over 300 subjects in another study thought they were simply describing the prevailing stereotypes of various cultural groups, until Eagly and Kite (1987) demonstrated how those national stereotypes were "more similar to stereotypes of the men than of the women of these nationalities" (p. 459).

Critics of the Enlightenment view maintain that the so-called impartiality of reason is a myth. Rather than being a God's-eye view of no one in particular standing nowhere in particular, this so-called impartial world-view reflects a socially and historically particularistic account. Critics insist that its claim to neutrality binds people today with often more insidious and hidden shackles – Blake's mind-forg'd manacles – than ever existed before the Enlightenment.

These critics of the Enlightenment view have loudly proclaimed on behalf of honoring, not suppressing, differences. They refuse to be melted down into a singular framework, and view all such melting-down as furthering only their oppression, not their liberation. These are the voices of women insisting on their differences from men; the voices of the gay and lesbian population insisting that they too have a special point of view that deserves to be heard; the voices of people of color who insist on being treated on the basis of their distinctive characteristics, not in terms of white male standards and rules; these are the voices of the elderly, the disabled, and all those groups that believe that the melting process perpetuates their oppression.

However liberating the Enlightenment understanding may have once been, it is used today to conceal a far greater truth: to deny people their own identities is to render them impotent to combat their oppression, further advantaging the dominant groups in society. Iris Young (1990) offers a persuasive defense of this position. She argues that the Enlightenment's case breaks down for two reasons.

First, to be blind to group-based differences between people – she includes differences based on skin color, physiology and cultural socialization – so that all can be treated equally on an individual basis brings new players into an already existing game, compelling them to test themselves against standards that already favor the dominant groups who have been playing the game for quite some time.

For example, a woman entering the workforce and seeking to climb the managerial ladder may find that while she possesses all the requisite motivation and ability, she has been socialized to adopt a less competitive and individualistic way of relating to other people than her male counterparts. For her to make progress in this managerial race, therefore, she must submit to the male standards. To follow her own cultural socialization would only push her further and further into the background, as more competitive and aggressive men walked over one another and her to get to the top. To be blind to this socialized difference by treating everyone alike, says Young, is to adopt a set of rules in which such women are decidedly disadvantaged. And to insist that the game can be played only by these rules, she adds, is to deny any other possibilities, thus further disadvantaging not only the woman in the example but all others whose socialization experiences may have cast them somewhat differently. (I return to this theme, and further examples, in Chapter 10.)

The passages quoted in Chapter 1 from Irigaray and from Cixous, among others, add further to this picture. In each case, in order to be heard, the woman must deny her own specificities and speak only as a man. To be seen and known, she must become in fact the character proposed by the dominating male gaze. As Catharine MacKinnon (1989) suggests, to be sexed, the woman must become what men's sexuality requires:

> The interests of male sexuality construct what sexuality as such means, including the standard way it is allowed and recognized to be felt and expressed and experienced. (p. 129)

> To be clear: what is sexual is what gives a man an erection. Whatever it takes to make a penis shudder and stiffen with the experience of its potency is what sexuality means culturally. . . . All this suggests that what is called sexuality is

the dynamic of control by which male dominance – in forms that range from intimate to institutional, from a look to a rape – eroticizes and thus defines man and woman, gender identity and sexual pleasure. (p. 137)

I touched above on Young's second argument. She suggests that currently dominant groups tend to believe they have no particularistic standpoint that marks them as separate and unique. This allows their own group's norms and standards to take precedence, while they never recognize that they too occupy a particular place. In other words, dominant groups tend to see themselves as having a God's-eye view from Nowhere and so fail to see the particular lens through which they too encounter the world. I am sure that the men in the managerial example, if asked, would not see that their way of taking on business is a *way* at all: it is simply how things are done.

Let us look at another example. We do not usually consider that a heterosexual orientation reflects any bias. Rather, we presume heterosexuality to be the normal and natural state of human sexuality, forming the standard against which all other sexual orientations are measured. This turns out to be a debatable position. John Money (1987), for example, a well-known researcher on sexual identity, has argued that monosexuality, whether heterosexual or homosexual, is the oddity – that bisexuality is the norm against which other patterns are to be measured. As Money has noted, this suggests that rather than adopting the heterosexual norm as though it were a neutral standard, we need to inquire about why any kind of monosexual pattern has developed into society's standard.[3]

The suppression of differences and otherness has thereby become a politics of domination by one group over others, carried out in the name of finding a single, unifying perspective from which all human experience can be evaluated. Although it is self-celebratory, it is more accurately depicted as an other-suppressing politics: it systematically seeks to deny, repress or transform all forms of otherness into the standardized, presumptively impartial categories of the dominant self-contained individual.

Identity and Difference

Not only has the challenge to the Enlightenment view found a receptive home among those groups for whom the suppression of differences has advanced the causes of their oppression rather than their liberation; it has been central to several academic-political critiques as well. I have found Adorno's (1973) critical theory and Derrida's (1974, 1978, 1981) deconstructionist views in literary criticism especially germane and relentless in their efforts to undermine the Enlightenment's identitarian thesis by revealing its fundamental incoherence.

Both Adorno and Derrida ask us to consider two contrasting positions. The first is associated with the Enlightenment and adopts an *identity thesis*. The second adopts a *difference thesis* and is currently associated with several group-affirming social movements (e.g. feminist, gay and lesbian, Third World, etc.) as well as being central to the critiques developed by Adorno and Derrida.

Identity

How are we to understand the nature of the objects and the categories by which we experience our world? The identity thesis adopts an essentialist view in responding to this question. Objects have their own essential nature or identity. This nature is self-possessed by the object; that is, it is an inherent property of the object and gives the object its recognizable identity as what it is. The coherence of the object through time, regardless of the many guises and forms in which its essential nature may appear, is assured by virtue of its possessing an identity-in-itself.

For example, there is an essential male, an essential female, an essential heterosexual, an essential homosexual, and so forth. Thus, we would argue that the essence of the male–female divide involves genitals and perhaps other biologically rooted characteristics such as chromosome typing: males have an XY pattern, whereas females are XX. Therefore, whether a male is strong or weak, tall or short, vigorous or passive, bearded or clean-shaven, bald or possessing long curly locks, we would nevertheless insist that this specimen before us is a male. We adopt what Kessler and McKenna (1978) refer to as "the natural attitude", believing that the world in fact consists of two clearly divided sexes, male and female, and that – in concurrence with Garfinkel's (1967) ethnomethodological approach – crossing lines is virtually impossible, or a symptom of pathology.

We can accept this essentialist view and simultaneously be socially and culturally sensitive – noting, for example, how society and history have produced different manifestations of *the same object*, or how the object's essential nature manages to shine through the societal and historical forces that have sought to distort its true form. For example, we could examine the fate of women throughout history, noting how they were once considered to be dangerously sexual objects and only later came to be considered nonsexual and pure.[4] Or we could focus on the manner in which different societies have treated homosexuality, noting how it was considered reasonable in Ancient Greece, only to be considered a punishable crime in later Western history.[5]

In carrying out this exercise, we treat the object as though it were the selfsame object throughout time and across cultural divides. It is simply dealt with differently in different times or in different places. The object, however, has an essential identity: it can be seen, felt, noted, observed and known for what it is, whenever it is and wherever it is. For this reason, for example, we hear claims that individualism, so rampant in today's society, also existed very clearly in early Greek and Roman times, so we should not consider it a new phenomenon (e.g. Waterman, 1981). After all, there is a common, natural thing known as the individual. Nothing really new under the sun here.

According to the identity thesis, the object is a kind of transcendent category of nature, with essential properties that make it what it is and permit us to identify it wherever we may encounter it. Obviously, if this or something close to it were not the case, then how could we ever hold meaningful conversations with different cultures or different eras? Without some sense of identity for the objects of our world, we would be unable to converse with others.

Difference

The contrasting difference thesis adopts a relational/dialogic view, arguing that no object is plainly and simply what it currently seems to be. Whatever anything is is always defined by what it is implicitly or explicitly being compared and co-constructed with. In other words, differences rather than essences render the identities we currently experience. Thus, rather than our viewing an essential woman who is transformed this way and that throughout human history, we would examine how women are defined, and according to what implicit comparisons – that is, compared to what others in various times and places. (I will have more to say about this in Chapter 10.)

For our present purposes, the crux of the difference thesis is its argument that the characteristics of all objects are defined relationally, usually in terms of implicit comparisons with other objects: whatever something is cannot be grasped without fathoming the nexus of comparisons which construct its qualities. Differences are critical to all definitions and all understandings. Whatever identity something has, it has by virtue of the differences that define it as such. This, of course, was Lutz's point in the example we considered above.

When Lutz tells us that we describe the child-rearing practices of Culture X as indulgent, her point is not that they are in fact – that is, essentially or intrinsically – indulgent, as though indulgence were a property possessed by Culture X. Rather, she is asking us to adopt the difference thesis and see how indulgence is a property built upon a comparison with Culture Y's formulation, taken as the implicit standard. In other words, rather than essentialist identities we have differences at the root. Furthermore, as the Lutz example suggests, the absent other that serves as the implicit standard is usually accorded privileged standing in the comparison.

When we describe Culture X as indulgent, we are not only implicitly making a comparison with Culture Y but granting privilege to the implicit standard represented by Y. The standard becomes an unexamined privileged term, providing the frame within which the comparisons are made while not itself coming under our scrutiny. We judge Culture X as an inferior representation of the superior qualities contained in Culture Y. This judgment is the conclusion of a process, yet it appears as a statement of pure, impartial description: Culture X *is* indulgent in its child-rearing practices.

We also saw this same process illustrated in Chapter 1 with the two paradigmatic cases we examined, gender and the American character. The argument there, as here, is that the male constructs his own character in terms of its implicit comparison/contrast with the female character he has constructed for that purpose. The male is dominant only in so far as the female is constructed as submissive; the male is autonomous only in so far as the female is constructed as dependent. What a man is, therefore, is not something essential or intrinsic to his sex but, rather, is constructed on the basis of implicit and necessary comparisons with the concept woman. Needless to say, woman has had little control over who she will be; man has called the shots and set the terms.

Morrison's (1992) analyses reveal a parallel process in the construction of the American character. In this case, that character is constructed on the basis of implicit and necessary comparisons with the African-American. The freedom of the white-American character is constructed, she argues, on the basis of the slavery of the African-American. Without the power to control the terms by which the African-American is known, the white-male-American character could not possibly be what it is. In each case, all definitions are relational and based on constructed differences, usually under the control of the dominant groups and designed to serve their interests.

At this point, let me anticipate the conclusion towards which I am heading, then call upon both Adorno and Derrida to lead us to that conclusion. There are two parts to the conclusion. First, if all identities are necessarily founded on differences, the identity thesis and all its corollaries must collapse into a difference thesis. The claim of impartiality, for example, based on the argument that the touchstone for identity is reality itself, fails, because what something really is is the outcome of a comparative process with a usually implicit evaluation – hardly an impartial and neutral description. Second, by virtue of the preceding position, the identity thesis itself is rendered incoherent: it must suppress what it needs in order to be itself. Now, let me build upon Adorno's and Derrida's accounts to move us to these conclusions.

Adorno

Adorno's (1973) negative dialectics, his refusal to permit any form of identity-thesis to remain in place unscathed, reflects his concern with the ideological consequences of sustaining an essentialist or identitarian position. This is how Adorno sees his task:

> Insight into the constitutive character of the nonconceptual in the concept would end the compulsive identification which the concept brings unless halted by such reflection. Reflection upon its own meaning is the way out of the concept's seeming being-in-itself as a unit of meaning. (Adorno, 1973, p. 12)

Or again, he tells us that "a fetish is made of the positive-in-itself. Against this, the seriousness of unswerving negation lies in its refusal to lend itself to sanctioning things as they are" (p. 159).

Adorno's message, like Young's – and, as we will see, Derrida's – warns us about the pitfalls that threaten when differences give way to abstractions, such as the abstraction of pure reason or the abstraction of the self-contained individual. Concrete, particularistic differences are central to Adorno's view and serve as a continual reminder and remedy for the problems of modern Western society's dominant, identitarian proclivities.

Sharing a great deal with those group-affirmative protest movements of our era, Adorno's understanding turns to politics and, indeed, to revolutionary transformation. As Buck-Morss (1977) notes in her examination of Adorno's theories, he frequently took issue with otherwise congenial colleagues, such as Erich Fromm, who sought to "construct a positive description of modern man . . . a new and lasting theory" (Buck-Morss, 1977, p. 186). For Adorno, "the desire to possess even a theory [runs] the risk of reproducing the commodity structure within consciousness" (Buck-Morss, p. 186). Adorno's was a negative dialectics seeking "to keep criticism alive" (p. 186) – a criticism, however, not for the sake of criticism alone, but for the sake of emancipation from the domination carried by the prevailing forms of the Enlightenment identity-thesis.

Adorno's negative dialectics yields the same kind of "quicksilver" that we will find in Derrida's insistent and incessant deconstruction: "just when you think you have grasped the point, by turning into its opposite it slips through your fingers and escapes" (Buck-Morss, p. 186). Yet Adorno's revolutionary goals were always apparent, whereas Derrida's often remain a mystery. Adorno's "relentless insistence on negativity was to resist repeating in thought the structures of domination and reification that existed in society, so that instead of reproducing reality, consciousness could be critical" (Buck-Morss, p. 189). The fact that people are continuing this quest today suggests how great is the distance still to be traveled, how difficult are the hurdles to be overcome, and how deeply engrained are the forms of thinking that suppress differences and otherness.

Derrida

Derrida challenges the idea that the author of a work is in charge of its meaning. He argues that concealed within any positive statement of meaning is an absent, other meaning, suggesting that difference rather than identity is necessary to our understanding. But since differences are as endless as the comparisons we can make, no single understanding will ever do – not even the author's own.

According to Derrida, our inherited Western tradition has led us to fulfill the Enlightenment search for something fundamental and unitary that provides a stable center or core on which to hang our understanding. In place of the variety we find on the surface, we seek a deeper-lying center or origin, a governing ideal beneath that provides the bedrock on which to build the edifice that is our knowledge. This governing ideal is treated as though it were a god, an origin without its own origin, a presence-in-itself requiring nothing beyond itself to account for its own being.

It is Derrida's view that our tradition has granted this privileged, originary quality to whatever appears to be most immediately present to us. He uses the distinction between speaking and writing to develop this point. Speech is presumed to be more privileged than writing because it lies closest to originary experience of the mind's operations at work, whereas writing is but a copy or replica of speech, and is thus mediated by speech. When we speak, Derrida notes, the sounds – presumably – directly reflect the operations of our mind; when we write, however, we are simply making a replica of those sounds of speech. Thus writing is considered secondary and mediated in comparison to the primacy and immediacy of speech.

By extension, says Derrida, all forms of identity, all objects which have an immediate presence to us, occupy the same position in the Western hierarchy as speech: that is, identity is privileged because of its presumed immediacy with the center, the origin, the governing principle of reality itself. Thus, it is the object itself rather than any replica, copy or trace suggesting the presence of the object that we consider to be primary and privileged. Its vivid, living presence, rather than anything that substitutes for its presence, is considered privileged.

For example, we come upon the tracks of a bear on the newly fallen snow. The privileged reality is the actual bear, not the traces of its presence left as tracks in the snow. These are but copies, replicas, representations of the truth which is the underlying reality, the immediacy of the bear-in-itself.

Derrida opposes this privileging of speech, presence, and essence. He argues that whatever we presume to be immediately present is always-already a trace structure. All presence is infused with absence, the trace, the copy, the replica. Without the latter, the former cannot exist. To put this in terms of our previous consideration, we would say that all identity is founded on difference. Only by virtue of the process by which we grasp whatever is immediately before us by means of a comparison with what it differs from – i.e. the absent other – can we experience the present object at all. Presence is built on absence; identity on difference; speech on writing.

In other words, each item we accept as having a substantive essence in its own right (i.e. each category, each identity, each immediate presence), and grant privileged status in organizing our understanding because of its assumed immediacy to some basic underlying reality, is always-already whatever it is by virtue of its relation to an absent other. Nothing thereby has privilege or essence; everything is based on differences. And so the Enlightenment project of erasing differences in its pursuit of some transcendent unity accomplishes this feat of erasure – but only by denying, suppressing and eventually oppressing the very other that is an essential aspect of its own being in the first place.

The essential reality of a given object can appear, says Derrida, only by virtue of the unstated other that is necessary for the object's identity to appear as such. In short, otherness is the basis for all identity, thereby undoing the essentialist view of identity and requiring that each identity be understood in terms of differences.

Therefore the Enlightenment's effort to suppress differences in the pursuit of a single, dominant framework in which to encase our understanding of our world and its people, to undermine group-based identities in order to find some common standard against which to measure all individuals, to try to find an Archimedean point, a God's-eye view of thoroughgoing impartiality, conceals the very differences that are required for any point of view to take on its positive presence.

We cannot describe something's existence without employing a framework in which that something's presence occurs by virtue of its being seen against an implicit background of something else from which it differs. Indulgent child-rearing is not an essence to be found within

Culture X, but rather reflects a relational judgment based on differences with another culture taken as the implied but absent standard. A homosexual orientation is not an essence found within certain males, but rather reflects a relational judgment based on differences with an implied heterosexual standard. Neither male nor female is a category-in-itself; each is defined by virtue of relational judgments based on treating one group – typically the male – as the standard, and the other as a comparison.

Thus, to adopt the heterosexual standard or the Western pattern of child-rearing or the white male socialization experience as the implicit norm and then to measure everything against this norm, while loudly proclaiming neutrality and impartiality in one's analysis, is to forget the hidden differences and relational judgments that are necessarily implicated in making any positive or affirming statement.

The deconstructive process requires that we return otherness and differences to their central place over the prevailing tendencies to privilege identity and essence. In deconstructing identity, for example, we search for the hidden differences that sustain it. I can illustrate this by calling upon Sedgwick's (1990) examination of the homosexual/heterosexual definition. Sedgwick comments that we have adopted the gender of object choice as the central, defining essence of the difference between homosexual and heterosexual males. She notes: "sexuality extends along so many dimensions that aren't well described in terms of the gender of object-choice at all" (p. 35); "our by now unquestioned reading of the phrase 'sexual orientation' to mean 'gender of object-choice', is at the very least damagingly skewed by the specificity of its historical placement" (p. 35).

In defining each of the preceding terms, why have we emphasized the gender of the object choice? Why not other dimensions of sexuality – including, for example, whether the choice is animal or human, adult or child, oriented to self or to other, directed towards one sexual object or several at once, and so forth? In other words, there is no essence to either term: that is, no essence either to homosexuality or to heterosexuality. Not only are they defined relationally (i.e. one exists only by virtue of having been employed as the standard by which the other term is measured) but also in a restrictive manner (i.e. in terms of the gender of the object choice) – all of which serves societal functions, usually of an other-oppressing sort.

In short, the self-contained view has been constructed on the ruins of a hidden otherness. To privilege the self-contained view parallels the privileging of the first or dominant terms in any of our culture's binary oppositions, including male over female, straight over gay, knowledge over ignorance, impartial over particularistic, white over people of color. In each case, we fail to see how the first term requires the second term if it is to be whatever it is. In each case, we fail to see how the first term constructs the second term in a manner designed to affirm its perspective over the alternative represented by the second term. I will return to these themes in Chapter 10.

Let me turn again to the two conclusions I introduced above. First: because all identities are founded on differences, the identity-thesis is placed under the more encompassing direction of the difference perspective. Second: the Enlightenment project of suppressing differences is rendered incoherent and a failure in that it seeks to undo what is required if its own thesis is to be sustained. Its failure also renders incoherent the belief that disputed claims can be settled by reference to the impartiality of some underlying governing principle (e.g. reason).

If each governing principle we proclaim is itself what it is by virtue of implicit comparisons with a standard from which it differs, we have no way of ever finally settling upon an impartial standard. The Enlightenment project turns out to have been – and, in its current use, to remain – a political position which is fundamentally incoherent and impossible to sustain, except by advancing the suppression of the very otherness that it requires as its own lifeblood.

To have an identity is not to have a special essence that is one's own, as the Enlightenment's creation of the self-contained individual and its search for a singular, unifying fundamental governing principle recommends. Rather, any identity builds upon its relation to other identities; nothing can be itself without taking into consideration the kinds of relationship by which its selfsameness is constituted.

Because we ignore differences, we search for something that is essential and substantial about the thing-in-itself rather than the thing-in-relation. In doing this, we achieve advantages for those groups that form the implicit standards against which other groups are described and evaluated. Thus, the only pathway to liberation for those groups disadvantaged by this forgetting of differences is to challenge any and all identities that are presented while seeking a more relational/dialogic understanding. We are now ready to move from the self-celebratory stance that transmutes differences into self-serving sameness to a celebration of the other, in which differences become central to our understanding. The dialogic perspective not only celebrates the other, but also leads us to a new agenda for the century ahead.

Notes

1. I have compressed into this one story line a literal cast of hundreds, led by some very familiar names: Chomsky (1957); Piaget (1929); plus the host of cognitive scientists I mentioned in Chapter 4.
2. Pascal noted that the heart has its reasons that reason does not know, granting a

special logic to the heart and the passions. In the context I am developing, however, it is useful to invert Pascal's formulation, recognizing that the logic of reason is based on a particularistic standpoint of which reason itself may be ignorant.

3. See also MacKinnon (1989).

4. Connell (1987) and several contributors to the collection edited by Caplan (1987) develop further details of this changing view of "woman".

5. Sedgwick (1985, 1990) develops this issue and theme.

Dialogism: Celebrating the Other

7

Celebrating the Other
The Dialogic Turn

What is it that we spend a great deal of our time doing when we come together with other people? We talk and we listen. We argue. We agree and we disagree. We negotiate and we compromise. We ask questions and we provide answers. We describe and we explain. We tell stories. We praise. We promise. We laugh. We cry.

In other words, what stands out when we look at what people do together is language as communication in action. Because we have become so intent on searching deeply within the individual's psyche for the answers to all our questions about human nature, we usually fail to see what sits right before us, a dominating feature of our lives with others: conversations. It is time now to take conversations seriously.[1]

Four features of conversations are of immediate interest to us. First, conversations take place between people; they are not events we can understand simply by probing inside any one person. Even when people are alone and wrapped in thought, their thinking occurs in the form of an inner conversation or dialogue.

Second, conversations are public rather than personal and private. They use a system of signs that is generally shared within a community and known to the people who are involved in the conversation.

Third, conversations involve addressivity: they are addressed by a particular person to another particular person in a specific situation. They are *"something we do* . . . in order to accomplish social actions" (Edwards, 1991, p. 517; original emphasis).

Finally, conversations encompass verbal, nonverbal, symbolic and written material. The author who writes and the reader who reads what is written are engaging in a conversation, as are two people whispering intimately together, or as is the solitary contemplator.

These four features link person and other in such an intimate way that disentangling the bonds that join them becomes an exercise in futility.

This dialogic turn transforms the dominant project of the Western world, its self-celebratory, other-suppressing stance, into a necessary celebration of the other. Dialogism's focus on the conversational quality of human nature marks an exciting direction for our inquiry, with profound implications for all that we are and all that we do. If we are dialogic, conversational beings, we cannot be understood by probing inside for personal and private processes taking place deep within each individual. All that is central to human nature and human life – and here I mean mind, self, and society itself – is to be found in processes that occur *between* people in the public world of our everyday lives.[2]

Although there have been many predecessors to the dialogic perspective on both sides of the Atlantic, and although a variety of investigators are currently involved in extensive programs of work in this area, I have found two usually separated bodies of work most significant in shaping my own understandings. The first would have to include Mead, Wittgenstein, Vygotsky, and the Bakhtin group.[3] The second would have to include the major contributions of feminist writers, especially Harding (1986) and Code (1991).[4] While a careful examination would discover points of disagreement among these contributors to dialogism, I am more impressed with the areas of agreement they share and the common vision of human nature that issues from their analyses.

In one form or another, these authors have responded to the self-celebratory, other-suppressing paradigm by challenging its inwardly focused, individualistic and – for the feminists – male-centered conception of human nature, insisting rather on the intrinsically social, historical and practical quality of the human experience. In one form or another, all have argued that the dialogic process that occurs between specific people in specific settings who are engaged in specific activities is the originating and ongoing source of mind, of self and of society.

Wittgenstein (1953, 1958) tells us that although our language habits confuse us into believing that there is a kind of mental substance lying within each individual that accounts for behavior, this very conception of a private inner realm of mental activities makes little sense. Our task is to examine how the language used in the public, social world of communication between people holds the key to our understanding.

Mead (1934) and Vygotsky (1978) let us see how the mind and its properties derive from the social process: in Vygotsky's terms, from the *intermental*; in Mead's terms, from *social interaction*. In both cases, the other is a central figure in the development of mindedness as well as its ongoing operations.

Bakhtin (1981, 1986) and Mead teach us that all meaning, including the meaning of one's self, is rooted in the social process and must be seen as an ongoing accomplishment of that process. Neither meaning nor self is a precondition for social interaction; rather, these emerge from and are sustained by conversations occurring between people.

We learn that social reality itself is constituted on the basis of dialogic processes. The conversations that people carry on together do not simply express the underlying fabric of their social world, but are the very processes by which that fabric is created and sustained or transformed.

The key to the feminist view of the dialogic basis of mind (and self as well, as we shall see) is to be found in the critique of the dominant epistemological position in which good knowledge is equated with objective knowledge, which is said to be abstract and removed from any concrete particularities: the God's-eye view from Nowhere to which I have referred above. This is the kind of knowledge that presumably grounds physics and also serves as the basis for the frequent illustrations that one finds in philosophical works – for example, knowledge that "the cat *is* in fact on the mat"; that "the house *is* in fact red"; that "this *is* in fact a rock". The argument is that once we understand how we know these simple objects/facts of our world, we will be able to understand how we know the more complex objects as well.

It is against this view that both Harding's initial treatment and Code's later treatment have been developed. In a manner that parallels Mead, Bakhtin and the others, they locate the dialogic paradigm at the root of *all* understanding, rather than treating it as relevant – if at all – only to a small, possibly peculiar segment of human knowledge and understanding. Code, for example, urges us to consider how we come to understand "others as friends" as the paradigm suitable to all knowledge and understanding:

> In fact, knowing other people is at least as worthy a contender for paradigmatic status as knowledge of medium-sized, everyday objects. Developmentally, recognizing other people, learning what can be expected of them, is both one of the first and one of the most essential kinds of knowledge a child acquires. An infant learns to respond *cognitively* to its caregivers *long before* it can recognize the simplest of physical objects. (Code, 1991, p. 37)

> it is surely no more preposterous to argue that people should try to know physical objects in the nuanced way that they know their friends than it is to argue that they should try to know people in the unsubtle way that they claim to know physical objects. (p. 165)

Wittgenstein's Challenge to the Private Inner World

There is a kind of general disease of thinking which always looks for (and finds) what would be called a mental state from which all our acts spring as from a reservoir. Thus one says, "The fashion changes because the taste of people changes". The taste is the mental reservoir. But if a tailor to-day designs a cut of dress different from that which he designed a year ago, can't what is called his change of taste have consisted, partly or wholly, in doing just this? (Wittgenstein, 1958, p. 143)

In this representative passage, Wittgenstein illustrates his case against the need to posit an inner mental world in order to explain human behavior. He argues that the meaning of the term "taste" in the quoted passage – where it is used "as the name of a feeling" (p. 144) – is not the same as it is when we refer to the taste of a beverage, for example. Unfortunately, our language habits lead us to confuse these two (and more) different uses, and so to believe that "taste" refers to some elemental mental quality within the individual that calls forth and explains a particular behavior, when in fact it does no such thing.

Wittgenstein offers another example involving Saint Augustine's attempt to define how one measures time, concluding that it is a truly puzzling thing. After all, one cannot measure the past, since it is over and done with, nor the future, because it has yet to arrive, nor the present, as it lacks extension:

> The contradiction which here seems to arise would be called a conflict between two different usages of a word, in this case the word "measure". Augustine ... thinks of the process of measuring a *length*: say, the distance between two marks on a travelling band which passes us. ... Solving this puzzle will consist in comparing what we mean by "measurement" (the grammar of the word "measurement") when applied to a distance on a travelling band with the grammar of that word when applied to time. (1958, p. 26)

In other words, when we come across puzzles of this sort, their solution usually involves probing further into the role of language in communication. Such probing will unravel the very thing that puzzled us in the first place. Measuring time is a puzzle only when we consider "to measure" to be to calculate as in length.

In a similar manner – but now applied directly to mental terms – Wittgenstein tells us that our language confuses us into believing that we are referring to a specific mental apparatus or activity, when in fact we have before us only grammatical usages in operation. "The thing to do in such cases is always to look how the words in question *are actually used in our language*" (1958, p. 56). And again: "The meaning of a phrase for us is characterized by the use we make of it. The meaning is not a mental accompaniment to the expression" (1958, p. 65).

Wittgenstein does not deny the mind, or mental concepts; he argues that they do have a definite use *in our language*. But it is their *use* in communication rather than their reference to some inner substance which is real independently of that social usage that he wishes to emphasize. He shows us in repeated examples how the substantive reference makes little sense, while the usage criterion holds the key to our understanding: "the grammar of those words which describe what are called 'mental activities': seeing, hearing, feeling, etc. . . . has deluded people into thinking that they had discovered new entities, new elements of the structure of the world" (1958, p. 70).

In turning to usage, Wittgenstein teaches us that the public, social world of shared practices is central to all understanding. Different social worlds with different practices and usages (i.e. different language-games) create different formulations.

By now it should be apparent that cross-cultural data are consistent with Wittgenstein's formulation. Our own language-games require the usage of mental terms that appear to refer to some personal, inner, private world containing real, substantive mental entities. This is not, however, because the terms refer to something substantive within us, but rather because we have evolved a form of living together in which such usages have become central.

As Gergen (1989) puts it: "When asked for accounts of self, participants in contemporary Western culture unflinchingly agree that emotions, ideas, plans, memories and the like are all significant. Such accounts of the mind are critical to who we are, what we stand for and how we conduct ourselves in the world" (p. 70). In true Wittgensteinian fashion, Gergen goes on to comment that none of these terms is "anchored in, defined by or ostensively grounded in real-world particulars" (p. 71); these terms do "not mirror or map an independent reality but [are] a functioning element in social process itself" (p. 71), "elaborated as various interest groups within the culture seek to warrant or justify their accounts of the world" (p. 72).

We have built our lives around these terms, but not because they are real, in the sense of being independent of the very social life and conversations within which they gain their meaning. Mental terms serve useful functions in accounting for, justifying and warranting our way of life – or, as Gergen implies, at least the way of life of dominant social groups within society. Other societies – the Baining we considered in Chapter 5, for example – eschew a similar mentalistic reference, yet get along quite well within the context of their society and its requirements for living together.

The Social Bases of Mind

There is perhaps nothing more peculiar or even contradictory for most of us than to consider mental processes to be "not bounded by the individual brain or mind" (Resnick, 1991, p. 1). Yet this is precisely the view advocated by both Vygotsky (1978) and Mead (1934), and currently entering with renewed vigor into the empirical investigation of cognitive development as a corrective to the more conventional cognitivist accounts such as those we considered in Chapter 4.[5]

Vygotsky's formulation is generally well known, although it has only recently been rediscovered by North American psychologists. Vygotsky's classic example of the social foundations of mind involves a young child who appears to be "pointing". The child makes grasping movements towards an object that lies beyond its reach. The care-taker enters the room and sees the child's actions, sensing that its gesture indicates its desire for the object:

> Pointing becomes a gesture for others. The child's unsuccessful attempt engenders a reaction not from the object he seeks but *from another person.* Consequently, the primary meaning of that unsuccessful grasping movement is established by others. Only later, when the child can link his unsuccessful grasping movement to the objective situation as a whole, does he begin to understand this movement as pointing. At this juncture there occurs a change in that movement's function: from an object-oriented movement it becomes a movement aimed at another person, a means of establishing relations. . . . It becomes a true gesture only after it objectively manifests all the functions of pointing for others and is understood by others as such a gesture. (1978, p. 56)

In short, what begins its life as an interpersonal process becomes transformed over time into an intrapersonal process:

> Every function in the child's cultural development appears twice: first, on the social level, and later, on the individual level; first *between* people (*interpsychological*) and then *inside* the child (*intrapsychological*). This applies equally to voluntary attention, to logical memory, and to the formation of concepts. All the higher functions originate as actual relations between human individuals. (p. 57)

In a strikingly similar manner, Mead (1934) presents us with a three-stage process involved in all social acts from which mental properties and mindedness are said to emerge:

> A gesture by one organism, the resultant of the social act in which the gesture is an early phase, and the response of another organism to the gesture, are the relata in a triple or threefold relationship . . . and this threefold relationship constitutes the matrix within which meaning arises. (p. 178)

We can use Vygotsky's grasping child to illustrate the three phases outlined by Mead. The child's grasping movements (the first phase) indicate a resultant state of affairs, namely holding the desired object (the second phase). In the case illustrated, this resultant initially exists in the social world of the care-taker, for whom the gesture indicates a desired resultant on the part of the child. The care-taker's response completes the social act and endows it with meaning (the third phase).

Both Vygotsky and Mead argue that these phases first exist in the social world involving other people; only later, when they call out in the child the same trio of phases as they call out in the care-taker, do they become the basis for meaningful social communication. In other words – as Vygotsky notes, and as Mead concurs – only when the child can indicate to itself what has previously been indicated only to the adult care-taker does a genuine intrapsychological process come into being. This internal conversation is called thinking and describes the person's carrying on internally a process that originated and remains rooted in the social world with others.

Both Vygotsky and Mead clearly emphasize the necessary social bases of human thinking, cognition, and mindedness. Indeed, rather than viewing the individual's mind as setting forth the terms for the social order, the reverse describes the actual event: the social process – namely, dialogue and conversation – precedes, and is the foundation for, any subsequent psychological processes that emerge. Furthermore, in so far as we always live and operate within a social world with others, mindedness remains rooted to that same social process.

One final point shared by Mead and Vygotsky involves their unequivocal emphasis on the central role that the other plays in the formation of all that we currently presume to be characteristics of the individual – including, for example, the individual's mind, thinking, memory, and so forth. It is the other's response that first endows the child's halting gestures with meaning. It is the other's response that completes the triadic social act and constitutes meaning.

In her original feminist challenge to the science question, Harding (1986) argued that because of their focus on the knowledge and understanding of people, the social sciences "should be the model for all science, and that if there are any special requirements for adequate explanations in physics, they are just that – special" (p. 44). As we have seen, Code (1991) has picked up on this theme, suggesting that our knowledge of other people should be taken as the paradigm for knowledge in general.

By insisting that an interpersonal model should become the model for all knowledge, both Harding and Code clearly affirm the Vygotskian and Meadian emphasis. In each case, learning in, through and about the other takes precedence, and would indeed serve us well as the model for all processes of knowing.

Code's ideas are especially useful to consider. I have been able to discern at least eight aspects of the cognitive activity involved in knowing other people that give us a very differently cast paradigm of knowledge.

1. There is a contrast between the multidimensional and multiperspectival quality of our knowledge of other people and the "stark simplicity of standard paradigms" (p. 37) of knowledge; this raises questions for Code about why we have granted such "exemplary status to the standard paradigms" (p. 37).

2. "[K]nowing other people, precisely because of the fluctuations and contradictions of subjectivity, is an ongoing communicative, interpretive process. It can never be fixed or complete; any fixity ... is at best a fixity in flux" (p. 38).

3. Because of the preceding, arriving at generalizations, let alone universal principles, is a very risky business. Knowing another keeps us on our "cognitive toes: the 'more or lessness' of this knowledge constantly affirms the need to reserve and revise judgment" (p. 38).

4. "Yet ongoing personal and political commitments cannot be left undecided; they require affirmation that people know one another well enough to be able to go on" (p. 38).

5. The knower/known positions are not fixed: "Claims to know a person are open to negotiation between knower and 'known', where the 'subject' and 'object' positions are always, in principle, exchangeable" (p. 38).

6. Under such conditions, "neither the self-conception nor the knower-conception can claim absolute, ultimate authority" (p. 38).

7. "The process of knowing other people requires constant learning: how to be with them, respond to them, act toward them" (p. 39).

8. "The crucial and intriguing fact about knowing people – and the reason why it affords insights into problems of knowledge – is that even if one could know all the facts about someone, one would not know her as the person she is" (p. 40).

Harding's point, as well as Code's, is that we have based our view of knowledge, cognition and mindedness on an asocial, distancing and abstract paradigm. While this paradigm might work well for physics – but apparently not really well there either, according to modern quantum physics – and while it may distort little when the issue involves knowledge about very simple objects of our world around which there is general agreement (e.g. this cup is red), it provides a poor paradigm for all knowledge, cognition and mindedness.

In this, then, several feminist critics of the masculinist quality of the prevailing paradigm join with certain philosophers (e.g. Mead and Wittgenstein), psychologists (e.g. Vygotsky) and literary analysts (e.g. Bakhtin) who, while not entering the debate over the male-centeredness of nondialogic formulations, have nevertheless proposed perspectives that are entirely congruent with such a formulation.

The Emergence of the Self

There is a scene in Sartre's (1946) play *Huis clos* (*No Exit*) that offers a useful example of the way in which a person's self is not only an emergent of social interaction but remains rooted as an ongoing accomplishment of social interaction. The scene involves Estelle, a particularly vain woman who finds herself trapped for an eternity without a mirror, and Inez, a second character also trapped together with Estelle for an eternity. Without a mirror to let her view herself as an object, and thus as others do, Estelle grows restive and deeply concerned about her existence. She pats her face to see if she really exists, only to realize that touching is a paltry substitute for her actual reflection through another person's eyes.

This is where Inez enters the scene, volunteering to be Estelle's mirror, in both a literal sense (permitting Estelle to step close enough to see her reflection in Inez's pupils) and a less literal sense (by commenting on how wonderful Estelle looks). Inez, recognizing that being Estelle's mirror gives her great power over Estelle, tells Estelle of a pimple that scars her otherwise perfect visage. But it is only a tease; there is no pimple. Yet how can Estelle ever know this without Inez to reflect her back to herself? Upset as Estelle is by this teasing, she is even more upset by Inez's threat no longer to look at her at all, and so to render her identityless.

This scene reveals the two *phases* of the self, the "I" and the "Me" that Mead posits. The "I" is that phase that is never directly knowable. Mead's point is that when we are doing something, we are unaware of what is going on until we can see our doings reflected back to us; that reflection back gives us ourselves as an object, a "me": "If you ask, then, where directly in your own experience the 'I' comes in, the answer is that it comes in as a historical figure. It is what you were a second ago that is the 'I' of the 'me'" (Mead, 1934, p. 243). And further on: "The 'I' is his action over against that social situation within his own conduct, and it gets into his experience only after he has carried out the act" (p. 244).

Bakhtin's analysis parallels Mead's in several respects. He too comments on the invisibility of the person's self, or what he terms the I-for-myself:

as a unique becoming, my I-for-myself is always invisible. In order to perceive that self, it must find expression in categories that can fix it, and these I can only get from the other. So that when I complete the other, or when the other completes me, she and I are actually exchanging the gift of a perceptible self . . . I get a self I can see, that I can understand and use, by clothing my otherwise invisible (incomprehensible, unutilizable) self in the completing categories I appropriate from the other's image of me. (In Clark and Holquist, 1984, p. 79)

As these passages indicate, both Mead and Bakhtin offer us a view in which the other plays a central role in constituting the individual's self. Without the other, our selves would be not only invisible to us but *incomprehensible* and *unutilizable*. The other endows us with meaning and clothes us in comprehensibility; the other engenders a self that we can utilize to function in our social world.

The argument, in short, is that we gain a self in and through a process of social interaction, dialogue, and conversation with others in our social world; that the only knowledge we can have of ourselves appears in and through social forms – namely, others' responses. Borrowing a term from Baier, Code refers to this process as our becoming *second persons*, beings created in and through our relations with others. None of this makes us passive, simple reflections of others; rather, the image conveyed by Bakhtin, Mead, Code and others is of a very active and ongoing process in which each party makes adjustments to the other's anticipated responses. I do not simply reflect your depiction of me, but rather adjust myself as I anticipate your responses, even while making responses to you that help to shape the very responses you are likely to offer back to me.

While we may feel sorry for poor Estelle captured for an eternity with Inez's teasing and threats, we should reserve that sorrow for another day. Estelle is very capable of employing whatever devices are at her disposal to gain the kinds of responses from Inez that she, Estelle, would most enjoy receiving. Estelle need not wait for Inez's responses in order to gain a desired identity; Estelle can play the situation as well, tempting Inez to come just a bit closer in exchange for a positive mirroring.

Mead and Bakhtin also agree on another feature of this addressive quality (to use Bakhtin's terminology at this point) of our selves. We address our own acts in anticipation of the responses of *real others* with whom we are currently involved; *imagined others*, including characters from our own past as well as from cultural narratives; *historical others*; and the *generalized other*, typically carried in the language forms by which a given community organizes its perceptions and understandings of its members, which we have learned to employ in reflecting us back to us. In each case, we adjust our own emerging actions in anticipation of the responses of these various others.[6] (The multifaceted quality of the self that is implied here will be examined more fully in Chapter 8.) The process by which our selves are constituted, however, is ongoing, never over and done with. As Bakhtin puts it, dialogues are not something that we can ever simply enter and leave; life itself is dialogic. We move from one to another, each shading into the next, and the next, and so on.

These processes by which our selves are socially constituted and sustained allow for either the kind of symmetry that both Mead and Bakhtin imply or for the kind of asymmetry that is so central to most feminist accounts – for example, those considered in Chapter 1 and those I take up in more detail in Chapter 10. Symmetry would exist if the parties – Estelle and Inez, for example – were equal contributors to each other's emerging identity. Asymmetry occurs whenever one of the parties has more power to determine the nature of the other's identity, and thus their own identity reflected through the other.

While many exchanges are undoubtedly more symmetrical than not, when the situation involves social categories that are in themselves based on power differentials (e.g. man/woman; black/white; civilized/primitive), asymmetry is more the rule than the exception. To put it simply: as most feminist analysts claim, nearly every male–female encounter is so saturated with power differentials favoring the male that asymmetry usually describes the processes by which the woman's identity is established so that she can be the serviceable other the male requires to achieve the identity he most desires.[7]

Constructing Social Reality

The argument up to this point is that mind and all its attributes, as well as personality and personal identity (i.e. self), are emergents of a dialogic, conversational process and remain socially rooted as an ongoing accomplishment of that process.[8] The third element in this analysis argues that social reality itself is likewise an emergent and ongoing accomplishment of the same social process: that the very categories by which we know, apprehend and experience the world in which we live are derivatives of a dialogic process occurring within that very world.

Voloshinov[9] illustrates this understanding in his example of hunger, noting that although we typically consider hunger to be a purely physiological event, its experience is basically dialogical: "Which way the intoning of the inner sensation of hunger will go depends upon the hungry person's general social standing as well as upon the immediate circumstances of the experience" (1929/1986, p. 87), which include the possible addressees who are involved.

More generally, Voloshinov argues:

> there is no such thing as experience outside of embodiment in signs. ...
> Furthermore, the location of the organizing and formative center is not
> within ... but outside. It is not experience that organizes expression, but the
> other way around – *expression organizes experience*. Expression is what first
> gives experience its form and specificity or direction. (p. 85)

It is clear that Voloshinov's position is that all experiences, of whatever sort,
are comprehensible and utilizable (to employ the previous terms) only in
and through social categories, and involve addressivity. Social categories,
however, are not merely the preexisting vehicles through which we
apprehend experience, but also the ongoing accomplishment of the very
dialogic process involved in their constitution. Dialogues both express and
constitute social reality. In other words, our conversations both express and
help to create the particular world in which we and others live.

This is how one author (Dominguez, 1989) stated what might otherwise
appear paradoxical: "through dialogue and discourse we may assume, or at
least come to believe in, the existence of something whose very existence is,
in fact, continually 'created' by discursive acts of signification in which we
participate" (p. 21). Our conversations both express and presuppose a
reality which, in expressing what is presupposed, we help to create.

Wittgenstein (1958) has his own way of stating this same central point.
He noted, for example, how the phrase

> "to express an idea which is before our mind" suggests that what we are
> trying to express in words is already expressed, only in a different language;
> that this expression is before our mind's eye; and that what we do is to
> translate from the mental into the verbal language. (p. 41)

He rejects this formulation, urging us rather to see how the very expression
(i.e. usage) constitutes social reality.

John Shotter (1990) puts this same point in the following way: "Mostly
we talk with the aim of creating and sustaining various forms of life" (p.
57). Edwards (1991) reminds us that we use our talking to construct a
social reality that we presume to be independent of the very talk that has
constituted and helps to sustain it. He notes, furthermore, how "What is
real, out there beyond the socially organized practices of knowledge, talk
and disputation, is precisely what all the talk is about" (p. 538). This is his
way of telling us that our conversations not only help to create the sense of
a shared reality, but often involve examining that very sense: evaluating
competing claims about its characteristics; settling disputes over who has
the right to set the terms by which our shared reality will be constituted.

What, then, does the dialogic turn teach us about us? First of all, we learn that we are fundamentally and irretrievably dialogic, conversational creatures, whose lives are created in and through conversations and sustained or transformed in and through conversations. We learn that the very processes of our mind – including how we think, how we reason, how we know, how we solve problems, and so forth – are best grasped by examining the conversations in the social worlds we inhabit, which we appropriate and use. We learn that the qualities of our personality and identity are likewise constituted conversationally and sustained through our dialogues with various others. We learn that the social reality in which we live out our lives is itself constituted conversationally; that much of our talk with others is both an expression of social reality and the means whereby social reality is created and sustained as an ongoing accomplishment of those very conversations with others.

But perhaps the greatest lesson of all, one that turns the tables rather completely on the self-celebratory project of the Western world, is simply that a celebration of the other lies at the heart of human life and experience. The other is a vital co-creator of our mind, our self, and our society. Without the other, we are mindless, selfless and societyless – hardly a fertile field, then, for continuing to celebrate much of anything.

Notes

1. Flax (1990, especially p. 228) questions the privileging of conversations that is central not only to my work but also to the variety of discourse theorists whose work I consider throughout this book.
2. To anyone familiar with his writings, it is apparent that I have appropriated the title and major chapters of G.H. Mead's (1934) book dealing with the symbolic and interactional basis of mind, of self, and of society.
3. Specific works will be cited and quoted in their relevant contexts; in general, however, I am referring here to the following: Mead (1934); Wittgenstein (1953, 1958; see also Bloor, 1983 as well as Monk's [1990] valuable biography); Vygotsky (1978; see also Kozulin, 1990; Wertsch, 1991); Bakhtin (1981, 1986; see also Clark and Holquist, 1984; Morson and Emerson, 1990; Todorov, 1984). I have included the writings of Voloshinov (1927/1987, 1929/1986) in Bakhtin's group, taking these works, written under his name, as being his, and sidestepping as irrelevant to my purposes whether or not they were really authored by Bakhtin, as some contend, or by Voloshinov, as others have maintained.
4. Many other feminist writers have also contributed to this understanding, including Braidotti (1991); Gatens (1991); Flax (1990).
5. There has been a recent upsurge of interest among some cognitive psychologists in the social bases of thinking, but especially in Vygotsky's ideas. One clear sign of this is the book *Perspectives on Socially Shared Cognition*, edited by Resnick *et al.* (1991) and published by the American Psychological Association. Other

works are also central to this recasting of cognitive psychology: Bruner (1990); Lave (1988); Rogoff and Lave (1984); Wertsch (1991); and, of course, the important works of Cole and his colleagues (e.g. Cole, 1988; Cole *et al.*, 1971; Cole and Means, 1981). See also Chapter 9 below.

6. The term *generalized other* is Mead's, and refers to the community-as-other that provides yet another position from which our "me" is constituted.

7. When I refer to "he" and "she", I am rarely referring to a specific concrete individual person, but rather to the collective male and to the collective female. In other words, any specific male or female may not fit this picture; collectively, however, the picture is all too accurate.

8. In using this phrasing here as previously, I am appropriating Garfinkel's (1967) ethnomethodology, in which social activity is studied as an ongoing accomplishment of actors' interactions. See also Cicourel's (1974) cognitive sociology, as well as the more current group of primarily European discourse analysts: e.g. Billig (1987); Edwards (1991); Harré (1984); Potter and Wetherell (1987). Needless to say, the idea that social reality is constructed conversationally also owes a great deal to Berger and Luckman's (1966) important book.

9. A reminder: as I previously noted, some suggest that Voloshinov is actually Bakhtin; others suggest that Voloshinov wrote under his own name. It is not central to my work to enter into this debate. I use Voloshinov as the author of record because that is the name on the book.

8

The Multiple Voices of Human Nature

The actual names, places or crimes do not really matter. A television documentary posed the problem. A woman had been convicted of a serious crime warranting a stiff prison sentence. However, psychiatric examination revealed that she was not one person, but several, possibly six. Who committed the crime? Was it Lola? Or perhaps Janet? Maybe Irene or Susan or Kathy or . . . ? With treatment, Janet became conversant with the many selves that seemed to dwell within her one frail body. She learned how to call forth each of her six or so separate selves, holding lengthy conversations with each one, including the criminal-self, Lola. Was it fair, wondered Janet, that she and all the others – including little 6-year-old Kathy – were incarcerated for a crime they did not commit! Surely, only Lola should be considered the wrongdoer, not Janet and company?

Although this case illustrates a serious problem, unfortunately, that problem was central neither to the TV documentary nor to Western beliefs about the self. The implication of the documentary is that a healthy individual contains but one central, core self – moody, perhaps, somewhat variable under trying conditions, shifting around a bit as we take on the many different roles we each play, but nevertheless, fundamentally integrated and whole. We insist that Janet *et al.* are pathological because her one body contains too many separately integrated personalities, violating the belief in an integrated whole, a core self.

Wetherell and Potter (1989) raised a question concerning whether this core idea or an alternative, more fragmented view predominates in Western understanding. They pointed to the prevalence of a cultural view of the self as a role-player. Since we all play many roles, we must have many different selves, not simply one integrated core.

While our character as role-players is widely recognized in the West, I maintain that most people continue to believe that beneath all this fragmentation lives their real self. Indeed, without this belief in a core, it would be difficult to complain that a particular role violated one's deeply felt sense of integrity. Despite their belief in a fragmented alternative, Wetherell and Potter's research lends support to my contention.

They studied the excuses that onlookers offered for the police riot that occurred in New Zealand in response to the demonstrations against the 1981 Springbok rugby tour. Some explanations excused police behavior by turning to role theory. Wetherell and Potter say: "The use of role discourse allows a split between the genuine motives and beliefs of the police and what they were required to do because it was their job" (p. 215). In other words, role explanations provide excuses – not because the self is fragmented and multiple, but rather because it is coherent and integrated around a core. It is because of this core that people – police in this study – faced conflicts with the roles they were forced to take on. It is because of this core that onlookers could excuse the police by arguing that while they did not really want to behave badly, their jobs required them to. And so, the alternative possibility notwithstanding, I continue to insist that the notion of an integrated core self predominates in Western understanding.

The serious problem that I see with this common cultural belief is its failure to take cognizance of the kind of multiplicity that necessarily comes into focus once we adopt the dialogic framework.[1] If people are constituted as who and what they are by the various conversations in which they engage throughout their lives, is it not far more reasonable to presume that we are each a multiplicity rather than a unity? I am not talking here about several fully integrated but separate personalities, such as the six that seem to live within Janet's frail body. Nor am I talking about people being the various roles they play, separating their real selves from the obligatory parts they are asked to take on. For the most part, these formulations presuppose an integrated, unified whole and then talk about departures from it – some relatively normal (e.g. role performances), others relatively pathological (e.g. Janet's multiple personality disorder).

If we begin very differently, however, by adopting the dialogic formulation of human nature, then we can readily see how multiplicity is the norm, while any apparent singularity of personality is an ongoing accomplishment of certain social forms and practices. In short, rather than beginning with the assumption of a unified core identity, one that traverses the many roles and situations people confront throughout life and ensures them a sense of unity and continuity, we begin with the assumption of an ever-shifting multiplicity and consider unity and continuity to be a particular social accomplishment. If we experience a core self, then, this is not because we have a core, but rather because we function in a society in which that formulation has become a dominant belief that is usually reaffirmed by everyday social institutions and cultural practices.

Some critical analysts have argued that those practices that accomplish a unitary core self do so on behalf of sustaining the dominance of certain powerful groups in Western society – primarily white and male – over others for whom multiplicity may be more typical. Irigaray's account of woman's specificity, for example, makes this argument. She notes that by suppressing multiplicity on behalf of a unitary conception of the person, woman's more multiply positioned body, sexuality and specificity are denied.

A similar view emerges from Pagels's (1981) discussion of the politics of monotheism. The Gnostic understanding of the multiplicity of God and of people was challenged by the monotheistic beliefs of the emerging Judeo-Christian tradition. Pagels tells us:

> As God reigns in heaven as master, lord, commander, judge, and king, so on earth he delegates his rule to members of the church hierarchy, who serve as generals, who command an army of subordinates; kings who rule over "the people"; judges who preside in God's place. (p. 41)

> If God is One, then there can be only one true church, and only one representative of the God in the community – the bishop. (p. 52)

The oneness of God thereby comes to represent the oneness of the entire hierarchy emanating from Him, including the fundamental oneness of man, made in God's image. As Pagels observes, this theme of oneness represents the view of primarily wealthy men seeking to gain power for themselves by capturing the religious frameworks of understanding. Their own interests were opposed to the more egalitarian and woman-recognizing Gnostic view. Needless to say, we all know the outcome of this early confrontation: oneness was victorious over multiplicity; male was victorious over female.

Whether we wish to join Irigaray and others who insist that multiplicity reflects woman's specificity as contrasted with the unity sought by man, it is clear that a more multiple view of the person remains a viable alternative conception. This multiplicity, however, is not based on fully formed but separate personalities, as in the multiple personality disorder; the latter emphasizes fully formed unities. Rather, the dialogic framework leads us to expect multiplicity within as well as between people, no one form of which is in itself unitary, integrated or whole.

In other words, we are asked to consider each of us to be composed of a rather thoroughgoing multiplicity, but not in the sense of several integrated personalities. Dialogic multiplicity refers to the diversity of voices with which we are all constituted, no one of which or combination of which marks a fundamental, real, central, integrated us. To think dialogically, we must dispense with our cultural belief in singularity and bounded wholeness so that we may see manyness without insisting that such manyness must consist of a collection of fully formed singularities. And we are asked to see the unity of a core self as a particular social accomplishment serving certain purposes – associated in the West, it seems, with male domination.

Genres and Heteroglossia

But how does dialogism understand multiplicity? The answer is to be found in Bakhtin's (1981, 1986) related set of conceptions: *genres*, *heteroglossia* and *chronotopes*. Let us return to the baseline, language. Considering language dialogically, as we know, means that our primary interest is not in language as a formal system, but rather in language as it is used by people communicating together in conversations. While each person's language use may appear to be a unique occurrence – and in some respects, indeed, may properly be so considered – "each sphere in which language is used develops its own *relatively stable types*. . . . These we may call *speech genres*" (Bakhtin, 1986, p. 60).

The scene that Bakhtin confronted had been dominated primarily by formalistic models of language. True to the Enlightenment project we previously considered, formalist linguists sought to uncover some under-lying and stable center for what was obviously a plethora of specific and unique vocalizations that comprised each individual's language perform-ances. Typically, this underlying center was sought in grammatical forms that could be examined as though they were a calculus, a formal mathematical system out of which the various observable features of all languages could be generated.

In short, Bakhtin faced a climate of linguistic study that sought to tame the diversity, uniqueness and particularity of each individual utterance by searching for an underlying formal system that was stable and universal. By contrast, Bakhtin argued that we could find whatever stability we required through the concept of speech genre. Each individualized utterance, however unique, nevertheless employed one or more speech genres. While these were extraordinarily diverse and "boundless because the various possibilities of human activity are inexhaustible" (1986, p. 60), genres were nevertheless stable forms that could be more systematically examined.

Basically, Bakhtin eschewed searching for some formal core lying beneath actual language usages among people communicating and living together; rather, he sought systematicity within the forms or genres of actual speech in use. Genres did not reflect or follow a formal calculus, nor did they form a quasi-mathematical system. Genres developed over time as people engaged together in the many activities of their collectively organized life. Genres were limited and coherent, but also boundless in that as the issues of collective life changed, so too would the genres.

When we talk with one another, we have a variety of speech genres available to us. As Bakhtin observes, we never just use language, but always languages in the plural. Every national language contains a diversity of speech styles and hence is heteroglot – this term refers to the varied *speechedness* that appears in any one national language: English, for example. For instance, there are genres of professions, generations, classes, areas of interest, ethnic groups:

> In fact, the category of speech genres should include short rejoinders of daily dialogue (and these are extremely varied depending on the subject matter, situation, and participants), everyday narration, writing (in all its various forms), the brief standard military command, the elaborate and detailed order, the fairly variegated repertoire of business documents ... and the diverse world of commentary (in the broad sense of the word: social, political). And we must also include here the diverse forms of scientific statements and all literary genres (from the proverb to the multivolume novel). (Bakhtin, 1986, pp. 60–1)

Although it is by no means complete, this listing should provide a good sense both of what Bakhtin means by speech genre and of the diversity of genres that people can employ in their everyday conversations. There is nothing esoteric at work here. When a father uses babytalk with his newly born infant, and moments later answers the telephone to carry on a conversation with a salesperson employing still another genre, and only moments after hanging up continues with the other adults in the room employing still a different genre, we have illustrated the variety of genres which we all employ every day.

Bakhtin illustrates another aspect of his analysis of speech genres with the case of a person who is in excellent command of language yet feels helpless in a given situation precisely because he lacks the speech genre that is appropriate to that situation. Consider, for example, the academic scholar who is very ill at ease in social conversation: "Here it is not a matter of an impoverished vocabulary or of style, taken abstractly; this is entirely a matter of the inability to command a repertoire of genres of social conversation" (1986, p. 80).

Bakhtin also tells us that "we speak in diverse genres without suspecting that they exist. Even in the most free, the most unconstrained conversation, we cast our speech in definite generic forms, sometimes rigid and trite ones, sometimes more flexible, plastic and creative ones" (1986, p. 78). We are somewhat like Molière's character, speaking in a specific genre without, however, being aware that we are doing so. Furthermore, as Bakhtin notes, the genre itself is constraining: it directs the manner by which we say whatever it is we are saying, however unique and individualistic our conversation might appear to be.

Any speech genre, however, is not simply a manner of speaking but, most importantly, a manner of viewing and experiencing the world, including self and other. When we employ a genre, therefore, we are casting our lot with a particular formulation of human experience – a theory, if you will – that provides its own particular accenting and intoning.

The point is an important one. For Bakhtin, genres help to shape our experience; each genre casts a somewhat different accent around our lives and our understanding. The person who employs a professional genre in dealing with others, for example, is not simply talking in a particular manner, but structuring both her own and others' experiences on the basis of that genre.

Although he approached this issue from a different framework, the interesting work of Basil Bernstein (1971, 1973) offers us one useful illustration of Bakhtin's point. Bernstein suggested that the different social classes he studied have different forms of speaking, or what he termed *codes* (i.e. genres), which provide them with different ways of understanding their situation. The *restricted code* that characterizes the working class constructs for its users a different social reality from the reality constructed by those of middle-class background who employ what Bernstein called an *elaborated code*. Here are some of the code-related distinctions noted by Bernstein.

Descriptions of people and events offered in restricted codes tend to focus more on concrete than on abstract matters. An illustration of this comes from another source, an interview study in which people of different social classes were asked about a tornado disaster that had recently hit their community (Schatzman and Strauss, 1955). Examination of the interviews indicated that the working-class subjects' descriptions were made entirely through the eyes of the person reporting, rarely offering any qualifiers to what was being said. By contrast, the middle-class descriptions not only included different points of view but also offered more qualified descriptions, calling upon the context within which their observations had been made.

A further distinction between the restricted and elaborated codes involves the way nonverbal information is integrated into the verbal messages. Bernstein's work suggests that the restricted code calls upon nonverbal markers to expand on the meaning of what is being said to a greater extent than the elaborated codes, which contain more richly varied verbal information and so require fewer nonverbal markers in order to get the message across to others. It is noted, for example, how middle-class children learn to look for clues in what their parents *say* in order to detect the meaning and pick up any changes in mood. Working-class children learn to look less at the verbal message and pay more attention to the kinds of nonverbal information that are being communicated.

Other research expands on this while further amplifying Bakhtin's point regarding speech genres. A fascinating study reported by Bourque and Back (1971), for example, examined the relationship between the availability of a language genre for dealing with intense emotional experiences of a mystical sort and people's ability to interpret and deal with such experiences. Data indicated that people whose genre included mystical experiences had less difficulty in describing and accepting intense emotional experiences compared with those for whom such a genre did not exist. The latter viewed intense mystical experiences as signs of pathology; they could not easily treat such experiences as normal or talk about them in a more routine manner.

Another illustration of the manner in which genres both structure and are structured by experience comes from some of the fascinating work reported by Maccoby (1990). Her studies of children's interactions reveal patterns that seem to be linked to the sex of the child. Girls favor what Maccoby refers to as an *enabling* style, whereas boys reveal a preference for a *restrictive* style. The former operates to advance the ongoing interaction, while the latter derails it. For example, the little girl responds to her partner's comments with a supportive statement that helps to keep the interaction going. The little boy, by contrast, responds critically, leading his partner either to withdraw and so bring the interaction to a close, or to escalate into a more conflictful encounter.

These examples call our attention to the way people placed differently in the social world develop different speech genres that structure their experiences even as they have been structured by their particular social locations. While these examples are useful for illustrating Bakhtin's point about the intimate connection between genres and experience, they may give an impression that is opposed to his point regarding multiplicity. That is, we may get the impression that each social class in Bernstein's project is stuck with one and only one genre, or that each gender in Maccoby's research is likewise genre-specific. In neither case, then, is multiplicity apparent.

While it is indeed not incorrect to note this possibility, and even to see it as one conversational mechanism by which a unity of identity is accomplished (i.e. by employing one rather than several speech genres), we must not lose sight of Bakhtin's other point, which indeed applies even in these examples. Boys are not entirely restrictive, nor girls entirely enabling; nor are members of a particular social class as entirely trapped as Bernstein's focus might lead us to believe.

Labov's (1966) classic study of New Yorkers, for example, while demonstrating social class differences in the use of higher-class vocal forms, also demonstrated shifts *within* each class in response to the nature of the situation: casual situations evoked lower speech forms than more formal situations in *both* upper-middle- and working-class subjects.

Other research likewise suggests a far greater flexibility in the generic repertoires available to most people, who slip into and out of each genre and thereby structure their experiences somewhat differently. Sociolinguistic research reported by Ervin-Tripp (1969), for example, offers numerous illustrations of genre flexibility as a function of specific social-situational requirements. She notes, for example, a switch from the familiar *tu* form of address to the more formal *vous* form when a worker is reprimanded by his or her supervisor. She also comments on Rubin's (1962) study revealing a shift among Paraguayan courting couples from Spanish before their vows to Guarani when their relationship became more intimate.

Research by Blom and Gumperz (1972) reveals a similar shift among the local residents of a Norwegian town who use standard Norwegian when enacting their roles as buyer and seller, but change to the local dialect if they want to initiate a private conversation on more personal matters. Each of these cases illustrates Bakhtin's point about the multiplicity of genres, and thus the potentially heteroglot quality of human nature.

Perhaps the most striking illustrations of this flexibility, however, appear in the body of research reviewed by Giles and Coupland (1991) involving the accommodations each of us makes in adjusting our speech genre to our addressee. They deal with two processes: congruence – when we change genres in order to speak like our addressee – and divergence – when we change to be more distinctive in our speech than our addressee. They report numerous studies in which both types of change were noted.

For example, Coupland reports one study in which travel agents adjusted their speech to converge with the social class of their clients. In another study, Bourhis and Giles (1977) report divergence among Welsh people whose strong beliefs in "their national group membership and its language" (see Giles and Coupland, 1991, p. 65) led them to broaden "their Welsh accents" when they were interviewed by a very English-sounding speaker who challenged their Welsh identity.

Giles and Coupland also report numerous studies in which the power of the addressee influenced the speaker's genre choice. One study in Quebec, for example, found greater convergence with the speech of an occupational superior than with that of a subordinate, while another, in Taiwan, showed sales personnel selecting a genre more suitable to their customers than vice versa. Once again, we see how each of us has a choice among numerous genres for encountering our world, never just one. Our choices reflect various "readings" we make of the situations we are in, the purposes we wish to accomplish, the people we are with. As growing bodies of research in the social psychology of language behavior increasingly demonstrate, we are truly heteroglot.

To summarize: genres are not simply ways of speaking but also ways of seeing, knowing and understanding. Different genres, then, place us in somewhat different worlds, or at least provide different accentings for experiencing our world, including our selves and others.

In general, the great diversity of genres that exist within any language and are available to language users creates a condition of *heteroglossia*: that is, varied speechedness as a normal condition of everyday life and experience. We have many different voices in and through which we speak, in and through which we relate to the world, in and through which we think. In that we are "the voices that inhabit us" (Morson and Emerson, 1990, p. 213), our many voices of heteroglossia offer us a manyness of selves, of thinking, of knowing and of experiencing.

The Chronotope

Bakhtin (1981) introduced the concept of the *chronotope* to add yet a further dimension to this picture: "We will give the name *chronotope* (literally, 'time–space') to the intrinsic connectedness of temporal and spatial relationships that are artistically expressed in literature" (p. 84). He viewed the chronotope as a basis for charting various literary and cultural genres. This concept involves generic variations of a historical and spatial-geographical nature, and also includes various conceptions of time. Paralleling his notion of heteroglossia, or the multiple languages of speaking, we have *heterochrony*, or *multiple timedness* (Morson and Emerson, 1990). Even as a variety of speech genres coexist at any one time, so too are we likely to find a variety of temporal–spatial world-views existing at the same time.

If we give it some thought, we are aware, for example, of a variety of temporal rhythms. Geological time is measured very differently from the sense of time that governs our individual biographies. Our lives begin and end in a tiny fraction of geological time. Indeed, the presence of humankind on earth is rather late and brief when considered against a geological timeframe. Yet both temporal chronotopes coexist.

Likewise, astronomical time, measured in light years, poses yet another formulation that differs dramatically from our sense of either personal time or even geological time. If we add to this the variety of temporal paces and rhythms of our everyday life, the picture becomes even more diverse. As Morson and Emerson (1990) comment:

> biological organisms may have their own special rhythms that are not

identical with astronomical ones or with each other. .... Furthermore, different social activities are also defined by various kinds of fused time and space: the rhythms and spatial organization of the assembly line, agricultural labor, sexual intercourse, and parlor conversation differ markedly. (p. 368)

Although most of Bakhtin's writing on the chronotope focuses on literary studies and genres, it is clear from both this writing and his overall work that his intention is not to restrict himself to literature alone, but rather to see how literary chronotopes help us to fathom the chronotopy of people's everyday lives and experiences. A sense of this wider use of the concept appears, for example, in Bakhtin's concluding statement, written towards the end of his life, noting how "every entry into the sphere of meaning is accomplished only through the gates of the chronotope" (1981, p. 258).

This passage appears after he has both illustrated literary chronotopes and briefly addressed the question of whether or not chronotopes appear in science and mathematics as they have in art and literature. His conclusion, clearly captured in the quoted passages, is that of course they must, for as soon as we are concerned with meaning – and when aren't we? – we must of necessity pass through the gates of the chronotope. In other words, even as the various speech genres of heteroglossia form different perspectives on the world, so too do chronotopes serve a similar function, providing the temporal–spatial frames within which our experiences achieve their meaning.

I will examine two somewhat different illustrations of Bakhtin's use of the chronotopic concept – not only to help clarify its meaning, but also to take us to the next necessary step: linking his ideas with some current work on narratives. The first example is based on Bakhtin's (1981) comparison of ancient and later chronotopes that formulate an autobiographical account of a person's life. He notes that in the earlier Greek view, autobiography and biography were hardly distinct; by contrast, later forms encouraged a separation of the public-biographical from the private-autobiographical form.

For example, the Greek consciousness of self was much more exterior and public than our own view: "Our 'internal' was, for the Greek's conception of man, laid out on the same axis as our 'external', that is, it was just as visible and audible and it existed on the surface, for others as well as for oneself" (Bakhtin, 1981, p. 135). In other words, "There is no mute or invisible core to the individual himself; he is entirely visible and audible. .... A mute internal life, a mute grief, mute thought, were completely foreign to the Greek" (p. 134).

Bakhtin (1981) tells us that although Plato "understood thought as a conversation that a man carries on with himself" (p. 134), that conversation was not private and internal in our terms, because it "did not entail any special relationship to one's self (as distinct from one's relationship to others); conversation with one's own self turns directly into conversation with someone else, without a hint of any necessary boundaries between the two" (p. 134).

Over time, and for reasons unspecified by Bakhtin, this chronotopic formulation was gradually transformed: "In following epochs, man's image was distorted by his increasing participation in the mute and invisible spheres of existence. He was literally drenched in muteness and invisibility" (p. 135). Bakhtin calls our attention to the growing interiority of the sense of the person and, with this move, the growing detachment of the private autobiography from the public biography. A person became known to self and others more through those private realms that were revealed in confessions, for example, or in accounts of personal, interior feelings, thoughts, and so forth, than through public accounts. Bakhtin speaks here of "the breakdown of this public exteriority of a man ... where the detached and singular individual's private self-consciousness begins to force itself through and bring to the surface the private spheres of his life" (p. 143). Similar understandings emerge from the collection edited by Carrithers *et al.* (1985) probing Mauss's concept of the person.

Bakhtin's contrast between these two chronotopes reveals how each offers a different account of a person's experiences. The Ancient Greek formulation employed a chronotope in which the melding of public and private made a person's own experience (as well as others' experience of that person) into a visible, audible, public story. If I were to share an account of my life, I would call upon the prevailing forms for doing this and so tell a story of my public experiences and activities. My view of myself would hardly differ from your view of me; we would both call upon what is publicly visible and available for both of us equally.

When that chronotope became increasingly interiorized, however, the separation between a public and a private perspective grew. In later times, my account of my life would not only build more upon private matters, known only to me, but would also consider these to be more essential in defining who I really was than any of my more publicly known activities.

Bakhtin's (1981) second illustration of chronotopes is more centrally focused on actual conceptions of time. This is illustrated in his analysis of what he terms folkloric time as contrasted with later chronotopes. Bakhtin presents eight features of folkloric time, referring here to the sense of time that appears especially among agricultural peoples: (1) time is collective and exists for the group rather than for the life cycle of the individual; (2) time is joined with work and labor, measured "by the phases of agricultural labor" (p. 207); (3) time involves productive growth, "blossoming, fruit-bearing, ripening, fruitful increase, issue" (p. 207); (4) time is "tensed toward the future" (p. 207) as "men sow for the future, gather in the harvest for the future, mate and copulate for the sake of the future" (p. 134); (5) "This time is *profoundly spatial and concrete*" (p. 208) – by which he means, that it is immersed in the earth and in nature: "The agricultural life of men and the life of nature (of the earth) are measured by one and the same scale, by the same events, they have the same intervals" (p. 208); (6) folkloric time is unified; it has not yet been abstracted from personal time, but is embedded in the life of the social whole; (7) this time "attracts everything into its orbit. . . . All objects – the sun, the stars, the earth, the sea and so forth – are present to man not as objects of individual perception . . . nor as objects of casual daydreaming, but exclusively as part of the collective process of labor and the battle against nature" (p. 209); (8) this time has a cyclicity to it, a kind of repetitiveness that "is imprinted on all events. . . . Time's forward impulse is limited by the cycle . . . growth does not achieve an authentic 'becoming'" (p. 210).

The folkloric chronotope is later differentiated into the forms with which we are more familiar. As society becomes increasingly stratified – for example, divided into diverse laboring and economic classes – and as the individual becomes increasingly differentiated from the collective, the individual's own time emerges as a new chronotope: "Out of the common time of collective life emerge separate individual life-sequences, individual fates" (p. 214). For Bakhtin, this new chronotope affects all facets of life: "Food, drink, copulation and so forth lose their ancient 'pathos' (their link, their unit with the laboring life of the social whole); they become a petty private matter" (p. 215). It is clear that these chronotopes do not refer simply to time as we might consider it today, but to the temporal and spatial accenting of all the activities and experiences of a person's life.

The two illustrations I have selected from the extensive array presented by Bakhtin demonstrate his meaning and usage of the chronotope concept while also revealing its importance to our understanding of the multiple quality of human experience. Both genres and chronotopes emerge from a people's collective practices and become available for use by individuals to frame their experiences and render their lives meaningful.

Since many different chronotopes/genres coexist in any complex society, we have a heteroglot array coursing through us, affecting how and what we think, know and experience. We are truly never a singular being with but one center, but multiple beings, without a unitary center or core. I will return to another facet of this point in Chapter 9 and again in Chapter 11. For now, however, it will prove useful to relate Bakhtin's concepts of chronotope/genre with some recent attempts to use a narrative approach in psychological inquiry.

Narrativism and Dialogism

Relatively recently, a narrative approach has found its way into several psychological analyses of human experience and behavior, providing us with an important link between Bakhtin's conceptions and some current work in psychology proper.[2] As some authors have stated the case, rather than continuing to pursue the image of humanity as a giant machine or a complex computer, we might do better if we were to change metaphors and consider people to be "*homo narrans*, humankind as story-teller" (Harvey *et al.*, 1990, p. *ix*).

This formulation teaches us that it is the stories that we learn to tell to frame our experiences, to explain us to ourselves and others, that are the central features of human life. The stories we tell about our lives "serve as vehicles for rendering selves intelligible" (Gergen and Gergen, 1988, p. 17); they give order, coherence and meaning to our experiences, and structure our relationships with others. Although we might be tempted to consider these narrative accounts to be like cognitive schemas that are created by individuals for their own private purposes, most narrativists emphasize the socially shared, cultural embeddedness of these stories and narratives.

Both Hewstone's (1989) and Moscovici's (1976, 1981) work illustrates the importance of social representations and collective beliefs in contrast to the typically individualistic view that most American social psychologists have adopted (e.g. Kelley, 1973; Schank and Abelson, 1977). As we noted in Chapter 4, for example, Moscovici's examination of the widespread use of psychoanalytic forms of explanation in French society is a classic illustration of this idea. These explanations gained currency and retained their force because they provided a narrative account that made sense within French culture. In other words, culture provides people with various narrative formulations which they grow up learning and employ to frame their experiences and understanding.

Gergen (1991) offers several additional illustrations in his lengthy list of elements out of which current narrative accounts in US society are composed, none of which existed until relatively recently. Thus, to explain a personal problem by locating it in a narrative about an identity crisis would hardly have made sense during the 1800s or, for that matter, find a receptive audience even now in a very differently framed culture. Likewise, to claim that my problems are related to a post-traumatic stress disorder or to fetal alcohol syndrome is to call upon elements of our modern storytelling. Neither is a condition that would be intelligible in prior eras or in different settings even today.

It is clear that Bakhtin's formulation of genres and chronotopes fits this narrativist formulation. After all, what is a genre or a chronotope but a form by which narrative accounts are framed in literature and in everyday life? Unlike most narrativist approaches in psychology, however, Bakhtin's dialogic emphasis alerts us to the degree to which various competing narratives, genres or chronotopes coexist today, as well as to the dialogic relationships that appear among them. For example, his approach contrasts with a prime example of similar-appearing work in psychology, Schank and Abelson's (1977) script theory, which we will examine shortly. Bakhtin tells us that we are not composed of only one genre in which to speak, nor of one chronotopic formulation of time, nor of one narrative account. All of us are composed of several, competing and often clashing perspectives.

While Bakhtin recognizes the press towards the unification of this diversity – he terms this the *centripetal* forces of all languages – he also insists that we pay our due to the competing press of diversity, the *centrifugal* qualities, as well: "Every utterance participates in the 'unitary language' (in its centripetal forces and tendencies) and at the same time partakes of social and historical heteroglossia (the centrifugal, stratifying forces)" (Bakhtin, 1981, p. 272). Bakhtin argues against any and all efforts to reduce human experience to what he refers to as "the dungeon of a single context" (p. 274). He insists on the thoroughly heteroglot and heterochronous quality of human experience, including human consciousness and understanding. These are not merely matters of literary genres, but matters involving the very terms by which we experience who and what we are, who and what others and our world are like. Unfortunately, narrativist accounts often align themselves with the centripetal world-view, and so part company rather quickly with Bakhtin's formulations.

In noting the more social and collective approach adopted by Hewstone and by Moscovici, and the more centrifugal emphasis in Bakhtin, I commented on their differences from the more typical individualistic and centripetal American view. A further, related difference involves the status of a narrative or genre. It is tempting, but incorrect, to see a narrative account as a kind of schema stored within the individual's mind, to be retrieved and employed more or less mechanically as the occasion warrants. Keeping in mind that dialogism speaks of an addressor and an addressee caught up together in an ongoing, mutually choreographed dance, it is far more accurate to see narratives (genres and chronotopes) as ongoing accomplishments of the addressor–addressee dialogue than as elements that precede that encounter and simply play out their lives within it.

The major difficulty with script accounts – such as that proposed by Schank and Abelson (1977), for example – is precisely this failure to operate in a genuinely dialogic manner. To speak of a script that a person follows, which might otherwise sound like employing a narrative, a genre or a chronotope, is to treat scripts as already existing plans rather than as events constituted on the basis of an ongoing dialogue with others in the setting of their usage.

Schank and Abelson speak of a restaurant script to illustrate what they mean, treating this as though it were literally a scenario that a person has learned to follow in a restaurant. What this deletes, however, is precisely what Bakhtin's dialogism insists must always be involved.

The use of a script in live interaction is less a matter of its simply flowing forth than of its being created, sustained or transformed in the ongoing restaurant transactions. My script might lead me to wish to appear sophisticated and worldly-wise, only to reveal my abysmal ignorance of what to do when I am presented with the cork of a newly opened bottle of wine I have just ordered. At that moment, my behavior may reveal many kinds of Goffmanesque (1959) "repairs" designed to return things to normal. None of this is a matter of my simply and routinely following a preprogrammed script.

Dialogues are too open-ended and ongoing to have to suffer the fate that script theorists and some more schema-oriented narrativists have in store for them. And needless to say, even when things in the restaurant move along so smoothly that it would appear that a preprogrammed script is actually in use, Bakhtin would have us remember that all routines are built upon an ongoing dialogic process in which others are always involved in profound ways.[3]

I have used Bakhtin's writings as my primary source for arguing against any unitary view of human nature and in support of its inherent multiplicity. Even when we pause to think and reflect, we do not do so in one voice only but always in a dialogue containing many different voices. When we interact with another person, although one genre may be primary, other genres lie at the ready to help us reformulate, reframe and newly understand our experiences. We are fundamentally many, never just one – not many in the sense of many thoroughly organized and coherent personalities; for that is the error of our current way of thinking about human nature. Rather, we are many because we are members of diverse conversational communities, with various perspectives on the world, ourselves and others with which to frame our experiences and render them, us and others meaningful.

Notes

1. Several other social psychologists, not all of whom are committed to a dialogic perspective, have nevertheless suggested a healthy multiplicity: for example Markus and Kunda (1986); Markus and Nurius (1986).

2. For example Bruner (1987, 1990); Gergen and Gergen (1988); Harvey *et al.* (1990); Howard (1991); Sarbin (1986). Work on everyday explanations, such as that summarized by Hewstone (1989) and by Gergen and Semin (1990), for example, is also relevant in this context.

3. I continue to refer to Bakhtin, but I could as well have involved Mead, and especially Garfinkel, in these statements.

9

Shared Ownership

Wertsch (1991) provides a helpful illustration of the question of ownership. He describes a 6-year-old girl whose toy is lost. She asks her father for help in finding it. Her father begins by asking her where she last saw it. She cannot remember. He next asks if perhaps she has left it in her room, or possibly outside, or even next door; maybe even in the car. At this last suggestion, the little girl brightens up. Together they go out to the car where, sure enough, they find the toy.

Wertsch asks us to consider the question "Who did the remembering?" Was it the little girl? The father? Neither? Both? This example leads us to consider the issue of ownership over qualities that most of us typically consider to be rightfully the individual's. Surely I am the owner of my memory and all my other psychological qualities. But the example suggests that ownership might better be seen as jointly shared – in this case not located in either the father or his daughter, but developed in conversations taking place between them both.

If memory and other similar psychological qualities are not possessed by the individual, what does this imply about the very nature of personhood in the first place? As Bakhtin insists, "neither individuals nor any other social entities are locked within their boundaries. They are extraterritorial, partially 'located outside' themselves. ... A person has no sovereign internal territory, he is wholly and always on the boundary ... always liminal, always on a boundary" (in Morson and Emerson, 1990, pp. 50–1). Both this view of persons as always liminal, and ownership over one's psychology as never the possession of the individual alone, challenge almost every time-honored belief that has guided Western understanding.

Let us consider several other cases of memory that further illustrate these points while contributing a few additional features. In the first place, we need to disabuse ourselves of the notion that remembering simply and entirely involves a calling forth of some stored trace located somewhere in the mind of the individual. Although there are those who consider memory in such terms and continue to search for the specific location in the individual's brain where we will find each specific memory locked away, a different approach, going as far back as Bartlett's (1932; also Shotter, 1990) pioneering work, emphasizes the constructive quality of the process of remembering.[1] When we remember something, we are not calling up a trace laid down somewhere in our inner computer banks; rather, we are engaged in a process of constructing an event in a current situation.

For example, Billig's research program (e.g. Billig, 1990a, b; Billig *et al.*, 1988) suggests that the social process within which memories are recalled often takes the form of a conversation, even an argument, in which the participants jointly construct "the positions for and against the topics of which they are talking" (1990a, p. 69).

Billig uncovered this shared ownership over memories in his study of an ordinary family's recall of the British Royal Family. He cites a piece of the family's conversation in which the father's egalitarian critique of the Royal Family's wealth is tempered by his recognition of how the pageantry surrounding them creates many new jobs:

> The father would probably be unable to identify the source of his economic assumptions . . . he is unaware what he is echoing, and perhaps indeed that his discourse is in a real sense not merely *his*, but is an echo of other nameless discourses. (1990a, p. 69)

In talking about the Royal Family and remembering bits and pieces of his experiences of them, the father echoes elements of common knowledge. These are picked up by other family members during the ongoing family conversation, making the memory more of an active, ongoing, joint production than anything residing within the mind of any one individual.

Take another example: someone asks us to recall an event from our childhood. In doing this, are we calling forth a memory trace of that event from the past that has been permanently stored somehow in our mind's memory banks? Or is this process better seen as a construction accomplished here and now in the current situation? Who has asked us to describe this event? For what purpose is this request being made? What has been our life course subsequent to the specific event that we are being asked to recall? Surely, if the request is from our analyst our responses might be quite different than if it were made by a prospective employer during an employment interview. And just as surely, events that followed the particular event in question cast it in a light very different from the one in which it might have been cast had those subsequent events not taken place.

Although they developed their work with a somewhat different agenda in mind, and although it does not involve recalling events from the distant past, Ceci and Bronfenbrenner's (1991) studies and conclusions are nevertheless consistent with this dialogic way of considering memory. Ceci and Bronfenbrenner asked children to bake cupcakes – some in the laboratory, others in their own homes. They reasoned that in order to know when the cupcake was ready to be removed from the oven, the child would have to remember to consult the clock; so they used this clock-checking behavior as their measure of remembering in the two different settings.

They found that there was 30 per cent more clock-checking in the laboratory than at home, as well as a different pattern of clock-checking in the two settings: children at home revealed a U-shaped pattern, checking a great deal initially, then very little, and then almost constantly during the final few minutes. This pattern suggested to Ceci and Bronfenbrenner that the children initially used the clock to calibrate some internal timekeeping mechanism which they then used later: "they allowed their psychological clocks to run on autopilot until the last few minutes, when they shifted back into a more conscious and effortful time-monitoring posture" (1991, p. 29).

This difference in memory behavior in the laboratory and at home reveals the key points that Ceci and Bronfenbrenner are making. As they comment, had they restricted their research to the laboratory, they would have missed some important forms of remembering. They emphasize this point because their purpose is to use this study in order to refute the claims made by those who insist that only laboratory research, not naturalistic studies, should be used to study phenomena such as memory.

For our purposes, however, what is most significant about this study are its conclusions about the important role that *context* plays in calling forth different patterns of psychological behavior – in this case, memory. Ceci and Bronfenbrenner ask: "What if the very essence of what is being studied is variable and systematically differentiated by the ecology in which it unfolds?" (p. 30).

Obviously, if the context calls forth very different kinds of psychological behavior, the question of where the behavior is properly located becomes relevant. Surely, it is as reasonable to locate it in the context as in the individual, and perhaps even more reasonable to suggest that the location lies somewhere in between. Admittedly, Ceci and Bronfenbrenner do not press this particular point, although I find it perfectly consistent with their findings and, indeed, with their entire research program, in which context plays a central role in all psychological phenomena, even defining the *essence* of the phenomenon.

In other words, if remembering is highly context-dependent, it may not simply involve calling forth a pure trace of the past or be entirely located inside the individual. It may be better to speak of a dynamic process located between person and other (including the context) rather than within the person.

Second: as the Billig example demonstrates, much that passes for both remembering and forgetting involves rather complex social processes well beyond the "mind" of any single individual. Indeed, the social dynamics of remembering and of forgetting make any restriction of memory to the individual seem seriously to have missed the whole point. The volume edited by Middleton and Edwards (1990a), for example, is devoted to the study of what they refer to as "collective remembering". This is how they frame the issue. First, they observe, as we have observed, that the focus of most work on memory "has been the study of memory as a property of individuals" (p. 1). Next, they comment that in the light of this approach, when social factors are considered, they are typically treated as background factors that affect a person's capacity or motivation for remembering rather than the process of memory itself. The focus of their work on collective remembering is designed to remedy these individualized approaches and reveal how "remembering and forgetting are inherently social activities" (p. 1).

Reread Ceci and Bronfenbrenner's conclusion. If the *essence* of memory (and other psychological processes) is a function of the context (ecology) in which it unfolds, then surely, such processes are inherently social activities that take place *between* people rather than *within* the individual's mind.

Middleton and Edwards (1990b) next argue that memory is not the recall of some neutral input but, rather, the product of conversations in which "the nature of the true original event is precisely the point at issue for the participants" (p. 43). In other words, the work of conversation is to construct what is remembered, not to play back the actual trace of the past. Therefore, memories "cannot be taken merely as windows upon individuals' mental representations, but have to be studied in their social, conversational context" (p. 36).

In addition to Billig's work which we considered above, research reported by Schwartz (1990) on President Lincoln and Schudson (1990) on President Reagan offers further examples of this social approach to the remembering process. Schwartz suggests that while both Washington and Lincoln are important historical figures in the American consciousness, the decrease in Washington's and increase in Lincoln's public image is a result of the play of broader social factors, specifically those involving the need to offer a tangible expression to governmental interventionist policies. In other words, Americans' memories of Lincoln serve recent social demands designed to justify government intervention more than they reflect anything that Lincoln actually did.

In a parallel fashion, Schudson places Reagan in a light that differs considerably from the actual policies enacted during his tenure as President. Schudson notes, for example, how we recall a highly popular president who entered office on a wave of buoyant popularity and departed in much the same manner. This memory occurs in spite of the survey findings that show that "during his first two years in office Ronald Reagan had the worst standing in public opinion polls of any newly elected president since the Second World War" (p. 108). Schudson traces the social dynamics involved in this kind of misremembering in a manner reminiscent of Russell Jacoby's (1975) earlier treatment of *social amnesia*: "memory driven out of mind by the social and economic dynamic of . . . society" (p. 4). All this is also quite consistent with the ideological dimension of memory that forms the centerpiece of several of Billig's projects.[2]

And yet, you insist, someday we will be able to record a change in the individual's brain when a memory has been stored. To refer to that change as memory, however, is as much to miss the point as it would be to argue that the little girl in the example at the beginning of this chapter is the holder of a memory that is actually realized socially, or that recalling a historical event is simply a replaying of something that actually took place in the past. In all cases, remembering is part of a social process; it involves conversations between people in specific situations for specific purposes.

To claim that memory is part of a social process is to open the door to the likely possibility that other psychological processes that we consider to be part of the individual's personal ownership are also subject to the same kind of social process. It is not just our memories that transcend us individually, and hence cannot be meaningfully considered to be our possessions alone, but literally all facets of our mind and our very beings. This, of course, recapitulates the argument developed in Chapter 7.

Coming at this same issue from a different perspective, Gregory Bateson (1972) described an ecological conception of the mind. He rejected the idea that the mind resides inside the individual's head, brain or body, and insisted that mindedness was a shared property of "systems". One of his illustrative examples involves a man using an axe to cut down a tree:

> Consider a man felling a tree with an axe. Each stroke of the axe is modified or corrected, according to the shape of the cut face of the tree left by the previous stroke. This self-corrective (i.e. mental) process is brought about by a total system, tree-eyes-brain-muscles-axe-stroke-tree; and it is this total system that has the characteristics of immanent mind. (p. 317)

Although he is critical of this particular example, Marshall Sahlins (1976) actually advances the case that I am making:

> The problem is that men never merely "chop wood" as such. They cut logs

for canoes, carve the figures of gods on war clubs, or even chop firewood . . .
they always enter into relations with the wood in a specific way, a cultural
way. (p. 91)

Rather than weakening my argument or Bateson's example, Sahlins
reminds us yet again of the important social location of psychological
processes that we otherwise insist are merely events taking place inside the
individual's mind.

An emerging focus of psychological theory and research has followed
these ideas, especially Vygotsky's view of the social location of mindedness,
to challenge all notions of cognition that locate the process inside one
individual's head. Resnick, Levine and Teasley (1991), for example, edited
a volume devoted to examining precisely this point, referring to *socially
shared cognition*, their term for this phenomenon:

We seem to be in the midst of multiple efforts to merge the social and
cognitive, treating them as essential aspects of one another rather than as
dimly sketched background or context for a dominantly cognitive or
dominantly social science. (p. 3)

In noting this, they call our attention to the intimate intertwining of what
were previously considered two separate realms, each of which could be
meaningfully studied on its own. On the one hand, the individual with her
mind and cognitive processes; on the other, the social world providing the
backdrop within which that mind played out its own story. We need only
recall the discussions of the cognitive revolution outlined in Chapter 4 to
see the operation of this conventional approach. The view that Resnick,
Levine and Teasley espouse, by contrast, sees the social permeating
thinking. Rather than serving as some backdrop within which individual
mindedness operates, the social world is an integral part of mental activity,
defining its very character, being the *essence* of the phenomena, as Ceci and
Bronfenbrenner comment.

Resnick (1991) observes:

mental work is rarely done without the assistance of tools. . . . Obvious tools
range from external memory devices and measurement instruments to tables
of arithmetic conversions and dictionaries, thesauruses, and maps. Cognitive
tools embody a culture's intellectual history; they have theories built into
them, and users accept these theories – albeit often unknowingly – when they
use these tools. (p. 7)

Here Resnick echoes a point made earlier by Vygotsky, for whom cultural
tools, including the external memory devices named by Resnick, are a
central element of the individual's mental activity, whether that activity is
rendered publicly or appears in moments of private cogitation.

Although many insightful studies based on this socially shared view of cognition are emerging almost daily, the work reported by Perret-Clermont, Perret and Bell (1991) is noteworthy both for challenging the traditional, individualistic account of cognitive activity and for setting forth, in no uncertain terms, the conversational basis of all mental activity. Perret-Clermont and her colleagues begin with the commonplace observation that the majority of research on the development of children's cognition in educational settings, for example, examines it independently of the very social contexts within which such cognitive activity appears.

Thus, if I were a Chapter 4 traditionalist interested in studying how well children deal with simple reasoning problems, I would present them with several problems and observe how they performed, hoping to discern a developmental sequence of cognitive ability as a function of the ages of the children being tested. In charting these psychological mechanisms of cognitive development, the one thing that I would definitely *not* pay attention to, at least in any systematic manner, would be the social situation and the social relationships involved. After all, if my interest is in how the child thinks and reasons, then I assume that this is a purely psychological matter to be discovered by focusing on the individual child's performance.

Perret-Clermont and her colleagues, however, adopt a very different perspective. They argue:

> First, the child's psychological functioning reveals itself within social relationships (e.g. with teachers and psychologists) that elicit certain types of behaviors, and these behaviors cannot be understood independently of the context in which they emerge. Second, identifying the cognitive and social processes that permit the transmission and learning of knowledge in culturally defined settings is a fundamental endeavor that raises vital questions concerning the nature of knowledge and culture. (p. 42)

In other words, from their perspective, one cannot meaningfully study cognitive activity independently of the social relationships involved in that activity. Their research with children demonstrated rather clearly that the child's:

> cognitive activity was often not so much a struggle with the logical and symbolic features of the task . . . but an effort to give meaning to the persons and task with which they were interacting and to make sense of the processes (notably conversational) that they were undergoing. (p. 43)

In this, Perret-Clermont and her associates echo Michael Siegal's (1991) conclusions. His research showed how the conversational rules and practices of a particular community affected children's cognitive activity. All this work provides rather strong support for the positions advocated by

Mead, Vygotsky, Wittgenstein and the Bakhtin group, as well as the more recent arguments developed by Billig (1990a, b; Billig *et al.*, 1988), Bowers (1991), Edwards (1991) and Shotter (1990). This work and this approach also clearly and strongly affirm the feminist position as argued by Harding and by Code, for example, in which the interpersonal setting is a central and, indeed, defining feature of mindedness.

Conclusion: remove the social from the cognitive and you end up with little on which to pin any understanding of how people think, reason, problem-solve or remember. In short, all those characteristics that we previously insisted could be understood only by focusing on events taking place inside the individual fail to lead us towards any real understanding. What is inside is simultaneously outside, and vice versa. The boundaries are by no means as neat as we had believed and, perhaps, as some continue to hope. The other, our conversational partner in specific social settings, plays too significant a role in what, how, when and even why we think ever to be deleted from our formula.

The Bakhtin group is very clear in this regard as well, using the term *transgredient* to sharpen our understanding (see Todorov, 1984). The term is employed in much the same manner as we would use the term *ingredient*. But unlike ingredients which we consider to be located within the individual – for example, as in the ingredients or elements that comprise the individual's psychology – the term transgredient leads us to consider elements that dwell not within but rather between individuals. But which qualities are transgredient? The conclusion is inescapable. Not only the so-called contents of mindedness but, as we have noted above, our very personality and self are not our possessions alone; they are shared within the socially organized groups in which we have membership.

Here is Voloshinov's (1929/1986) statement of these ideas:

> In point of fact, *word is a two-sided act*. It is determined equally by *whose* word it is and *for whom* it is meant. As word, it is precisely *the product of the reciprocal relationship between speaker and listener, addresser and addressee*. . . . A word is a bridge thrown between myself and another. If one end of the bridge depends on me, then the other depends on my addressee. A word is territory shared by both addresser and addressee, by the speaker and his interlocutor. (p. 86; original emphasis)

Bakhtin (1981) – not surprisingly if, as some claim, he and Voloshinov are one and the same author – reaches much this same conclusion in describing the role of language in constituting individual consciousness. Language (and hence consciousness) "lies on the borderline between oneself and the other. The word in language is half someone else's" (p. 293). We find this same perspective in Mead's thoughts as well. He insists that both mind and self are not things whose ownership is the individual's alone; they are invariably co-owned, shared, joint.[3]

This dialogic position challenges the primary Western understanding of ownership over one's own psychology, over one's mind, self and personality. Although, when I speak, it is my vocal cords that are vibrating, the voices which I use – the words, if you will – are never mine alone. As Billig (1990a) notes, citing both Halbwachs (1980) and Moscovici (1983), we are all echoes. Furthermore, we not only speak in many voices but participate in a process that is always jointly constructed and jointly sustained or transformed. How can I own myself, my mind or my personality, if all that is presumably mine requires you for its completion?

Two important points are being made. First, although psychological processes may take place using the individual's apparatus and mechanisms – as in the vibrating vocal cords or the individual's hand holding the pencil that writes the answer to the problem – if we begin and end our search for understanding inside that individual, we will fail to understand just how much the individual never operates independently of the social world within which she or he is embedded. The words that are formed by my vocal cords are not simply my words; they are words with a life, a story, a history, a society, an echo that I appropriate and use and, in so doing, reveal as much about when and where I am as we erroneously assume they reveal only about the individual psychology that I am:

> the word does not exist in a neutral and impersonal language (it is not, after all, out of a dictionary that the speaker gets his word!), but rather it exists in other people's mouths, in other people's contexts, serving other people's intentions: it is from there that one must take the word and make it one's own. . . . Language is not a neutral medium that passes freely and easily into the private property of the speaker's intentions; it is populated – overpopulated – with the intentions of others. (Bakhtin, 1981, p. 294)

Bakhtin reminds us that only the biblical Adam could avoid this collective situation, for only an Adam who entered an "as yet verbally unqualified world . . . could really have escaped from start to finish this dialogic inter-orientation" (p. 279). In short, strictly speaking, our words are never ours alone, but always-already populated by a long tradition and history in which we are immersed and from which we draw in formulating our usage.

Although I was the one who selected these specific words from among the many alternatives that were available, even that selection is never an entirely personal, private act that is mine alone. I make my selections with you, my addressee, in mind. And once I have made my selection, I am then swept up into a story that is also never entirely mine. It is your response that renders my words meaningful. In addition, the very words themselves have the accents of their own life story – or, in Bakhtin's terminology, they have the *taste* of some genre: "Each word tastes of the context and contexts in which it has lived its socially charged life; all words and forms are populated by intentions. Contextual overtones (generic, tendentious, individualistic) are inevitable in the word" (1981, p. 293).

The second point asks us to focus intently on the other, the addressee. Both Bakhtin and Mead agree that the major responsibility for completing the gesture which the individual initiated lies with the other. The other thereby holds the key to its meaning. Here first is Bakhtin (1981):

> In the actual life of speech, every concrete act of understanding is active . . . and is indissolubly merged with the response, with a motivated agreement or disagreement. To some extent, primacy belongs to the response, as the activating principle: it creates the ground for understanding, it prepares the ground for an active and engaged understanding. Understanding comes to fruition only in the response. Understanding and response are dialectically merged and mutually condition each other; one is impossible without the other. (p. 282)

Then Mead (1934):

> The response of one organism to the gesture of another in any given social act is the meaning of that gesture, and also in a sense responsible for the appearance or coming into being of the new object . . . so, in the social act, the adjustive response of one organism to the gesture of another is the interpretation of that gesture by that organism – it is the meaning of that gesture. (p. 180)

In calling our attention to the other's central role in constituting meaning and understanding, both Bakhtin and Mead – as we saw in Chapter 7 – tell us about the socially shared quality of mind, self and personality. In addition, they inform us about the degree to which "control and mastery", two concepts that rank high up on the Western ladder of cultural values, are never properties that the individual can personally manage. Our inherent interconnectedness with others, with our addressees, means that we cannot be masters in our own home, but not for the reason that Freud noted: that is, not because we have an unruly unconscious living inside us.

Rather, we cannot be masters in our own home because our own home is never quite ours alone: you live there as well; we share our home together. As my addressee, you help to shape my anticipations and preparations. Your responses complete the actions that I initiated in the first place. I address myself with you in mind and so adjust myself in terms of the response I anticipate receiving from you. Once your response appears, another round of adjustments is set in motion, as I now have what you did to contend with, not simply what I anticipated your doing. Your response might confirm or deny the course of action that I initiated, leading me to make still further adjustments. As I commented, because we share our home together, I am never entirely in charge. As my addressee, you play a central role – so central, in fact, that we must reconsider all our cherished conceptions of personal, private ownership and of individual mastery and control over our psychologies.[4]

In previous chapters I introduced three ideas relevant to our current discussion of ownership. The first pertains to the doctrine of possessive individualism; the second to the transformation of the public person into its private counterpart; the third to male domination of the very concept and practice of ownership. All three help us to understand our current cultural view of ownership better without, however, explaining "why" it happened this way.

Recall that Macpherson (1962) used the concept of possessive individualism to describe the position developed in seventeenth-century English debates over voting rights. The doctrine insisted that if a man were to vote, he must be free. For a man to be free, he must not be beholden to anyone else or subjected to another's will. For this condition to be realized, a person had to be the owner of his own capacities and attributes. Any other situation – for example, a shared ownership over one's person – would undermine the entire political structure built on the possessively individualistic model.

The second process that is also part of the current Western view of self-contained and self-possessed individualism can be seen in Bakhtin's (1981) discussion comparing early Greek with later views of the person. Bakhtin's account compared the Greeks' emphasis on the public nature of persons – linking biography with autobiography – with a view that emerged with special force around the Middle Ages and subsequently, in which the person's private interior came to dominate understanding. As Bakhtin argues, when autobiography is biography, the public man and the private man are one and the same thing. This means that there is little or no difference between the point of view one adopts to one's self (as in autobiography) and the point of view others adopt (as in biography). It also means that purely personal and private events (e.g. feelings, thoughts) known only to the individual lack political and social significance as compared with the profound importance attached to publicly known events and experiences.

Bakhtin charts the slow breakdown of this public person and the growth of interiority: where the personal and private autobiographical world-view is separated from the public and shared biographical world-view; where the self is increasingly located inside the person as something private and intimate. It is clear that along with possessive individualism, this trend has also contributed to our current understanding. We locate psychological qualities inside the individual and treat them as the keys to the person's life. We consider public qualities to be mere masks that conceal what is truly important about the person.

From the feminist point of view, our current conception of ownership is restricted to the kinds of ownership available primarily to the privileged, the dominant social classes and gender groups – in the West, primarily white males. Those who are kept in subordinate positions, who have been constructed by the dominant groups to service them and their needs, have rarely been granted ownership over much of anything, least of all their own psychological interior.

Gatens (1991), for example, adopts a very clear position against the appropriateness of Macpherson's conception of possessive individualism to describe women's lives:

> In neither a legal nor an economic sense could women be seen as sole proprietors of their persons or capacities in a market relation. Men are socio-economically placed such that Macpherson's description is a theoretically coherent account of relations between men as individual owners of their persons and free contractors of their capacities. Women, however, are not analogously placed and . . . cannot legitimately be described as individuals at all. (p. 35)

In short, the currently dominant conception and practice of ownership has been developed by and for men (collectively); it has not been applied with equal force (or at all) to women and others held to be lesser objects. Given the insistently dialogic quality of most feminist accounts, it seems unlikely that they will heartily endorse the male conception of ownership, either for men or for women.

Dialogism inverts the prevailing (and probably masculinist) understanding by insisting on the intrinsically shared quality of human experience. Thus dialogism poses a serious challenge to the dominant Western world-view. Dialogism, however, is not a return to the Greeks' entirely public person, nor to several nonWestern cultures' undemocratically communitarian focus. Both individuality and interiority can and do indeed exist for dialogism, but *not* as a personal, private territory with no links to the publicly shared world.

A person's interior is conversationally constituted and conversationally sustained. The presence of others is invariably involved. Although the process may be invisible and mute as we gaze at the individual, it is nevertheless fully social and based on a publicly shared culture. The conversational framework is sustained whether we focus on external conversations held with others or on internal conversations held with one's self. Dialogism is no enemy to interiority. At the same time, however, this interiority is built around others, and is therefore hardly personal and private as we have come to understand these terms.

An example may help to clarify this point. Take jokes. From a Freudian perspective, jokes appear to reveal the operation of the individual's unconscious as it makes unique connections between various ideas that heretofore have never been joined. From a dialogic perspective, a joke works because it communicates to others, to an audience. In other words, jokes and humor operate by the principles of all conversation and communication between people: they are significantly influenced in their formation by the anticipated nature of the audience's response. The process is one that involves an addressor and an addressee and does not simply take place entirely inside the head of the individual joke-maker-and-teller. Here, then, we have an illustration of a process which, while it has an interiority about it, has a very clearly external, dialogic form as well.

Who, then, owns the joke? In the dialogic formulation, it is not the property of the individual's unconscious in operation. Jokes, like all forms of human experience and expression, are shared by virtue of their fundamentally dialogic quality. They are, in effect, the property of both addressor and addressee, not the addressor's alone. Once we insist on a dialogic perspective, then, we insist on viewing all matters of personal psychology in terms of voices involved in communicating, whether the communication is an internal dialogue or one carried on externally. We are squarely within a world of shared ownership.

As Code (1991) comments:

> Even the ability to change one's mind is learned in a community that trains its members in conventions of criticism, affirmation, and second thinking. (pp. 83–4)

> A knowledge claimant positions herself within a set of discursive possibilities which she may accept, criticize, or challenge; positions herself in relation to other people, to their responses, criticism, agreements, and contributions. (p. 122)

Here, then, is a full-bodied recognition of our intrinsically dialogic nature, even when we are carrying on those internal conversations we call thinking.

Mead has formulated much this same idea, agreeing that our lives must be a shared story, never entirely ours alone. For example, even as Code notes, the internal conversations that occur when we are alone and thinking by ourselves involve specific others to whom we are addressing ourselves and from whose perspective we respond. It is common to say such things as "I debated the issue before finally deciding not to accept the job with Lockheed", describing the internal conversation in which we mulled over the issue and came up with a decision. Who were those others involved in our inner dialogue? The cast of possibilities is extensive and may include actual figures in our lives (e.g. I looked at the decision from my wife's point of view) as well as hypothetical figures (e.g. I considered what someone at my age and stage should do).

Mead introduced the notion of *the generalized other* to represent the abstract addressee reflecting our particular group or community. He argues that our inner dialogues are often addressed to this generalized community other – for example: "What would other women think of my decision to remain at home rather than pursuing my career at this time?" The presence of that generalized other to whom we address our thoughts – even the most abstract of thoughts, says Mead – ensures that another is always present, even in our most personal and private moments. Once again we see that the way we frame our experiences is not ours alone, but always a shared enterprise.

Although Bakhtin does not speak of a generalized other as such, he does introduce us to the *superaddressee*: "Each dialogue takes place against the background of the responsive understanding of an invisibly present third party who stands above all the participants in the dialogue" (in Morson and Emerson, 1990, p. 135).

Morson and Emerson (1990) offer the following example:

> In everyday speech between two people, one might turn to an invisible third person and say about the person actually present: "Would you just listen to him!" Or one of the two may gesture: roll up his eyes or put his body into a questioning position, as if asking some invisible person for guidance in understanding the recalcitrant other. At times, we speak to someone as if our real concern is with a possible listener not present, one whose judgment would *really* count or whose advice would really help us. (p. 135)

There is an affinity between Mead's notion of the generalized other, Habermas's (1984; also McCarthy, 1978) notion of the ideal speech situation, and Bakhtin's concept of the superaddressee. In all three cases, the dialogue does not merely take place with specific others as addressees, but is also framed with regard to someone or something that goes beyond the present situation and provides a larger standard for judging the current dialogue.

I speak of a similarity despite the fact that Bakhtin's superaddressee apparently occupies the kind of position one envisions for God, while Mead's generalized other is based on the organized social groups to which a person belongs, and Habermas's concept involves his efforts to find some external standard for judging the validity of any truth claims. In spite of these differences, all three impress me because they have sought to include in their conversational models of human nature something that is outside and beyond the immediate conversation taking place here and now, a third perspective that would allow yet a further angle from which to view the current conversation.

Somewhat paradoxically – but understandably, given the long history of silencing – radical feminists have taken on superaddressee functions, standing outside the *malestream*[5] and providing another voice – in this case, a critical voice and standpoint from which to view the currently dominant forms of dialogue.

Notes

1. The January 1991 issue of *The American Psychologist* devoted a significant portion of its pages to the "debate" over the nature of memory. The several articles published in this special section reflect various sides on this obviously still contentious and unsettled topic.
2. For example Billig (1982, 1990a, b); Billig *et al.* (1988).
3. In Voloshinov's and Bakhtin's quoted passages, reference is made to "the word". It is important to observe that in so far as "the word" – that is, language – is the centerpiece of all human experience, when they refer to "the word" as "territory shared" or as "half someone else's" they mean that all facets of the individual's psychology are shared events, never simply the individual's alone.
4. See also Gilligan (1982); Jordan (1989); J.B. Miller (1984, 1987); Noddings (1984) for a not-too-dissimilar understanding.
5. The term *malestream* was used by Code (1991), who attributes it to Mary O'Brien (1980).

10

Power and the Suppression of the
Other in Dialogism

We are at a key crossroads. On the one hand, in the view of some of its major proponents – e.g. Bakhtin, Mead and most current American, British and continental discourse theorists[1] – dialogism asks us to consider the other as our friend, the co-creator of our mind, our self and our society. This led Clark and Holquist (1984), citing Bakhtin as their source, to note that "the self is an act of grace, a gift of the other" (p. 68). As I have argued, we are not set off over and against others, but are essential aspects of each other's very being. Our selves, our minds – and, indeed, the society in which we live – are all co-created projects, never solo performances in which we have star billing and others are mere background. We celebrate the other, for without the other there is no existence for us either.

Yet on the other hand, human history and the everyday experiences of many of the world's peoples do not portray the self–other relationship in such glowing, egalitarian terms. Rather than a friend and equal partner, much of the story of human endeavor involves dominant groups constructing serviceable others. Rather than dialogues, we have monologues masquerading as something other than what they are.

In other words, there is a gap between what some of the major dialogic theorists tell us and the actual terms of living for the majority of people. One of the paradigmatic cases I have been considering throughout this book, man's construction of woman as a serviceable other, reveals this gap rather clearly. We do not have a genuine dialogue taking place between men and women, but rather a carefully crafted monologue in which the dominant male speaker repeatedly encounters himself in the mirror of the other, while the subordinated woman must struggle to discover who she actually may yet be. It would seem, then, that power and domination are missing from the master dialogic accounts.

Until we enter power into the dialogic equation, we will find that we have adopted an overly optimistic portrait of human relations that contributes to enshrining the very conditions that a true dialogism hopes to undo. Chapter 6 examined one aspect of power in considering the other-suppressing quality built into the Enlightenment view. In this chapter we must come to terms with many of these same issues, but now understood dialogically. Although dialogism celebrates the other, this is a celebration that has not yet been extended to most real people.

The Challenge

Dialogism is simultaneously both correct and incorrect. It is correct in leading us away from a merely self-celebratory stance and permitting us to see just how intimately intertwined self and other are. Dialogism is incorrect, however, in assuming that self and other are always equal contributors to the co-constructive process. Some have more power to set the terms of co-construction than others. The history of human relationships can be seen as a playing out of this differential.

Of the many current challenges that illustrate how power undermines genuine dialogism, I have selected two to examine in more detail. The first continues the issues introduced in Chapter 1, based on the feminist critique. The second introduces us to another paradigmatic case developed especially in the postmodern anthropological understanding of the self–other relationship.

Each case illustrates the various ways, often subtle, by which dominant groups both wield their power and ensure its maintenance by engaging in monologues masquerading as dialogues. Since a genuine dialogue requires the co-constructive processes that can occur only when two distinct points of view meet, this masquerade effectively undermines this possibility by placing all the constructive power in the hands of the dominant side. Like ventriloquists operating their dummies, those in power manage the portrayals of the other and so manage who they too will be.

The Feminist Critique

There is no monolithic body of work known as feminist theory. We would do better to speak of feminisms, in the plural, granting full recognition to its diversity – its liberal and its radical formulations; its views of class, race and culture.[2] Writers in this genre evidence as much diversity and disagreement as one finds in almost any other body of scholarly endeavor. There is, however, the generally shared understanding that women's lives and experiences have been shaped to their detriment by an oppressive patriarchal system that has constructed them as serviceable others:

> A theory is feminist to the extent it is persuaded that women have been unjustly unequal to men because of the social meaning of their bodies. Feminist theory is critical of gender as a determinant of life chances, finding that it is women who differentially suffer from the distinction of sex. Compared with men, women lack control over their social destinies. (MacKinnon, 1989, p. 37)

Without exception, the various feminisms tell us of an unrealized dialogue. There cannot be a genuine dialogue between two parties, men and women, one of whom decides who the other will be.

Women at Work

As we have already seen, feminist writers have been among the most vocal in arguing that the characteristics attributed to women have been shaped by the agenda of men.[3] The historian Joan Scott (1988), for example, provides both argument and supporting historical documentation for the thesis that male and female are not natural categories so much as categories shaped by the steady hand of the male, creating the kind of other he needs to suit his own particular purposes.

In this, Scott echoes numerous other feminist writers, including the pioneering themes so eloquently stated in the 1940s by Simone de Beauvoir (1949/1989), who reminds us that "Representation of the world, like the world itself, is the work of men; they describe it from their own point of view, which they confuse with absolute truth" (p. 143). Thus, "One is not born, but rather becomes, a woman" (p. 267), and does so rather clearly through the eyes and in the service of the male perspective.

Scott has been especially keen to demonstrate how this process has operated to construct a gendered workforce:

> In the nineteenth century, for example, certain concepts of male skill rested on a contrast with female labor (by definition unskilled). The organization and reorganization of work processes was accomplished by reference to the gender attributes of workers, rather than to issues of training, education, or social class. And wage differentials between the sexes were attributed to fundamentally different family roles that preceded (rather than followed from) employment arrangements. In all of these processes the meaning of "worker" was established through a contrast between the presumably natural qualities of men and women. (p. 175)

Scott urges us to consider critically the various categories by which we order the world, seeing them not as essences but rather as relationally and historically based. There is no such thing as "the female worker", she tells us; what we have is a historical process in which such a worker is constituted by men in order to provide the contrasting requirements of their own situation. One of the many cases Scott offers documents this process among the Parisian garment workers in the mid 1800s.

In the political context of that time and place, garment workers were trying to defend their craft traditions against efforts to transform their jobs and affect pay, security and respect. Part of this defense called upon a distinction between genuine craftsmen with special training and skill and otherwise similar workers who, however, were not as deserving because they lacked the requisite skills of the true craftsman. Scott argues that most other discussions of this period of labor history have failed to examine how representations of both the family and sexual differences were deployed in the debates defending the craftsman's demands.

Scott specifically notes how a gendered interpretation was built into the distinction between garment work carried out in the shop and conducted primarily by men, and work carried out at home and done primarily by women:

> skilled work and the shop became synonymous. Those who worked at home were, by definition, unskilled. (p. 100)

> men working at home were demeaned by an implicit association with femininity. In this way, the defense of the *atelier* secured the masculinity of skill and the political identity of tailors as skilled workingmen. (p. 102)

In other words, men sought to gain political and economic advantages by exploiting the very definition of women as other, and they had the power then (as now) to shape reality to fit their desires. Women's work became a category defined by male workers to distinguish their own skilled from her less skilled work performances. This case illustrates the operation of power within what otherwise appears to be a dialogic formulation. It alerts us to question critically all social categories – especially those that seem to be most natural – in order to see how the objects defined by the categories are constituted to serve certain group interests. Those groups that have the political clout to set the terms by which self and other are known deploy the definition of the categories so as to serve their groups' interests.

Women and Humanity

A second illustration appears in Denise Riley's (1988) analysis of "woman". According to Riley, there is no object out there known as "woman" whose collective life course can be followed through time and place: "no originary, neutral and inert 'woman' lies there . . . . Some characterisation or other is eternally in play" (p. 98). Riley is especially concerned with examining how that characterization of "woman" has been "discursively constructed, and always relatively to other categories which themselves change" (pp. 1–2).

While it is recognized that there are concrete and specific women, and thus that women in this sense exist as something quite real in the world, the manner by which women have been characterized to serve the interests of the dominant male has a history that renders the entire concept, woman, problematical, "an unstable category" . . . [with] a historical foundation" (p. 5). As Riley comments:

> If being a woman is more accurately conceived as a state which fluctuates for
> the individual, depending on what she and/or others consider to characterise
> it, then there are always different densities of sexed being in operation, and
> the historical aspects are in play here. (p. 6)

Riley develops a case to support her contention that several different characterizations of women exist historically, each based on a specific and shifting relational understanding. Two examples are developed: (1) women versus human being; (2) women versus the social. Each characterization of women is set contrastively against the characterization of men. The male stands for the human and the political in contrast to the not-quite-human female, whose social concerns make her apolitical. The specific characterization of the female in each case serves to define what the male thereby is, providing a different description for both in different historical periods.

Riley's examination of the period between the seventeenth and eighteenth centuries suggests a time when the contrast was drawn between women and humanity. Although the earlier Aristotelian thinking about woman had been abandoned by 1600, Riley notes how in that period women were nevertheless assigned to a lower category of being: "woman as a misbegotten male . . . at once a kind of systematic exception and not necessarily of the same species as man. Indeed an anonymous work of 1595 enquired as to whether women are or are not human" (p. 24).

Writing in the late 1940s, de Beauvoir suggests that little has changed:

> In actuality the relation of the two sexes is not quite like that of two electrical
> poles, for man represents both the positive and the neutral, as is indicated by
> the common use of *man* to designate human beings in general; whereas
> woman represents only the negative . . . it is understood that the fact of being
> a man is no peculiarity. (1949/1989, p. xxi)
>
> Thus humanity is male. (p. xxii)

The several examples noted in Chapter 6, based on the work of Broverman *et al.* (1972), Eagly and Kite (1987), Gilligan (1982) and Miller *et al.* (1991), suggest that while women may at long last be considered "human" – quite an advance over 1595, and perhaps even the 1940s – men remain the implicit standard for judging mental health, moral reasoning, and so forth.

Riley next examines the historical links connecting women with the social. Because the social was equated with the feminine, the social was presumed to be of lesser standing than other areas of human endeavor. The social pertained to the family, health care, education, fertility, and so forth. These were the territories associated with women, not with men. Today, we would call these "women's issues"; and although we would consider them of political interest, even now they do not carry the same weight as the "real" political issues of war and finance – men's concerns.

Because the social was dissociated from the political (the arena of power, politics and men), it was clear that women were not considered political beings: "In the 1930s the unemployed working-class man was seen as emasculated within his family. But the woman as a mother was understood not to be in a relationship, but to be pursuing an occupation" (Riley, 1988, p. 58). And when women pursued political aims – for example, by challenging motherhood as an occupation – they were accused of seeking benefits for their own sex and failing to be considerate of the social whole, a selfish point of view clearly detrimental to the wellbeing of society: "if woman's entanglement in Nature had held her apart from Humanity, so did her newer entanglement in 'the social', since the latter was constructed so as to dislocate the political" (Riley, p. 66).

Walking a Tightrope

Riley, de Beauvoir, Scott and countless others help us to see how the category woman has been so thoroughly employed by men as their necessary other that the pathway to liberation is fraught with difficulties. One problem involves how to free women from their situation without destroying the very concept and distinct reality of woman herself. Riley calls our attention to a point that many others have also made. If women seek to mute their differences with men, to reject men's portrayal of them and to become just like men, then the very category woman may disappear. As Irigaray has suggested, this move may be genocidal for women. If, on the other hand, differences are highlighted, an invitation to further submersion at the hands of dominant males seems probable. The twistings and turnings involved in this issue have come to light in numerous settings. Scott traces them in an employment discrimination case pitting the Equal Employment Opportunity Commission against Sears Department Stores. A second case, Hoyt versus Florida, provides an equally dramatic illustration of the dilemmas involved.[4]

Gwendolyn Hoyt came to trial in Florida for killing her husband. After she had been convicted by an all-male jury, her attorneys appealed, claiming that because of the sex of the jurors, Hoyt had not received a fair trial by her peers. Florida law permitted women to be exempt from serving on juries because of their far greater importance to the domestic world of home and children. This meant that the pool of jurors available for any trial typically had a vast preponderance of men.

In pleading its own case before the US Supreme Court, the State of Florida argued that if women and men were truly equal, then the sex composition of the jury would not matter. In other words, if differences are muted, the category woman gets fully subsumed under the category man, and the conclusion is "reasonably" drawn that sex composition for a jury is thereby irrelevant. But Florida also argued the "differences" position in order to justify its decision to exempt women from jury duty: because of their obvious (natural) domestic talents, women are needed at home to shop, take care of the children, cook dinner, and so forth. So, in highlighting differences, a potentially discriminatory practice is kept in place.

In the light of these twistings and turnings, Riley suggests that women must be willing to challenge any and all male efforts to capture them as *their* particular other, and "to develop a speed, foxiness, versatility" (1988, p. 114) that will allow them simultaneously to be woman and not to be woman. This also describes the *dissonance* to which Braidotti (1991) refers in describing women as acrobats who must learn to "jump long and jump high, and still land on our own two feet" (p. 284). I will shortly return to this dilemma in considering MacKinnon's contributions.

Women and Male Sexuality

As we have seen, the key to all feminist accounts revolves around the power of dominant social groups, primarily white males, to construct woman as a serviceable other, thus undermining any genuinely dialogic possibilities. At least one major account, developed by Catharine MacKinnon (1989), locates the center of this process of domination and inequality in male sexuality:

> Women and men are divided by gender, made into the sexes as we know them, by the social requirements of its dominant form, heterosexuality, which institutionalizes male sexual dominance and female sexual submission. If this is true, sexuality is the linchpin of gender inequality. . . . Male and female are created through the erotization of dominance and submission. The man/woman difference and the dominance/submission dynamic define each other.

This is the social meaning of sex and the distinctively feminist account of gender inequality. . . . The feminist theory of knowledge is inextricable from the feminist critique of power because the male point of view forces itself upon the world as its way of apprehending it. (pp. 113–14)

As MacKinnon argues, it is not simply that female specificity has been lost in the shuffle, but what a female is has been so thoroughly determined by male sexuality that she (and he) have no sense whatsoever of who she is except as defined by his sexual requirements, aided fully by the legal supports provided by the liberal state.

Women have become what men's sexual desires require them to be. The system of gender differentiation, says MacKinnon, is a system of power with far-reaching consequences. Women are economically exploited, pressed into domestic slavery and forced motherhood, sexually objectified, abused and denigrated, given neither voice nor culture, and excluded from public life: "Men as men have generally not had these things done to them; that is men have had to be Black or gay . . . to have these things done to them as men" (p. 160).

MacKinnon also observes what so many others have noted: that men's desires have so transformed women that many enjoy being what they have been made into; or, if they do not enjoy it, at least many compliantly accept their fate, even buying into the male theories of the *naturalness* of the hierarchy that places them in an inferior position. MacKinnon takes us back to the themes we first encountered in Chapters 1 and 2, which Scott, Riley and Braidotti (and others) speak of as the acrobatic, tightrope act required of woman: to be and not to be at the same time.

To be: this describes the identity charted for women on the basis of male sexual desires. It refers to the fate that befalls all who have been constructed as serviceable others by the dominant groups in society. For a woman, this means to see and to identify herself and her own sexuality in terms set forth by the male point of view.

MacKinnon takes each element of the classic female stereotype, including such qualities as vulnerability, passivity, softness, and so forth, and shows how "each element . . . is revealed as, in fact, sexual" (1989, p. 110). To be vulnerable is to provide easy sexual access to men; to be passive is to be receptive to male advances and to be unable to resist. Overall, she argues, "femaleness means femininity, which means attractiveness to men, which means sexual attractiveness, which means sexual availability on male terms" (p. 110).

THE IDEA IS THE REALITY

MacKinnon argues that women become, in both idea and reality, the image portrayed for them by male sexuality and male use. In other words, their

gender reflects the power of the male to construct the world and its objects
in terms of his interests, needs and desires. MacKinnon is not talking
simply about the male construction of *the idea* of woman, but of his
construction of *the reality* that woman has become. Male power resides in
man's ability to create *in fact* a world (of women) who conform to his
fantasies and to make this factual reality hold.

In this, then, MacKinnon departs from those theorists, feminist and
otherwise, who find themselves eternally wandering in the world of mere
representation. She argues that the lines between representation and reality
have been too neatly drawn when it comes to women's lives, citing other
instances in which words as representations are essentially acts. For
example, to say the word "Kill!" to a trained attack dog is not merely to
utter a word, but to carry out an action. The sign "Whites Only" is not
merely a representation, but an act with definite material consequences for
the lives of many people: "It is not that life and art imitate each other; in
sexuality, they are each other" (p. 199).

Although MacKinnon's main referent here is pornography, her more
general argument is that when sexuality is the core of male domination,
permeating nearly every facet of the gendered system within which both
men and women live, then representation and reality cannot be as neatly
separated as male desire might wish. The pornographic pictures of women,
for example, are not simply representations of male fantasies; they are the
actual realities by which women's lives are lived:

> Pornography is not imagery in some relation to a reality elsewhere
> constructed. It is not a distortion, reflection, projection, expression, fantasy,
> representation or symbol either. It is sexual reality. . . . The way pornography
> produces its meaning constructs and defines men and women as such.
> (MacKinnon, 1989, p. 198)

As I commented above, following MacKinnon on this point, the
separation between idea and reality does not hold for those who lack the
power to sustain such a separation (e.g. women, people of color,
African-Americans, and so forth). In the hands of those with the power to
make the idea real, what is thought about subordinate groups can and does
establish the actual realities by which they live.

Not to be: at the same time, however, MacKinnon argues that women
must learn not to be what they have become. This involves adopting the
feminist stance of being able to critique the conditions that have produced
one's life and identity, to engage in the struggle against being what one has
been constituted to be. The dilemma, then, from MacKinnon's perspective, is to be and not to be at the same time, thus capturing the dissonances
and acrobatic tightrope act to which others have likewise referred.

MacKinnon's career as a feminist lawyer and professor of law has put her in an especially key role to examine and attempt to transform the legal system. She argues that by denying the sexual basis of inequality, the law and the liberal state affirm men's interests, all the while appearing to adopt a stance of neutrality and gender-blindness. She focuses most of her attention on laws in the United States involving pornography, abortion and rape. In each case, she argues, the law serves male interests and male domination while presenting itself as a gender-neutral body of legal decisions.

Rape law, for example, is based on the idea of consent: with consent, it is sex; without consent, rape: "Under law, rape is a sex crime that is not regarded as a crime when it looks like sex" (p. 172). Yet, argues MacKinnon, "If sexuality is relational – a power relation of gender – consent is a communication under conditions of inequality" (p. 182). How can consent be given under such conditions? "Rape law assumes that consent to sex is as real for women as it is for men" (p. 169); their inequality, however, makes this a lie.

By defining abortion as an issue of privacy and adopting the liberal state's view that privacy is a matter that does not fall under state concern, once again, argues MacKinnon, we see the law adopting the perspective of the male while presenting itself as neutral: "The right to privacy is the right of men 'to be let alone' to oppress women one at a time" (p. 194).

Privacy laws entered an already existing system of inequality. To refer to such laws as neutral because they do not intervene in people's private affairs is, under conditions of inequality, to be interventionist, not neutral. The intervention involved in such "nonintervention", however, adopts the perspective and interests of the dominant groups in an already unequal arrangement. Not intervening is to intervene on behalf of male interests in sustaining their domination.

While pornography, says MacKinnon, seems to pit freedom of speech and expression against censorship, pornography laws deal with the freedom of men to express their sexuality, to possess and consume females, whose only freedom is to be possessed and consumed: "the fight over a definition of pornography is a fight among men over the terms of access to women, hence over the best means to guarantee male power as a system" (p. 203). MacKinnon sees pornography as an act of male supremacy, producing women who "live in the world pornography creates – they live its lie as reality" (p. 204). In other words, pornography is harmful to women in that it affirms the system of inequality that keeps them subordinated to male desires. MacKinnon worked to change these laws; she has been successful in the case of Canadian pornography legislation, and as yet unsuccessful in the United States.

Anthropology's Concern with the Self–Other Relationship

In Chapter 1, I introduced a second paradigmatic case involving the white-American construction of a serviceable African-American other. Once again, the possibilities for a genuine dialogue are thwarted by the ability of the dominant group to set the terms by which the nondominant group is known and lives. A perusal of the literature of anthropology reveals that this process is restricted to the construction of neither women nor African-Americans. The dominant groups in the Western world – American, British and continental – have a long history of constructing serviceable others, defining themselves and their own civilization by its contrast with these "primitives".

By its very nature, the field of anthropology has been concerned with the other – in this case, other peoples and other cultures. Until relatively recently, anthropologists have treated the other as a real object with real properties. With the postmodern turn to relational and dialogic approaches, however, several anthropologists came to see the other as a category constituted on the basis of the investigator's own cultural framework, usually designed to make a point about the natural excellence of the home culture.[5]

The idea that other cultures are primitive while the Western world is civilized has occupied an important position in anthropological work. But as several have noted, the primitive is not a category of being that exists out there in the world as such; the primitive is a creation of the Western world, serving as a constant reminder of how far "we" have come:

> A discourse employing terms such as primitive, savage (but also tribal, traditional, Third World, or whatever euphemism is current) does not think, or observe, or critically study, the 'primitive'; it thinks, observes, studies *in terms* of the primitive ... *primitive* is a category ... of Western thought. (Fabian, 1983, pp. 17–18)

As McGrane (1989) comments, primitives were not factually discovered but, rather, *made* on behalf of Western needs and conceptions:

> The very identification of and naming of the non-European Other as "primitive", as "primitive mentality", as "primitive culture", presupposd a theory (language) of rational progress, of progress in and by reason ... the European [was taught] that his condition was that of "an advanced civilization". .... Progress produces primitives. (McGrane, 1989, p. 99)

McGrane continues his argument by developing a brief history of how the Western world created a serviceable other. Initially, the non-European other was conceptualized in terms of Christianity's concerns with demonology. Thus the other was possessed by demons, whereas the good Christian had been saved from this scourge.

The Enlightenment shifted the focus from defining self and other in terms of a religious theme to a concern with the use of knowledge and rationality to distinguish between self and other. McGrane suggests that during this period, otherness was defined in terms of ignorance – that is, the absence of rationality and knowledge, which in turn, of course, implied that the European possessed these traits.

In the nineteenth century, McGrane continues, otherness became the more familiar "primitive", defined now in terms of an evolutionary theory of progress. European civilization represented the evolutionary pinnacle; primitives were employed as demonstrations of how far Europeans had come.

Finally, says McGrane, the concept of "culture" forms the center for today's definitions of self and other. The other is culturally different from us, making us, of course, just one of several kinds of difference that exist. As the material of this and several other chapters suggests, however, I am less sanguine than McGrane seems to be about this current stage in the West's treatment of the other. The ongoing battles between the dominant forces in society (i.e. primarily white, primarily male, primarily upper- and upper-middle-class) and its others, whether these be people of color, women, persons of differing sexual orientation or whatever, suggest that we have not yet accepted otherness as merely a different way of life. The demand to control how the other will be constructed remains too firmly implanted. Dominant groups are not yet prepared to see themselves as simply another other.

I suspect that McGrane recognizes that this is an ongoing issue. The stakes are indeed very high: "A culture which 'discovers' that which is alien to itself also thereby fundamentally reveals that which it is to itself" (McGrane, 1989, p. ix). If the other is the vehicle through which I come to understand myself, then controlling how that other is to be known seems too important for those with the power to do so not to intervene on their own group's behalf.

Recall MacKinnon's argument. The issue is not simply one of words and ideas. The construction of a serviceable other is a real construction, with real consequences. Both the dominant groups' and the subordinate groups' everyday lives are shaped by the power of the dominant groups to create a reality that fits the image they desire. Even as women become in fact the ideas that men hold of them, primitives become in fact the ideas that dominant Euro-Americans hold of them. Changing what we think or say without changing the actual conditions of living, then, may be one step in a process, but it can all too readily become a step that leads nowhere.

Dominguez's (1989) examination of the construction of selfhood and peoplehood in contemporary Israel offers a further illustration of some of these ideas. She demonstrates how confrontations over who is and who is not a Jew are designed to define the true Jewish self by controlling how the other is defined. In none of this is there a factual discovery of a person's characteristics. Rather, dominant groups, or those aspiring to political dominance, strive to set the terms for their own existence by defining the nature of the other.

Several of the debates that Dominguez describes in Israel are very reminiscent of current debates in the United States over how a person's racial or ethnic category is to be defined. This determination in the United States is relevant to concerns over affirmative action. The same issues – albeit with a very different outcome – were also relevant to Nazi Germany's attempts to determine the required percentage of "blood" that defined someone as a Jew.

Dominguez points out that there has been an ongoing debate in Israel over whether the Falashas, the black Ethiopians, are really Jews. In 1972, Israel's Chief Sephardic Rabbi ruled in the affirmative. Yet a few years later, when many other rabbis questioned the Jewishness of the Falashas, it was stated that they "would have to undergo a process of ritual conversion before intermarrying with other Jews" (p. 74). The issue is relevant and the stakes are so high because how the other is defined signals how the self is to be known as well. If "they" too are Jews, then what can be said about "my" own Jewishness?

Clifford's (1988) examination of the Mashpee Indians' legal travails on Cape Code strikes a similar chord. The issue centered on defining who was and who was not a Mashpee Indian, and whether or not the tribe had any real existence any more. Settling this issue was no trivial matter: the claims to a fortune in real estate were at stake. Clifford notes that at least one tribal member wondered how it was possible for a white majority to decide who is or is not a member of the Mashpee tribe. Surely, this is a matter best left to the tribe. Yet the outcome was too important to the dominant groups to leave in the hands of anyone claiming to be a Mashpee.

To complicate the picture further, it was difficult to determine if the tribe itself had the kind of reality that was needed to claim standing in the law courts:

> The related institutions of culture and tribe are historical inventions, tendentious and changing. They do not designate stable realities that exist aboriginally "prior to" the colonial clash of societies and powerful representations. The history of Mashpee is not one of unbroken tribal institutions or cultural traditions. It is a long, relational struggle to maintain and recreate identities that began when an English-speaking Indian traveler, Squanto, greeted the Pilgrims at Plymouth. (Clifford, 1988, p. 339)

The clash involves two very contrasting conceptions of what it means to be a tribe, and the difficulties the West and its legal system has – as MacKinnon notes – in dealing with relational, dialogic definitions of the sort that the quoted passage suggests. One side is searching for a real other that has a coherent history and an unbroken line of development; the other side (represented by Clifford's own views) sees the other always as relationally determined by the ever-shifting vicissitudes of power relations in society.

The Suppression of Dialogism

The Mashpee issue, like the issue of the Jew in Israel, involves the themes we have been considering throughout this chapter in the analysis of woman as man's other. In each case, the other is held captive by those with the greatest power and resources to define the terms by which they will be known and their lives lived. The primitive has served the West well. As Said (1979) has commented, so too has the *Oriental*, another invention of the West designed to serve the West's own purposes. Much the same could be said for all others whose paths have crossed and been crossed by the dominant West.

What, then, is our situation? We know that the self needs the other in order to be a self at all. We know that when those selves are dominant in a given society, they can construct the other so as to affirm a particular kind of self for themselves. We also know that in the current situation, many of these others have risen up to have their own voices register their character, no longer bowing to the will of the dominant groups in society or in the world.

The gift that the other gives us is our own selfhood. Yet when the other declines our offer to roll over and play dead, this is a gift we may not want to receive. As long as the others quietly submitted to our own determination of who they were, we could gladly accept the gift of our selfhood that they provided: women who remain in their proper place; people of color who fit our view of who they must be; primitives who remain exotic and quaint; gay and lesbian groups who remain securely in the closet. All these provide us a gift of ourselves that we rarely need to examine critically. It is when the other's gift forces us to take a second look at ourselves, however, that many balk at the selfhood they are now asked to consider.

The point is simple: if I find myself in and through you, but no longer control the you that grants me my self, then I am forced to deal with a self that is beyond my control, and I may not always enjoy this self with which I must now contend. Several authors, for example, have commented on the meaning to male domination of accepting a homosexual orientation as an alternative lifestyle rather than an aberration or a defect (see Caplan, 1987; Connell, 1987; Kitzinger, 1987; Sedgwick, 1990).

The initial definition of the homosexual as an identity rather than a specific set of behaviors appeared within the Western world around 1870. It described a category of defective male identity, permitting nondefective males to experience themselves as normal by comparison. It is one thing to be a male facing defective males and females; it is a very different matter to be a male who faces an alternative male lifestyle that challenges the ideals on which masculinity itself had been based, or an alternative female lifestyle that excludes the need for men.

Temporal Suppression

Although some approaches employed by dominant groups to construct serviceable others and suppress a genuine dialogism seem outrageously apparent, finesse and subtlety also frequently appear. Fabian (1983) has pursued one such case through his analysis of the different *timeframes* disciplines employ for grasping the other. His suggestion is that even well-meaning and otherwise sophisticated postmodern anthropologists find themselves trapped by their conception of time into defining the other in terms that give them, the anthropologists, the very power over the other that they seem to be eschewing.

Fabian tells us that when time was assumed to be a sacred matter, the time of the other – of the pagan savage, for example – was measured by the distance between the other and the saved Christian world. Under this temporal canopy, at least the other was a *candidate* for salvation rather than something entirely alien. When time became secularized, however, Fabian contends, the other was henceforth understood to be of a rather different category from the self. This is how he describes the difference: "The pagan was always *already* marked for salvation, the savage is *not yet* ready for civilization" (p. 26).

This different conception of time, says Fabian, involves a *denial of coevalness*: a refusal to recognize that we and the other share the same moment in time. However much we act as though the other is simply different from us, by adopting a secularized timeframe that disallows the other a presence in our world (i.e. a denial of coevalness) we avoid being confronted by the implications of otherness for ourselves. In other words, at that very moment when we might indeed be transformed in and through our relational encounters with the other, we avoid this possibility by continuing to distance the other from ourselves, treating the other as a creature that "lives in another Time" (p. 27), not really a part of our world.

I believe that Fabian's denial of coevalness describes a denial of dialogism: both denials attempt to sustain a monologic relationship with the other, to manage the terms of this relationship in a way that minimizes the impact on the dominant self doing the managing.

I will return to further aspects of Fabian's views in Chapter 12. For now, however, the importance I attach to his analysis lies primarily in what I see to be the striking parallels between his concept, denial of coevalness, and the concept introduced here involving a denial of genuine dialogism. Coevalness defines a simultaneity of being together in the here and now and recognizing how that moment constitutes the joint reality of the participants. When this simultaneity is denied in favor of a distancing between the time of the self and the time of the other, we have a denial of coevalness and a repression of dialogism.

Fabian contends that it is precisely this denial that marks most anthropological work. The denial of coevalness is most evident in earlier work in which the other was self-consciously distanced and transformed thoroughly into the terms defined by the investigator. But it is even apparent in more current works that try to capture the "native's" own experiences, but do so as an afterword – that is, as translated into the investigator's language which distances the actual time in which the native and the investigator met together and constituted the event the investigator is describing. The native's world is described as though it existed entirely apart from the very dialogic, temporally coeval moment of its constitution.

Listen to Pierre Bourdieu's (1977, 1990) parallel rendering of this point:

> Objectivism constitutes the social world as a spectacle presented to an observer who takes up a "point of view" on the action, who stands back so as to observe it and, transferring into the object the principles of his relation to the object, conceives of it as a totality intended for cognition alone. . . . This point of view is the one afforded by high positions in the social structure, from which the social world appears as a representation . . . and practices are no more than "executions" . . . or the implementing of plans. . . . It is possible to abandon the sovereign point of view from which objectivist idealism orders the world, without being forced to relinquish the "active aspect" of apprehension of the world by reducing cognition to a mere recording: it suffices to situate oneself *within* "real activity" as such, i.e. in the practical relation to the world . . . that active presence in the world through which the world imposes its presence, with its urgencies, its things to be done or said, things "made" to be said and said "to be done", which directly command words and deeds without ever deploying themselves as a spectacle. (1977, pp. 96–7)

Oneness and the Suppression of Dialogism

Other accounts refer to a similar repression of dialogism, this time focusing not on a temporal denial, as in Fabian's analysis or in the kind of similar distancing revealed by Bourdieu, but rather on a suppression based on a desired fusion into oneness. Geertz, Bakhtin and many feminist accounts directly address this form of dialogic suppression.

Geertz's (1979) classic paper on "understanding from the native's point of view" urges us "not to achieve some inner correspondence of spirit with your informants" (p. 228), but rather "to figure out what the devil they think they are up to" (p. 228). The latter does not involve fusing with the other, for in doing this – if we ever really could – we would fail to understand much of anything. What we need, rather, is a "continuous dialectical tacking between the most local of local detail and the most global of global structure in such a way as to bring both into view simultaneously" (p. 239).

Bakhtin's ideas offer us a genuinely dialogic position that situates his thought most clearly in the same position adopted by some of the radical feminists whom we have previously considered and by some of the new breed of postmodern anthropologists. Bakhtin reminds us that the emphasis in dialogism is on dialogue. For a dialogue to occur, at least two differing points of view must be engaged. Anything that tries to fuse these different perspectives into one undoes the truth of dialogism. Bakhtin is especially keen to challenge the idea of empathy as a kind of fusion between self and other, because such fusion offers yet another device for making a monologue out of a potential dialogue.

We have already seen this same message appear in the feminist challenge to patriarchal domination. In this case, a true dialogue cannot occur so long as woman is defined from the male standpoint. That standpoint produces a monologue in which the dominating speaker controls what both he and the other will be like, thereby avoiding any possibility of learning about either himself or the other on the basis of this seemingly dialogic encounter. Of course, that is precisely the point of the dominant groups' control. Their advantage is lost when true dialogues occur.

In short, differences are valued for the possibilities of dialogue they provide. These are enlightening possibilities for all parties to the dialogue. If I try to understand you by losing me, then we will both fail. Or if I try to understand you by denying our differences, then once again, we will fail. In both cases, our failure derives from our having lost the edge of awareness that differences provide. But as I have been arguing in this chapter, much of that desire to repress dialogues – or to deny coevalness, to use Fabian's analysis – or to see others as though viewing a spectacle – to employ Bourdieu's framework – serves the purposes of domination of the other by those in power. Dialogism threatens domination; in monologism lies the heartland of Western domination. These are themes to which we return in Chapter 12.

Thomas v. Hill

At this point, let me turn to a case that I believe illustrates several of the themes with which we have been dealing in this chapter: the 1991 special Senate hearings on the confirmation of Clarence Thomas to be an Associate Justice of the US Supreme Court.

The special hearings were called just days before the full Senate vote in order to respond to allegations of sexual harassment on Thomas's part. The allegations were made by a female law professor, Anita Hill, who ten years previously had worked for Thomas in two government agencies. Ostensibly, the hearings were designed to discern which of them was telling the truth. Was it Thomas, who adamantly denied that any of Hill's allegations were true? Or was it Hill, who adamantly claimed that her allegations of harassment were true?

One of the issues raised during the hearings involved male Senators' difficulty in understanding Hill's point of view. Why had she waited some ten years before making these allegations public? "If I had been as rudely treated as she claims she was," says one Senator, "I would have complained, and loudly at that time." Why had she followed Thomas to another governmental job? "If I had been so badly treated as she claims she was," says one Senator, "I would never have followed him anywhere, let alone to another job." Why had she maintained contact with him for years after the alleged incidents, calling him on the telephone, seeking his assistance in various matters, and so forth? "If I had been treated in such a disgusting manner as she claims she had," says one Senator, "then I surely would have broken off all further contact with the man."

From their perspective as men, Anita Hill was not to be believed, because in her shoes they would have behaved differently. Her perspective was reduced to theirs and found wanting. They did not engage her perspective in a dialogue with theirs, but rather continued to reflect on her situation entirely through their eyes, as though she had no eyes of her own, no voice of her own that might differ from theirs. There is but one way of thinking, of seeing, of experiencing, and this is shared by everyone, isn't it? That Anita Hill seems not to have shared this in one way reflects poorly on her veracity, leading one Senator to describe her testimony as a clear case of perjury. A dialogue was reduced to a monologue and the Senators never had to deal with the results of a genuine encounter with her as other.

Differences without Hierarchy

A question that is central to any dialogic account – especially relevant given the past and current status of human relationships – is whether it is possible ever to have a genuinely dialogic meeting: that is, a meeting of two differently situated persons, neither one of whom occupies a dominating position. The issue is made even more complex by the realization that differences are socially constructed, not natural formulations. Is it possible, then, to have differences which, though socially constructed, are not hierarchically arranged? While history and current events suggest otherwise, we must operate on the assumption that a genuinely dialogic possibility exists.

Whenever we find differences between people, we are dealing with a social mapping of the human world, not a natural one. What is considered to be the same or different, then, is the outcome of a social process in which even qualities that appear to be facts of nature are sufficiently acted upon by social dynamics to give them the character they come to possess. The examples are legion. All people must eat, but what they deem to be edible and what they shun are based on a complex social process that divides objects into the two categories: edible versus inedible.

As Marshall Sahlins (1976) observed, there is nothing inherent in the object – cow or dog, for example – that makes the former edible for us, while the latter is not. This categorization is based on a socially constructed difference, not something we will find in the objects themselves, no matter how long or how closely we examine them. Indeed, as Sahlins comments, even our conception of what is natural and what is social is a socially constructed categorization.

Bourdieu's (1990) rendering of this point takes the form of challenging all substantialist approaches that seek certain invariants in nature and so mask the active process by which social reality and its objects are constructed. He comments on the importance of recognizing how the very cognitive structures by which we structure our world "are themselves socially structured, because they have social origins" (p. 131). In other words, rather than searching within nature for the constitution of differences, we need to direct our gaze towards the society and its practices by which different objects and their categorizations into same and different are accomplished.

It would appear, therefore, that differences are connected to a society's particular ways of creating and organizing the objects that come to inhabit its universe. The reasons why any organized social group would divide its world into a particular set of similarities and differences are undoubtedly as variable as there have been organized social groups. Of course, a Marxian view would emphasize an economic basis for social differentiation, whereas a nonMarxian feminist view would focus on gender and sexuality, matters that are ignored in classic Marxian analyses. Still other possibilities and theories exist (e.g. sociobiological theories).

Important as economic differentiation has been in dividing societies and establishing the foundation for the hierarchical organization of differences,

I find myself persuaded by feminist accounts. It is abundantly clear that far back in Western history, and regardless of the particulars of the economic system involved, gender has served as a central basis not only for marking differences but also for ranking them in a hierarchy. And while economic advantage was a definite part of this process, other aspects of power were also clearly involved. In other words, male economic dominance is but one part of a much more complex picture.

If we were to adopt Irigaray's (see Whitford, 1991) position, we would argue that "the whole of our western culture is based upon the murder of the mother. The man-god-father killed the mother in order to take power. . . . And if we make the foundations of the social order shift, then everything will shift. That is why they are so careful to keep us on a leash" (p. 47). In other words, gender is a marked and hierarchic social category because it reflects the male's matricidal acts, their rejection and repudiation of the maternal process of creation and the installation of themselves as the only true creator. In this view, a kind of jealousy has led men to use their power to dominate women and claim the generative process for themselves.

A variant on this theme appears in the thesis developed by Freud in *Moses and Monotheism* and in Code's and Harding's (and others') arguments concerning the preferred male form of knowing. Freud contrasts sensuous knowledge of the sort that stems from maternity with the more abstract kind of knowledge that stems from paternity, which requires an inference that the former does not. In Freud's view, the latter is a higher form of knowledge than the former, thereby building a gendered hierarchy based on the "facts" of birthing.

Code and Harding find a compelling correlation between male dominance and the kind of disembodied, abstract and transcendent form of knowledge that Freud describes and we have come to consider properly scientific and objective. Basically, we have come to esteem a form of knowledge that denies its parentage: that is, knowledge that is anonymous, has no name, no heritage, no parents, applying everywhere and to everyone.

It is intriguing to consider that males, lacking the same certainty about the issue of parentage that females possess, have used their power to propose that their uncertainty marks them as not only different from women but superior to women. They have translated their concern with certainty into an obsession with obtaining certainty by finding that God's-eye view. They have made a virtue out of a vice – or, if not a vice, at least out of a differently certain role in the process of creating life.

On the other hand, if we adopt MacKinnon's view, we would stress the central role of male sexuality in undergirding gender inequality and all forms of male domination. In her colorful way of phrasing matters, she suggests that "part of the male interest in keeping women down lies in the fact that it gets men up" (p. 145). She is not being facetious here, but rather continuing to affirm her thesis that all forms of power and all forms of domination, in whatever sphere they may lie, are rooted in men's sexuality, in the eroticization of dominance and submission.

Fascinating as these speculations are – Flax (1990) would consider this desire to find the origins of male domination an especially male concern – they have taken us away from the question with which I opened this section. Can we have differences without hierarchy? Differences breed hierarchy only in a system in which hierarchy is a requisite of the system's maintenance. If it were possible magically to eliminate all oppressive social arrangements, differences would not vanish; rather, what would disappear would be either the erasure of differences or their division into good and bad, superior and inferior. We have not yet seen a utopian world like this, but if someday the efforts of those who have been marginalized prove effective, then we will indeed encounter diverse people engaged in genuine dialogues.

Much of what I am noting here is food for a different book. All I am attempting to say at this point, however, is that (1) differences will continue to be evident, issuing from society's ongoing life; and (2) differences need not inevitably produce an oppressive arrangement of people. As I noted previously, efforts to mute, suppress or deny differences by setting up a monologic account of human nature reflect a continuing oppressive desire to achieve hegemony for one point of view without ever submitting that point of view to the very scrutiny it warrants.

Notes

1. While some discourse theorists address power (see, for example, Chapter 1, Note 10), in many other cases, power often simply describes how people in low power positions accommodate to those in higher power positions, and therefore tends not to adopt the more critical stance for which dialogism calls.
2. For example Braidotti (1991); Flax (1990); Gatens (1991); and MacKinnon (1989), offer useful summaries of some of these differences.
3. In addition to those authors whose works I cite directly, numerous others have contributed to the feminist challenge: e.g. Brownmiller (1975); Chesler (1978); Chodorow (1978); Dworkin (1981); Firestone (1971); Flax (1990); Friedan (1963); Millett (1972).
4. I base this discussion on an article, written under the by-line Karen J. Winkler, that appeared in the 20 November 1991 *Chronicle of Higher Education* (pp. A9, A13). Scott (1988) provides a very informative discussion of similar issues in the EEOC v. Sears employment discrimination case.
5. Some of those who have been instrumental in this dialogic turn in anthropology include Geertz in his early work (1973), but also Fabian (1983) and McGrane (1989); and Clifford (1988); Clifford and Marcus (1986); Marcus and Fischer (1986). Although this list is by no means exhaustive, these offer a good sampling of the relational/dialogic turn in the anthropological treatment of the other.

PART IV
Implications

11

Dialogic Ethics
On Freedom, Responsibility and Justice

When am I most free? When I can do what I want without worrying about you? When you are not so tightly woven into my space that sometimes I feel unable to breathe? When people just let me be without imposing their demands and their agendas on me, disrupting my own plans? When I can think for myself, decide for myself and act for myself without always worrying about you?

One of dialogism's greatest challenges is directed to this understanding of freedom and responsibility. Our current view is built around a self-contained conception of the individual, around the cultural hero, the *autonomous man* (Code, 1991). Shatter that conception, as dialogism does, and a new understanding is required.

As I argued in Chapter 3, most of us have learned that human freedom is based upon people's ownership of their own capacities and characteristics, and the consequent autonomy that this allows them. Conditions that limit freedom are recognized; but these are understood to be the result of contractual arrangements among rational individuals who for their own good agree to submit themselves to others' rule.[1] The bottom line, however, is that freedom depends on autonomy – that is, independence from subjection to another's will; this requires possession of one's own capabilities and characteristics. Only a self-contained individual has these requisite qualities of personal boundedness and personal ownership.

Lorraine Code (1991) refers to this as our *autonomy obsession*:

Autonomy and dependence tend to be polarized as the terms of a stark dichotomy, so that self-reliance and reliance on other people are constructed as mutually exclusive and the achievement of self-reliance is thought to require a complete repudiation of interdependence. (pp. 73–4)

Dialogism undermines this understanding. There is no such creature as the self-contained individual, meaningfully abstracted from others and set apart as a wholly self-possessed being. We are, says Bakhtin (see Morson and Emerson, 1990), *liminal* creatures whose very essence is not contained within us, but always lies on the border between us and others. Because all that we claim to be ours owes a continuing debt to others, we are forever being "intruded upon", "imposed upon", and "interfered with" by others. Of course, the terms "intruded", "imposed" and "interfered" all come from a self-contained discourse. Dialogism finds little sense in these terms as we commonly understand them.

These terms, however, have a clear and familiar place in our everyday understanding. We know all too well what each means, and consider ourselves free to the extent that the events they describe do not rule us. It is not an intrusion upon my turf if I have *chosen* to invite you over. Nor do I consider it an imposition when I have *agreed* to help you out. I consider it neither an interference nor a threat to my personal freedom when I really *want* to work on a project with you. To choose, to agree and to want all make your involvement in my affairs an appropriate and proper matter. Their absence, however, suggests a threat to my personal freedom and autonomy. It is when I do something I have not chosen or agreed to or want to do that I am most unfree.

As our previous considerations – especially in Chapters 6 and 10 – suggest, however, this autonomous ideal tends to be restricted to the dominant groups in society; the rest do not have this luxury, not even of choosing who and what they will be. And as we shall see, even the dominant groups live a lie: their autonomy rests upon their power to construct nonautonomous others. Even they are dependent on these others, without whom their illusory autonomy would vanish, as Hegel so clearly reminded us.

What becomes of these understandings and obsessions with autonomy under the dialogic frame? Because dialogism teaches us that we are in ongoing, co-constructive relationships with others, it makes little sense to speak of freedom as independence from others. Independence from others is an illusion, hardly descriptive of the real quality of human nature, yet it is an illusion that is very real for those who are required to play their parts in its maintenance.

What can it mean to speak of your intruding upon my turf, when *my* turf is necessarily *our* turf? How can you impose upon me, when that *me* has been significantly constituted by you? What is the meaning of being interfered with, when our relationship is essentially mutual and co-constructive?

It is clear that we must develop a very differently cast understanding of what it means to be and to act freely. The old formulation that is built on self-containment will no longer suffice. Freedom cannot mean a freedom *from* others, but must of necessity be recast as a freedom to work jointly with others on projects and towards ends that we mutually agree upon: i.e. a freedom *because of* others.

But this is not an easy task; it creates a dilemma both for those on top and for those far below in the social hierarchy. For those on top, the dilemma involves dialogism's demand that they recast their understanding; they must come to see what they have spent their entire lives so actively repressing: their inherent dependence on others for their very being. For those far below on the social hierarchy, for whom dependence on others is only too well known, dialogism's dilemma becomes how to avoid making a virtue out of what has become their necessity.

The task is also made difficult because our scientific views of freedom are based on the ideal of the autonomous man, and have therefore encouraged an erroneous understanding. Several years ago, for example, a social psychologist, Jack Brehm (1966; also Brehm and Brehm, 1981) introduced the concept of *reactance*. He argued that in order to preserve their sense of freedom when it was being threatened by another person's demands, individuals react back to demonstrate just how free they really are.

Another social psychologist, Elliot Aronson (1988), offers two examples. A student who is flunking his course gives him a lavish birthday present, leading Aronson to feel uncomfortable. After all, the gift could be construed as trying to limit his freedom to grade the student's work as he sees fit. Reasoning in this manner, Aronson decides to grade the student's work even more harshly than he would otherwise in order to demonstrate his personal freedom. Reactance. Another example cited by Aronson involves a salesman who tries a hard-sell approach, leading Aronson to want to leave the store just to demonstrate how free he really is. Reactance.

But it is not only in reactance theory that we see the cultural narrative writ large. The majority of developmental theories chart a rather clear course of separation and individuation, resting comfortably only after the growing child has fully and finally extricated himself (and herself?) from the mother and become his (and her?) own person.[2]

These ideas are clearly founded on the autonomous ideal and the meaning of freedom as a freedom *from* others. They depict a situation which is very familiar to most of us. We too have grown up in a culture in which this captures the essence of human freedom: the freedom to determine one's own fate independent of the wills of others; a freedom based on the ability to grow apart from others.

Dialogism asks us to turn things around. It tells us that our freedom cannot be based on our independence from others, primarily because *we are not independent of others*. Our lives and others' lives are so intricately and intimately intertwined that to base our sense of freedom on breaking those bonds is to fly in the face of this fundamental quality of human nature. Dialogism requires us to redefine freedom in terms of our mutual responsibility to work with others to shape our common, shared destinies. Anything that undermines this collective possibility would be unfreeing. In effect, conditions that undermine the possibilities for dialogue threaten human freedom.

Human freedom involves the rights of individuals collectively to determine their mutual fates. Since who and what I am are joined with you, to define all that is central about my life in terms oppositional to you, creating a situation of individual versus other, is to deny your importance to me and mine to you. What we need, therefore, is to build our meaning of freedom around collective units, individual-and-other. We share collective responsibility for one another; neither of us can be us alone. We are both free, then, only in so far as we can work collaboratively to define who and what we are and who and what we will be. Not surprisingly, all monologic accounts warp this meaning and undermine the very freedoms they promise. *I* cannot be free. Only *we* can be free.

I believe that this is John Shotter's (1990) message in referring to the kind of practical–moral knowledge that all persons must develop in order to work together as morally accountable citizens. It is also the point developed in Derek Edwards's (1991) analysis of what he terms a discursive psychology and I have called dialogism. And it is also clearly the message contained in most feminist accounts for which the autonomy obsession works to no one's long-term advantage, no matter how compelling its imagery may appear for those on top and in control and perhaps even for those further down the ladder, whose dependence may seem temporarily comfortable.

Shotter (1990) presents a dialogic model that recognizes how:

> in our social lives together, the fact is that we all have a part to play in *a major corporate responsibility*: that of maintaining in existence the communicative currency, so to speak, in terms of which we conduct all our social transactions. . . . It is this responsibility that modern psychology has ignored, and which has led it, mistakenly, to give professional support to the view "that 'I' can still be 'me' without 'you'". (p. 21)

The responsibility of which Shotter speaks is a *responsibility of communication*: "the responsibilities between people involved in maintaining our social constructions as the constructions they are" (pp. 69–70). Linking our lives with others demands that we act responsibly by following standards that sustain the intelligibility and legitimacy of our actions. In short:

> if our forms of rationality are socially constructed, and if one knows this to be the case, then one cannot rationally deny in one's talk the (moral) grounds

upon which one's rationality depends – while still claiming, at the same time, that one's denials are rational. (pp. 75–6)

Edwards's (1991) discursive psychology recognizes the importance of talk in our everyday lives, and of the moral responsibilities that are thereby embedded in everything we do. Talk is not something idle that we do simply to pass the time of day; it is in and through talk that we constitute the objects of our world, including ourselves and others (see Chapter 7). This recognition gives us a profound sense of shared responsibility. It is our working together that makes us who and what we are. We share responsibilities together for these achievements.

Since we do *in fact* and necessarily operate jointly, we are *in fact* and necessarily members of an ongoing collectively self-and-other determining process. A recognition of this feature of our being would bring along with it a recognition of the responsibilities we share for whatever outcomes we each have. As Shotter and Edwards note, the self-contained conception flies in the face of this understanding of human nature. In addition, the individualized (i.e. self-contained, monologic) account establishes a basis for human freedom – as freedom from – that undermines the possibility for people to act in a responsible manner. By denying our mutual responsibility for one another's lives, we have formulated a view of human nature that speaks about responsibility while virtually making responsible actions impossible.

Several of the feminist accounts we have been examining favor the dialogic understanding of freedom and responsibility. When Irigaray (1974/1985, 1977/1985), for example, urges us to uncover and operate in terms of woman's uniquely embodied specificity, she is not urging each person to function alone and independently of one another. Rather, her claim is that only when we can have two fully upstanding, positively defined persons engaged in a dialogue can either realize his or her genuine potential and so work together collaboratively.

Likewise, when Code (1991) asks us to consider friendship as the paradigm for knowledge and moral action, she too embraces the dialogic view of human freedom and responsibility. She speaks of "the moral requirements of relationships" (p. 75) – all too easily lost when we begin and end our story with the autonomous man:

> Emphasis on the *rights* of autonomous individuals, together with the minimal significance accorded to the responsibilities of people to and for one another, produces a tension, for moral agents, between claims of impartiality and of particularity. . . . Learning about morality is learning about the responsibility, care, and concern one owes to . . . specific other people. It is not easy to believe that such a training would "naturally" generate an ideal of moral impartiality. (p. 76)

Noddings's (1984) development of a feminist ethics, based on the notion of caring, adopts a similar perspective. Noddings argues that because we are so intimately intertwined with one another, a merely contractual bond, built around the self-contained individual, distorts the actual conditions of our lives together: "What we seek in caring is not payment or reciprocity in kind but the special reciprocity that connotes completion" (p. 151).

When it has been shorn of its male bias, Code finds Aristotle's treatment of friendship a more realistic model for human relationships than the autonomous-man theories that mark both other philosophical treatises (e.g. Descartes, Kant) and our current cultural ideals. She argues that Aristotle not only turns to friendship – which he sees to be as much a constituent of the human being as rationality and language – but in so doing makes "friendship central to good character development" (p. 98):

> Aristotelian friendship can point the way to a relational analysis of subjectivity that is at once morally accountable, politically engaged, and located in "second person" dialogues. (Code, 1991, p. 101)

There are striking parallels between Code's and Noddings's accounts and both Shotter's and Edwards's views.

Certain aspects of the ecology perspective, including the ecofeminist movement, add further to this picture.[3] All are based on a relational paradigm rather than the self-contained paradigm that currently holds sway in the Western world. All introduce us to a revised conception of ethical concerns and a revised agenda for human action.

Listen to an ecofeminist treatise proclaim that:

> In an ecofeminist society, no one would have power over anyone else, because there would be an understanding that we're all part of the interconnected web of life. Such a worldview requires some radical changes in perspective (not to mention behavior), since the whole world becomes part of one's self – not something Other to win, conquer, exploit or get ahead of in the hierarchy. (Van Gelder, 1989, p. 61)

Murray Bookchin (1982), expressing similar sentiments, insists on viewing people and their environment as interconnected parts of a larger relational whole. If we set our designs on mastering the environment as though it were a distant and alien other, says Bookchin – an idea similar to that proposed years earlier by Horkheimer and Adorno (1944/1969) – we end up mastering ourselves to the detriment of both ourselves and our environment.

The ecological view of a person-determining environment and an environment-determining person captures this relational understanding.

We are not free because we cannot do as we wish to the environment as our other, without profoundly affecting ourselves as well.

Once again, Shotter (1990) has aptly described this ecological view while placing it into the conversational framework that is so central to dialogism:

> the rights and duties associated with being a 1st-person speaker, a 2nd-person listener, or a 3rd-person observer, are quite different from each other. As a 2nd-person one has a status quite different from that of a 3rd-person: one is involved in and required to maintain the action; we do not have the right to step out [of] our personal involvement with the speaker. (p. 201)

When we approach the environment as master to other, we adopt a third-person relationship and so do not see our responsibilities for any jointly created outcomes. We are merely observers or operators effecting a change in a mute and lifeless other. Ecological thinkers such as Bookchin and the ecofeminists ask us to adopt a more dialogic view, seeing ourselves to be like first-person addressors relating to the environment as our second-person addressee, sharing mutual responsibilities and fates.

If I am to act responsibly, I must understand that we are mutually self-determining. But under the current regime, not only does this threaten my sense of being a free agent beholden to no one but my self-contained self; in addition it undermines my ability to construct the very kind of world that permits this other image to be sustained. Yet I cannot both be free and act responsibly under the auspices of the self-contained formulation. Not only is this formulation factually in error in its view of human nature; it also creates a contradiction that makes it impossible for people to realize the freedom they are promised while simultaneously behaving in a socially responsible manner.

Dialogism offers us a way out of this incoherent impasse. Not only does it provide us with a correct view of how human nature is formed and sustained, but in addition, in linking person with other as mutually determining beings, it recasts the meaning of freedom: we are free jointly to construct our lives together, and are therefore of necessity responsible beings by virtue of this feature. "I" cannot be free; only "We" can be free. This builds upon the recognition that the only possible meaning for freedom involves a recognition of the jointly shared responsibilities we and others have.

We currently consider both freedom and responsibility negatively. We are free in so far as another's will does not impose itself upon us. We are acting responsibly in so far as we do not harm others, intrude upon their "space" or infringe on their own freedom. Dialogism insists on recasting both of these in positive terms. We are free, not because we are detached from others, but literally because we and they are interconnected. We are responsible, not in order to avoid harming others or intruding upon their turf, but because we and they are mutually involved in one another's completion as human beings and in sustaining the very social world that makes our lives and its values even possible to consider.

Up to this point, I have focused primarily on ideas of freedom and responsibility, contrasting the self-contained, monologic with the dialogic understanding of these concepts and practices. There is another arena, however, in which value-laden, ethical issues are ever present: justice. When we think of justice, the prominent image is of a blindfold woman whose blindfold is the guarantor of impartial judgments carried out without knowledge of the particular characteristics of the parties involved. Like freedom, justice is conceptualized in terms of the self-contained ideal. Can justice, however, be blind and yet operate in a just manner?

As we first saw in Chapter 6 and encountered again in Chapter 10, the dialogic answer is a resounding "no". It became clear in Chapter 10, for example, especially in the views developed by MacKinnon, that a blind justice and a neutral state are not blind, neutral or just: they reflect the standpoint of the dominant groups in society, freezing their advantages into place. Both Iris Young (1990) and Michael Sandel (1982) offer somewhat parallel arguments critical of individualistic and differences-blind conceptions of justice.

If we are fundamentally relational beings, defined in and through our embeddedness in social networks which not only constitute our identities but to which we owe ongoing responsibility, a blind justice must deny this very feature of our lives in rendering so-called just decisions. And yet, as I previously commented, blindness under these conditions does not guarantee impartiality, but rather the operation of the unexamined position of those groups that are dominant in society masquerading as impartial.

Where differences matter, their denial in the pursuit of a differences-blind policy is unlikely to promote justice, unless by justice we mean the perpetuation of policies that advantage some groups and disadvantage others. Consider Young's (1990) definition of justice:

> A goal of social justice . . . is social equality. Equality refers not primarily to the distribution of social goods, though distributions are certainly entailed by social equality. It refers primarily to the full participation and inclusion of everyone in society's major institutions, and the socially supported substantive opportunity for all to develop and exercise their capacities and realize their choices. (p. 173)

It is her argument that differences-neutral or differences-blind approaches fail to achieve this goal precisely because their blindness attempts to subsume everyone under one framework (typically the implicit framework of already dominant groups) and so must deny the very particularities of life experiences on which differences are based and on which group needs must be considered. In short, justice-as-blindness undermines the dialogic possibility of diverse perspectives and points of view by trying to assimilate all differences into one perspective: for example, positing a general interest, which, as Young notes, tends to "systematically ignore, suppress, or conflict with the interests of particular groups" (p. 189). So, rather than a dialogue ensuing between persons differently situated in the social fabric, we have a monologue in which those in charge employ their perspective to continue to stifle any serious consideration of other voices.

The major targets of Sandel's somewhat parallel critique are all individualistic, nonconstitutive (i.e. monologic and nondialogic) formulations of justice, especially the popular Rawlsian (1971) account. Sandel's constitutive individuals are our familiar dialogically constituted persons, who have no existence prior to or apart from the socially organized communities that define and give them their character and to which they have ongoing commitments and allegiances:

> Allegiances such as these are more than values I happen to have or aims I "espouse at any given time". They go beyond the obligations I voluntarily incur and the "natural duties" I owe to human beings as such. They allow that to some I owe more than justice requires or even permits, not by reason of agreements I have made but instead in virtue of those more or less enduring attachments and commitments which taken together partly define the person I am.
>
> To imagine a person incapable of constitutive attachments such as these is not to conceive an ideally free and rational agent, but to imagine a person wholly without character, without moral depth. For to have character is to know that I move in a history I neither summon nor command, which carries consequences none the less for my choices and conduct. (Sandel, 1982, p. 179)

Once again, we see a vision of people as fundamentally attached and connected, as constitutive beings who are defined in and through their relationships with others, never having a life, a character, a psychology apart from these relational bonds. There can be neither freedom nor justice without due consideration of this fundamental feature of human nature.

Therefore, a blind justice attempts to deny the very qualities that make people the people they are, turning to some abstract principle that denies the very rootedness that defines who and what we are. A justice that issues from such blindness is more likely to reveal a concealed partiality than the impartiality that we have incorrectly assumed such blindness will provide. Justice needs to see again, and more clearly than ever – not so that justice, standing apart and removed from the affairs of humanity, can issue her decrees, but so that people from within their very differently cast worlds can meet together and reach agreements made in the light of their differences.

Genuine dialogue requires at least two differently situated persons who recognize their mutual embeddedness in one another's lives, who meet and work together. Conditions that thwart this possibility, whether based on a refusal to recognize the embedded nature of persons or on power arrangements that transform dialogues into monologues held by the powerful in order to rule the rest, undermine any serious hope that justice can prevail.

Young (1990) hints at the dialogic possibility when she adopts the "city" rather than the "community" as her normative ideal of a just society. She rejects the ideal of "community" because it is built on sameness and unity rather than on the great diversities on which her thesis (and dialogism's) is based. She sees city life offering:

> a vision of social relations affirming group difference ... without exclusion. ... If city politics is to be democratic and not dominated by the point of view of one group, it must be a politics that takes account of and provides voice for the different groups that dwell together in the city without forming a community. (p. 227)

In other words, the city serves as a more apt metaphor than does the ideal of community. A city encompasses teeming diversity without requiring that such diversity be tamed or reduced to the unity of the single common interest or point of view that we find in most versions in which the image of "community" is invoked.

I have suggested that our understanding of freedom, responsibility and justice is transformed once we move from the currently dominant monologic formulation and develop the full scope of the dialogic view. Whereas freedom and responsibility are defined negatively within the monologic world-view and justice is defined oppositionally, the dialogic framework helps us to realize the flaws in defining our major ethical concepts in this way.

We are obliged to work together with others in a responsible manner because who and what we are and who and what they are are intimately and inextricably linked. We cannot be us, nor can they be they, without one another: our responsibilities, then, are not simply to avoid the other but, of necessity and in recognition of this inherent bonding, to work together on our collective behalf. We cannot define freedom negatively as a freedom from, or justice oppositionally as a balancing of individual versus society. There can be no justice when we pit one against the other. We are not free by virtue of having insulated ourselves from the reaches of the other; we are free only in so far as we and the other can operate together in a democratically egalitarian manner.

We are led away from a view of justice as blind and as based on the individual and towards not only a justice that sees clearly but one in which groups meet as equals with different voices to negotiate issues of their shared concern. The conditions that promote such dialogues are necessarily democratic, even as dialogism itself promotes the conditions of democracy. This, then, is a perfect bridge to Chapter 12.

Notes

1. This was Hobbes's (1651) contribution to our understanding. If people failed to reach a rational agreement to submit themselves to constraints, we would have a war of all against all as individuals did as they wished. The US Constitution's Bill of Rights, outlining the protections each individual has from unwarranted governmental intervention, and thus the freedoms each possesses, offers us the other side of this same issue. Governmental intervention can go only so far; people retain individual rights that no greater power can deny except under extraordinary circumstances.
2. In addition to Erikson's (1959) well-known ideas, perhaps the clearest emphasis on individuation stems from the writings of Mahler *et al.* (1975).
3. I am referring here especially to the works of Berman (1981), Bookchin (1982) and Merchant (1980). Devall and Sessions (1985) and Van Gelder (1989) are also relevant.

12

Democratization and Human Nature

At this point, there can be little doubt remaining: the monologic view of human nature that has thus far dominated our understanding is fundamentally undemocratic in its promotion of inequality. Yet while only a dialogic approach can offer us a more securely democratized understanding of human nature, its realization requires a more egalitarian society.

Monologic views unashamedly adopt a singular perspective for negotiating the diversity of human experience. They make little or no pretext about being democratic or egalitarian: the experts know; others are there to find out. Dialogism's view of the essentially embedded quality of human experience is inherently democratic. But as we have seen, even a dialogue can all too readily be transformed into a monologue when the powerful construct serviceable others and so return again to themselves wherever they look.

In stating this, I am *not* suggesting that all those who have devoted their energies to developing the monologic view are undemocratic in their intentions or desires. Far from it. Some of the staunchest defenders of democracy are to be found among proponents of a perspective that I believe in itself carries undemocratic seeds. The undemocratic quality of which I speak is to be found within two related elements of the monologic framework: first, its insistence on distancing itself from the very objects of its study as the preferred device for gaining objectivity; second, its division of the world into those who know – the experts – and those who are ignorant – the people, the subjects, the other.

By distancing the researcher from the objects studied (i.e. its other) monologic approaches exclude, deny and erase their own involvement in constituting their knowledge of the self–other reality that is of interest to them. They try to become third-person observers of a phenomenon that has been created by the dialogic encounter between themselves as first persons with their subject-others as second persons. As a result of this initial distancing, monologic approaches create a world in which they not only stand apart and outside but occupy a hierarchically superior position as "those who know" – that is, as experts. Both features establish the necessarily undemocratic, inegalitarian characteristics of all monologic approaches.

Let me illustrate certain aspects of this argument by calling upon the remarks made by a highly esteemed psychologist and former President of the American Psychological Association, George Miller, in his 1969 Presidential Address to the American Psychological Association.[1] Miller introduced a frequently quoted democratic appeal: he urged psychologists to discover "how best to give psychology away" (p. 1074) to the people.

Miller believed that psychology had developed some rather powerful insights about human nature, and that these insights were simply too valuable not to share more broadly with a public who needed to know. Keeping knowledge privy only to a handful of professionals who read scientific journals would deny knowledge to those for whom its application might serve extremely useful purposes. His goal was to let nonpsychologists practice psychology, at least in the sense of having available our "secret" recipes and formulas.

Miller argued that "scientific psychology is potentially one of the most revolutionary intellectual enterprises ever conceived by the mind of man" (p. 1065). He commented that once the people had access to what we professionals have learned about their behavior, they would be armed with both a changed conception of themselves and a different view "of what is humanly possible and what is humanly desirable" (p. 1066).

Miller's remarks do not appear to contain even one hint of their fundamentally undemocratic character. Indeed, his desire to share scientific knowledge more broadly so that the people can know what we experts also know seems on the face of it to be the very basis for a democratic view. Wherein lie the undemocratic themes that I announced at the outset of this chapter? I believe they are to be found in the very understanding of science on which Miller has built his case – a monologic rather than a dialogic formulation. To see this point more clearly, we need to see Miller's perspective as a plea to democratize the *outputs* of psychological science, where those outputs (e.g. knowledges about human experience and behavior) have been gained by the very distancing and hierarchization which, I argue, are fundamentally undemocratic.

Miller's notion of giving away the fruits of our science conforms to most conceptions of the proper role of the scientist-citizen in a democratic state: what is to be given away are the outputs or products of research – that is, discoveries about human nature and the understanding of what they mean.

These discoveries emerge after we have applied the appropriate techniques of our science to learn about the nature of the world – in this case, about human nature itself. Scientific knowledge is privileged over everyday common-sense understanding because it has been obtained by the distancing process of the prevailing scientific method. With this process comes a privileging of the expert over the citizen.

Psychological science is urged to give away its discoveries, products and outcomes to help correct the erroneous common-sense views of the everyday citizen. I favor Lave's (1988) term here, referring to the latter as jpfs or "just plain folks". The argument is that the privilege of the experts is based on their providing a better, more accurate, more objective representation of reality than jpfs' folk psychology.

Lopes (1991) demonstrates this privilege through a study that examined citations to articles published between 1972 and 1981 involving decision-making, judgment and problem-solving. She notes that citations to papers that presented jpfs as *poor* performers appeared about 27.8 times, whereas citations in which jpfs were seen to be good performers appeared only 4.7 times. The jpfs were said to be poor performers measured against the standard of good performance – namely, the forms of reasoning and problem-solving employed by the very scientific experts conducting the research in the first place! As Lopes says: "In claiming that most people make foolish errors, and in demonstrating that even the reader may do the same, authors suggest that they have superior knowledge or insight into difficult decision situations" (p. 79).

Thus, it is argued, our scientific methods give us access to the true nature of psychological reality which we are then urged to give away to the people, the jpfs, so that they too will know what we know about them. Because our methods permit us to discover the actual terms by which reality itself exists, our voice, naturally, should occupy a privileged standpoint over the voice of those who, while purporting to refer to reality, are actually referring to wishes, opinions and values concerning reality, but not to the real thing itself.

Pick up almost any psychology textbook and see how clearly it draws a line separating psychology's scientific knowledge of human nature from everyday common-sense knowledge: "our commonsense or even the so-called 'wisdom of the ages' provides us with a confusing picture of human social relations" (Baron and Byrne, 1987, p. 6). While we agree that such information is not useless, because "it can serve as a rich source of suggestions for further study" (p. 6), it is obvious we cannot accept it because "it fails to provide an adequate basis for fully understanding the complex nature of our social relations with others" (p. 6). The authors' recommendation: "accurate and useful information about human social relations can be readily acquired through the use of scientific methods" (p. 7).

This position is not peculiar to the authors whose work I have quoted. The majority of psychologists and other social scientists would agree that common-sense understandings are flawed, and only proper scientific methods permit psychology to obtain a more accurate and useful view of human nature. Billig (1990b) has summarized this view in commenting that textbook writers justify the scientific discipline with the "contention that ordinary common sense is unsatisfactory and that social psychologists must labor hard to correct its imperfections, or, better still, to replace it by a new form of knowledge" (pp. 52–3).

Several ideas presented by Shotter (1990, 1991) and by Fabian (1983), some of which we previously considered, help us to understand better why this monologic point of view is in itself flawed and, in my view, undemocratic. In great measure, their arguments and mine turn on the failure of monologic accounts to deal with the fundamentally dialogic basis of all human knowledge and understanding. What is fundamentally dialogic is transmuted into a monologue. This requires distancing the scientist's self from the other who is to be subjected to the scientist's scrutiny. In this manner, the scientist hopes to gain a handle on the truth and reality that constitute the basis of their privilege. What began its life as a dialogue becomes a monologue that privileges one side over the other and so encourages an undemocratic relationship.

Shotter's argument is centered around his understanding of the way in which truth-claims are warranted. The science of psychology attempts to provide this warrant by claiming that the facts speak for themselves, and that is why we should believe in scientific assertions based on such facts. This argument seems to make sense and, as I have noted, clearly serves as the basis for Miller's argument that psychology should share these gems of truth with the people.

But, says Shotter, this view fails precisely because "if we want to have what *we* say evaluated by *them* as intelligible, rational and legitimate . . . then we must ourselves also, eventually, evaluate our talk in the same way as they do" (1991, p. 497). Despite this situation, the science of psychology seeks its warrant in conditions that transcend those by which any warrants can be evaluated in the first place. In this, therefore, psychological science hopes to accomplish what it cannot ever possibly accomplish. Its claims must be redeemed, as are all claims, in the very talk and conversational practices that comprise any organized social group.

Here is Fabian (1983) on this same point:

> all sciences, including the most abstract and mathematized disciplines, are social endeavors which must be carried out through the channels and means, and according to the rules, of communication available to a community of practitioners and to the wider society of which they are a part. (p. 109)

Yet this is precisely what the science denies to itself. That is, psychology
and the other sciences dealing with human nature *use talk to construct a sense
of a talk-independent reality.*[2]

Our talking with one another does not represent a reality that is
independent of that talk. It is through talk that we establish and warrant a
sense of living together in a shared world that exists independently of those
very practical activities of talking together on whose existence it depends.
Scientific psychology's talk ignores this feature; it ignores "the contextual-
ized, constructive and rhetorical dimensions in how all versions of the
world are produced" (Edwards, 1991, p. 535) – especially its own.

In other words, scientific psychology's claims reveal its own rhetorical
strategies for talking about reality in a way that constructs a reality which
appears to be independent of those very activities of talking. Thus, when
psychology says that it is better than common sense, it can demonstrate this
claim only by destroying the very fabric of common sense that makes its
claims intelligible. It claims privilege for a form that cannot have special
privilege and still operate in society. This creates a situation in which
expert knowledge tries to dominate jpfs' knowledge without any basis
except the very erroneous beliefs contained in the experts' own claims –
hardly a basis for a democratic giving away of its special insights.

As we first noted in Chapter 10, Fabian's (1983) challenge focuses
primarily on his analysis of the temporal distancing that is built into the
typical scientific method applied to the study of human beings. While his
arguments are complex, in my reading they center, as do mine, around the
notion that all knowledge is the result of a co-constructed, ongoing dialogic
process; to deny this feature by seeking various distancing strategies,
including temporal distancing, produces a politically oppressive, undemocratic science.

Fabian probes temporal distancing in his field, anthropology. His
arguments can be applied, however – as Bowers (1991) has applied them to
cognitive science – to any of the social and behavioral sciences for which a
similar conceptual underpinning appears. Recall from our earlier discussion that Fabian focuses on the denial of coevalness that characterizes the
preferred methodology of those sciences that deal with human life:
"coevalness aims at recognizing cotemporality as the condition for truly
dialectical confrontation between persons as well as societies" (Fabian,
1983, p. 154); [thus to deny coevalness is to engage in a] *"persistent and
systematic tendency to place the referent(s) of anthropology in a Time other than
the present of the producer of anthropological discourse"* (p. 31; original
emphasis).

In other words, whereas knowledge is necessarily constituted dialogically
and hence in terms of the cotemporality or coevalness of the knower and
the known (i.e. self and other), monologic views deny and suppress

coevalness, creating "a science of other men in another Time" (p. 141) removed from the time of the scientist. Scientists place themselves as third persons *vis-à-vis* an other located in a different temporal zone, thereby failing to recognize their participation as first persons to second persons in the production of the very knowledge of which they speak.

For example, the ethnographer obtains field notes based on dialogic encounters with the other, but then takes them back home to another time (and place), where they are transcribed in a manner that denies the very conditions of their creation in the first place. Fabian is especially keen to remind us throughout his work of the definite linkage between the denial of coevalness and implicit (or explicit) domination of the other. Two points are relevant. First, by being located in a time other than that of the investigator, the other is created in the terms set by the fieldworker, as though the other possessed qualities as objects of observation independent of the dialogic, temporal relation by which those qualities were constituted in the first place.

Interesting findings reported by Eleanor Maccoby (1990) in a very different context join with my previous discussion of the feminist thesis to lend both credence and concreteness to this point. She found that when two little girls were paired together in a play situation, they tended to act in a much more aggressive and assertive manner than appeared when a little girl was paired with a little boy. In the latter case, the little girl tended to behave very passively, even submissively. Is the little girl aggressive or passive? Maccoby tells us that by ignoring the interactive event, we are likely to misrepresent the actual little girl, who is both. In other words, we forget how the object, little girl, has been constituted in and through a dialogic encounter, in this case with another little girl or little boy; she does not possess either of these characteristics in herself.

Fabian's second point linking political domination with the denial of coevalness observes how the distancing between the time of the scientist and the time of the other permits scientists to exclude themselves from being subjected to the very principles they apply to the other. The knower is removed from whatever is uncovered about the object that is known, by virtue of having separated the times they occupy. The knower claims privilege for herself because she stands outside the stream of time in which the known has been located; and by implication, her outsiderness is the key to her objectivity and her ability, thereby, to know what is truly taking place – things of which the known cannot be aware.

Bowers (1991) has used some of Fabian's ideas to examine cognitive science critically, noting that although experimental psychologists may not act precisely as ethnographic fieldworkers, they manage to accomplish much the same denial of coevalness, and much to the same ends of domination. In speaking of the experimenter's subjects arriving for their appointed session with the investigator, for example, Bowers comments that they "must be let in but not for too long. If they were to stay, they might force a bewildering and unmanageable multiplication of representations of themselves" (p. 561). Bowers uses this to illustrate how the temporal management of the experimental situation permits investigators to restrict representations to only those pieces of the other they want to see.

Bowers continues by noting that actions and events are carefully managed so that the information gleaned can be neatly packaged and taken away for later scrutiny. For example, it is the experimenter's slicing up of the array of potential events presented to the subject that is of central interest, not the subject's own slicing. Subjects are asked to attend to what the experimenter deems important, not what they may or may not consider relevant to them.

In addition to the points that Bowers makes, we should note that because the vast majority of experimental studies continue to employ professors (or their assistants) as researchers and college students as subjects, we have a situation that is intrinsically fueled with power differentials, perhaps of an even more potent sort than one typically finds among the anthropological fieldworkers of whom Fabian writes.

Finally, I must also note the significant overlap between these several arguments and those we first encountered in Harding's and Code's feminist critique of the predominantly masculinist scientific method. The paradigm of friendship of which both speak, the idea that all knowledge is based on the knowledge of others that we obtain as second-person partners, not as third-person observers, carries the feminist critique and the feminist message.

By now it should be apparent that this feminist critique is dialogic in my terms and agrees as well with the position and arguments set forth by Fabian, Shotter, Edwards and Bowers. If there is any distinction to be made among these various approaches, it would have to center around the feminist and my dialogic emphasis on the fundamentally undemocratic quality of all nondialogic perspectives – an emphasis to which the others tend to give somewhat less prominence.

Where, then, do we stand? I have suggested that because monologic formulations base their expertise and authority over others on an argument that must deny the very terms by which its knowledge is formed and its claims to rationality are warranted, these approaches give away truths that may better reflect a particular group's self-interest than anything else. Although experts in those sciences whose subject matter is distinctly separate from their own lives may indeed make claims to possess expertise and so base their authority on these warrants – but see Code's and Harding's challenges here – the issue is much more troublesome for those who claim expertise over human nature by acting as though they are not part of the very human community over which they possess this expertise.

In this they manage expertise in a duplicitous, self-interested manner – hardly the currency of a genuinely democratized process.

The outputs of psychological science cannot be neutral statements about human nature. They have been generated by positioned and interested scientists who must call upon forms of warranting that persuade members of the wider community in which they too have membership. In so far as psychology helps to formulate and disseminate the prevailing self-understandings in a nonreflective, uncritical manner by simply reporting its findings as though they were disembodied facts, the discipline helps to perpetuate current systems of domination and group advantage. Data are presented as though they were ahistorical facts about nature rather than facts about conditions that have a history and a politics. Such data have been both obtained and warranted dialogically. Denying this in order to claim special privilege for one's own knowledge is an incorrect portrayal of the actual processes that are involved, and serves undemocratic and inegalitarian purposes.

So when we hear Miller urging psychologists to democratize the outputs of their knowledge, sharing the truths about people with those people, what we may actually be accomplishing is the perpetuation of oppressive arrangements: that is, presenting as facts items whose history reveals precisely for whom such facts serve useful advantages. Sharing outputs of this sort does not accomplish a genuine democratization of our knowledge of human nature.

If the first element of my argument has been that monologic approaches are inherently undemocratic, and that their pleas to give away the outcomes of psychological science to the people merely advance that undemocratic quality, then the second element of my argument focuses on the dialogic perspective's inherently democratic perspective. Dialogism insists both that genuine democratization must deal with the *inputs* to knowledge, not merely the outputs; and that these must be understood dialogically – that is, as jointly created by knower and known, scientist and jpf. And I will continue to make these claims for dialogism in spite of the critique I developed in Chapter 10. Whereas a monologic perspective can never be anything other than undemocratic, at least dialogism offers the hopes for a genuinely democratic possibility – often unrealized, but nevertheless possible.

Ethnopsychology

A view that has been emerging in anthropology, referred to as ethnopsychology, when it is joined with a view in psychology that emphasizes "everyday cognition", directs us to the kind of democratization of inputs which, I believe, is essential to any genuinely democratic approach to the sciences dealing with human nature.[3] Lutz (1985) defines ethnopsychology as being "concerned with the way in which people conceptualize, monitor, and discuss their own and others' mental processes, behavior and relationships" (p. 36). Among the other proponents of the ethnopsychological perspective, Lutz argues that only by employing the formulations of the people themselves can we minimize the ethnocentric and undemocratic bias that otherwise creeps into our work. The ethnopsychological view is contrasted with the more conventional understanding of cross-cultural research.

The typical cross-cultural researcher, for example, takes a conceptual framework resident in her or his own culture and seeks to extend its generality by studying its shape in other cultures. In doing this, investigators do not allow the other culture to communicate *its own* terms for understanding human experience. Rather than conducting a dialogue, conventional investigators carry on a monologue in which their version must necessarily win out.

For example, Lutz (1988) contrasted our way of understanding emotional concepts with the Ifaluk's way. Her data led her to conclude that there is no biological event that is simply labeled or expressed differently in the two cultures. Rather, she says, the understanding of emotions differs markedly between the two cultures. She lists several Western or Euro-American views of emotion to set the stage for this comparison, including *our* tendencies (1) to separate emotion from thinking; (2) to consider emotion irrational and out of our control; (3) to believe that emotional expressions put us at a disadvantage, making us vulnerable to others; (4) to view emotion as a part of nature, not culture; (5) to consider emotion more female than male. Not every understanding of emotion separates the Ifaluk from our way. There are sufficient differences in each of the preceding formulations, however, to suggest that we would profit from adopting an ethnopsychological rather than a conventional cross-cultural approach.

Lutz's view has been supported by several other investigators, while it has been challenged by still others.[4] Her contention, however, is that before we presume that our terms and our understanding of emotion apply universally because they are founded on "nature" or "biology", we had better first carry on a dialogue with others and attempt to discover points of agreement and points of disagreement. To do otherwise is to subsume the other and thus to accomplish domination without recognizing that we have even done so.

We have seen much this same way of thinking in Bakhtin's (1981) work as well as in the feminist analyses we have examined. When Bakhtin argues that our contemporary understanding of the person differs from the ancient Greeks' view, he is asking us to carry on a dialogue with them in order to understand both what they meant and what we mean. Feminist analyses adopt much this same argument – in this case, however, suggesting that the male standpoint has so overwhelmed the definition and reality of woman that no genuine dialogues are yet possible. Yet were the inequality that roots the gender system undone, the ensuing dialogues would undoubtedly prove eye-opening for both men and women.

To examine a culture's own system of understanding requires us to become familiar with the culture in *its* terms, rather than our own. This demands a dialogic rather than a monologic approach. We must carry on a dialogue with the other culture. In this dialogue, our framework and theirs meet. Out of that meeting a newly cast understanding of both them and us is likely to emerge. At a minimum, a dialogue can reduce the chances that we will impose our view on theirs or subsume theirs under our own.

Note how different this outcome is from the outcome of the more conventional, monologic approaches. Because dialogism recognizes how both parties are created in and through their dialogic encounter, it can try to minimize the likelihood that one view will win out. The monologic encounter, by contrast, is designed to avoid producing precisely this kind of knowledge. Third-person observers who conduct research hope to use their distance from the other as the vehicle for better seeing the other's reality unfold. There is no desire to be involved; no obligation to be a participant; no recognition of the mutual determination of self and other. As we have seen, however, these very failures create the illusion of distant experts commenting on what is observed from afar, failing to see their own complicity in constituting what is seen and what is known.

Everyday Cognition

Although they have not examined the exotic cultures of primary interest to most anthropologists, a group of psychologists have focused on the everyday cognitions of Lave's just plain folks, offering us a perspective and conclusions very similar to those of their anthropological colleagues.[5] Lave, for example, examined how people carry out everyday arithmetical operations while grocery shopping or beginning a diet program. She compared their problem-solving in these settings with their performance in the laboratory. Her data revealed such striking differences between the kinds of cognitive activity that occurred in these different settings that she formulated a situation-specific "social anthropology of cognition" (1988, p. 1) in which the culture of the setting plays a key part in shaping the nature of the problem-solving processes that will occur. I noted in Chapter 9 how proponents of collective and ecological concepts of psychological processes – such as Ceci and Bronfenbrenner, for example – make much this same point and provide very similar data.

Lave tells us of a grocery shopper deciding on which of two products to select, comparing a five-pound bag of sugar costing $2.16 with a ten-pound bag costing $4.20. Lave noted that the choice was not dictated simply by the rules of mathematical proportions, but took into consideration a range of issues involving food management: for example, how much sugar one could feasibly use, how much shelf space was available for storage, an evaluation of upcoming menus, when the next trip to the grocer's was planned, etc. Is it acting foolishly for the shopper to consider these factors in making a decision? Or is it, as Lave insists, that the problem-solving operations of everyday life follow different rules of practice from those typically discovered in the laboratory, on which much of our understanding of cognitive processes has been founded?

If a community's social life, its conventions of belief and practice, provide the terms by which human experience is organized and self-understandings are accomplished; if those conventions have emerged and are sustained in historical contexts and in particular places, and work to structure experience in one way rather than another; and if there is no grounding for these conventions in a reality that can be described independently of those very conventions that propose it in the first place, then we are surely obliged to enter into a collaborative, dialogic relationship with our "subjects" in order to discern how they function in their world. In this, we have necessarily democratized the very inputs of our science. The next step – sharing our conclusions, the outputs of our work – would then accomplish the kinds of genuinely democratized process that Miller and others hope to be the heritage of psychology and the other human sciences.

I have been arguing that dialogism is inherently democratic in that it recognizes that the knowledge we have about human experience and behavior is jointly produced by self and other, knower and known. Unlike monologism's division of the world into experts who know and objects of their scrutiny who are there only to be known, dialogism cannot privilege one side or the other. Neither the expert's view nor the everyday common-sense view can occupy a privileged position. This means that the expert's perspective on the situation is *essential* to consider, but by no means the only view or the correct view. It also means that the perspective of the performers, the cultural members, is likewise essential to consider, but in itself is also neither privileged nor correct.

What is called for is a dialogic encounter among and between these two different positions and others that may enter the arena for consideration. Surely this is what Clifford (in Clifford and Marcus, 1986) meant when he advocated our entering into a collaborative relationship with our subjects and becoming, along with them, the co-authors of their life stories. Surely this is also Geertz's (1979) point when he insists that we become expert fieldworkers who are adept at carrying on a dialogue with our subjects.

Surely this is likewise Irigaray's desire to see woman's unique specificity engage man's in an equal dialogue. Surely this is MacKinnon's demand that we overthrow the guise of gender neutrality so that we may not only disclose its point of view but, in so doing, open the doors to a genuinely dialogic encounter among people equally but differently situated in the social world.

If we privilege either side of a dialogue, we miss the point. In our current society, the tendency has been to privilege the side of the dominant groups and so to create a monologue, usually among experts, rather than a dialogue with our subjects. Too often critiques of our current view are also flawed, as they urge us to abandon entirely our own perspective and so thoroughly enter into the other's world that we can never carry on a proper dialogue.

A proper dialogue, however, in which each side benefits from its encounter with its other, requires a democratic and egalitarian context in which to operate. Not only does democracy issue from dialogism, but without a genuinely democratic and egalitarian society, dialogues themselves are not possible. We are much more familiar with dialogues gone sour than with those that work, especially in cultures that pride themselves on being democratic.

A genuinely democratic society is one in which both experts and nonexperts alike contribute to the understandings – in this case, understandings about human nature – that are eventually settled on, at least until additional dialogic partners enter the scene to take us on yet another voyage of mutual adventure and discovery. What our adventures teach us, of course, is not something fundamental about human nature, other than its grounding in dialogue and conversation. We learn how many possibilities there are, how open we must be to this diverse range, and how no one voice can be quieted without losing the greatest opportunity of all: to converse with otherness and to learn about our own otherness in and through those conversations.

Notes

1. Aspects of this argument and this chapter were originally developed in "The democraticization of psychology" (Sampson, 1991).
2. This is a point that is also central to the work of Edwards (1991) as well as to Garfinkel's ethnomethodology (1967).
3. Again, there are numerous contributors in anthropology – Clifford (1988); Clifford and Marcus (1986); Geertz (1973); Heelas and Lock (1981); Marcus and Fischer (1986); Rosaldo (1989); Shweder and LeVine (1984); Stigler *et al.* (1990); White and Kirkpatrick (1985) – and in the study of everyday cognition –

Gergen and Semin (1990); Lave (1988); Ochs (1988); Ochs and Schieffelin (1984); Rogoff and Lave (1984); Schieffelin (1990).

4. Robert Solomon (1984), for example, makes an especially strong case in support of Lutz's position, commenting that "an emotion is a system of concepts, beliefs, attitudes, and desires, virtually all of which are context-bound, historically developed, and culture-specific (which is not to foreclose the probability that some emotions may be specific to *all* cultures)" (p. 249); and, further: "the concepts that make up virtually all emotions are essentially tied to the community and its conceptual apparatus" (p. 251). Both Averill's work (1983) and Harré's edited collection (1986) lend support to Lutz's views. James Russell (1991), on the other hand, offers somewhat less complete support, noting that while "people of different cultures and speaking different languages categorize the emotions somewhat differently ... there is great similarity in emotion categories across different cultures and languages" (p. 444). This leads him to question Lutz's claims.

5. See Note 3 above.

Bibliography

Adorno, T.W. (1973) *Negative Dialectics*. New York: Seabury Press.

Arbib, M.A. and Hesse, M.B. (1986) *The Construction of Reality*. Cambridge: Cambridge University Press.

Aronson, E. (1988) *The Social Animal*. New York: W.H. Freeman & Co.

Averill, J.R. (1983) "Studies on anger and aggression: Implications for theories of emotion". *American Psychologist*, 38, 1145–60.

Bakhtin, M.M. (1981) *The Dialogic Imagination*. Austin: University of Texas Press.

Bakhtin, M.M. (1986) *Speech Genres and Other Late Essays*. Austin: University of Texas Press.

Baron, R.A. and Byrne, D. (1987) *Social Psychology: Understanding human interaction*. Boston, MA: Allyn & Bacon.

Bartlett, F.C. (1932) *Remembering: A study in experimental psychology*. London: Cambridge University Press.

Bateson, G. (1972) *Steps to an Ecology of Mind*. New York: Ballantine.

Bellah, R.N., Madsen, R., Sullivan, W.M., Swidler, A. and Tipton, S.M. (1985) *Habits of the Heart: Individualism and commitment in American life*. Berkeley: University of California Press.

Berger, P.L. and Luckman, T. (1966) *The Social Construction of Reality: A treatise in the sociology of knowledge*. Garden City, NY: Doubleday.

Berman, M. (1981) *The Reenchantment of the World*. Ithaca, NY: Cornell University Press.

Bernstein, B. (1971) *Class, Codes, and Control, I: Theoretical studies towards a sociology of language*. London: Routledge & Kegan Paul.

Bernstein, B. (1973) *Class, Codes, and Control, II: Applied studies towards a sociology of language*. London: Routledge & Kegan Paul.

Bernstein, R.J. (1983) *Beyond Objectivism and Relativism: Science, hermeneutics and praxis*. Philadelphia: University of Pennsylvania Press.

Billig, M. (1982) *Ideology and Social Psychology*. Oxford: Basil Blackwell.

Billig, M. (1987) *Arguing and Thinking: A rhetorical approach to social psychology*. Cambridge: Cambridge University Press.

Billig, M. (1990a) "Collective memory, ideology and the British Royal Family". In D. Middleton and D. Edwards (eds), *Collective Remembering*. London: Sage.

Billig, M. (1990b) "Rhetoric of social psychology". In I. Parker and J. Shotter (eds), *Deconstructing Social Psychology*. London: Routledge.

Billig, M., Condor, S., Edwards, D., Gane, M., Middleton, D. and Radley, A.R. (1988) *Ideological Dilemmas*. London: Sage.

Blake, W. (1946/1968) "London". In A. Kazin (ed.), *The Portable Blake*. New York: Penguin.

Blom, J.P. and Gumperz, J.J. (1972) "Some social determinants of verbal behavior". In J.J. Gumperz and D. Hymes (eds), *Directions in Sociolinguistics*. New York: Holt, Rinehart & Winston.

Bloor, D. (1983) *Wittgenstein: A social theory of knowledge*. New York: Columbia University Press.

Bookchin, M. (1982) *The Ecology of Freedom: The emergence and dissolution of hierarchy*. Palo Alto, CA: Cheshire Books.

Bourdieu, P. (1977) *Outline of a Theory of Practice*. Cambridge: Cambridge University Press.

Bourdieu, P. (1990) *In Other Words: Essays towards a reflexive sociology*. Stanford, CA: Stanford University Press.

Bourhis, R.Y. and Giles, H. (1977) "The language of intergroup distinctiveness". In H. Giles (ed.), *Language, Ethnicity and Intergroup Relations*. London: Academic Press.

Bourque, L.B. and Back, K.W. (1971) "Language, society and subjective experience". *Sociometry*, 34, 1–21.

Bowers, J.M. (1991) "Time, representation and power/knowledge: Towards a critique of cognitive science as a knowledge-producing practice". *Theory & Psychology*, 1, 543–69.

Braidotti, R. (1991) *Patterns of Dissonance: A study of women in contemporary philosophy*. New York: Routledge.

Brehm, J.W. (1966) *A Theory of Psychological Reactance*. New York: Academic Press.

Brehm, S.S. and Brehm, J.W. (1981) *Psychological Reactance: A theory of freedom and control*. New York: Academic Press.

Broverman, I.K., Vogel, S.R., Broverman, D.M., Clarkson, F.E. and Rosenkrantz, P.S. (1972). "Sex role stereotypes: A current appraisal". *Journal of Social Issues*, 28, 59–78.

Brownmiller, S. (1975) *Against Our Will: Men, women and rape*. New York: Simon & Schuster.

Bruner, J. (1986) *Actual Minds, Possible Worlds*. Cambridge, MA: Harvard University Press.

Bruner, J. (1987) "Life as narrative". *Social Research*, 54, 11–32.

Bruner, J. (1990) *Acts of Meaning*. Cambridge, MA: Harvard University Press.

Buck-Morss, S. (1977) *The Origin of Negative Dialectics*. New York: Free Press.

Cahoone, L.E. (1988) *The Dilemma of Modernity: Philosophy, culture, and anti-culture*. Albany: State University of New York Press.

Caplan, P. (ed.) (1987) *The Cultural Construction of Sexuality*. London: Routledge.

Carrithers, M. (1985) "An alternative social history of the self". In M. Carrithers, S. Collins and S. Lukes (eds), *The Category of the Person: Anthropology, philosophy, history*. Cambridge: Cambridge University Press.

Carrithers, M., Collins, S. and Lukes, S. (eds) (1985) *The Category of the Person: Anthropology, philosophy, history*. Cambridge: Cambridge University Press.

Ceci, S.J. and Bronfenbrenner, U. (1991) "On the demise of everyday memory: 'The rumors of my death are much exaggerated': (Mark Twain)". *American Psychologist*, 46, 27–31.

Chesler, P. (1978) *About Men*. London: Women's Press.

Chodorow, N. (1978) *The Reproduction of Mothering: Psychoanalysis and the sociology of gender*. Berkeley: University of California Press.

Chomsky, N. (1957) *Syntactic Structures*. The Hague: Mouton.

Cicourel, A.V. (1974) *Cognitive Sociology: Language and meaning in social interaction*. New York: Free Press.

Cixous, H. and Clément, C. (1975/1986) *The Newly Born Woman*. Minneapolis: University of Minnesota Press.

Clark, K. and Holquist, M. (1984) *Mikhail Bakhtin*. Cambridge, MA: Harvard University Press.

Clifford, J. (1988) *The Predicament of Culture: Twentieth-century ethnography, literature, and art*. Cambridge, MA: Harvard University Press.

Clifford, J. and Marcus, G.E. (1986) *Writing Culture: The poetics and politics of ethnography*. Berkeley: University of California Press.

Code, L. (1991) *What Can She Know? Feminist Theory and the Construction of Knowledge*. Ithaca, NY: Cornell University Press.

Colby, A. and Damon, W. (1983) "Listening to a different voice: A review of Gilligan's *In a Different Voice*". *Merrill-Palmer Quarterly*, 29, 473–81.

Cole, M. (1988) "Cross-cultural research in the socio-historical tradition". *Human Development*, 31, 137–57.

Cole, M., Gay, J., Glick, J.A. and Sharp, D.W. (1971) *The Cultural Context of Learning and Thinking*. New York: Basic Books.

Cole, M. and Means, B. (1981) *Comparative Studies of How People Think: An introduction*. Cambridge, MA: Harvard University Press.

Connell, R.W. (1987) *Gender and Power: Society, the person and sexual politics*. Stanford, CA: Stanford University Press.

Coote, R.B. and Coote, M.P. (1990) *Power, Politics and the Making of the Bible*. Minneapolis, MN: Fortress Press.

Cushman, P. (1991) "Ideology obscured: Political uses of the self in Daniel Stern's infant". *American Psychologist*, 46, 206–19.

de Beauvoir, S. (1949/1989). *The Second Sex*. New York: Vintage.

de Lauretis, T. (1987) *Technologies of Gender: Essays on theory, film, and fiction*. Bloomington: Indiana University Press.

Derrida, J. (1974) *Of Grammatology*. Baltimore, MD: Johns Hopkins University Press.

Derrida, J. (1978) *Writing and Difference*. Chicago: University of Chicago Press.

Derrida, J. (1981) *Dissemination*. Chicago: University of Chicago Press.

Devall, B. and Sessions, G. (1985) *Deep Ecology*. Layton, UT: Peregrine Smith.

Dominguez, V.R. (1989) *People as Subject, People as Object: Selfhood and peoplehood in contemporary Israel*. Madison: University of Wisconsin Press.

Dreyfus, H.L. and Dreyfus, S.E. (1987) "From Socrates to expert systems: The limits of calculative rationality". In P. Rabinow and W.M. Sullivan (eds), *Interpretive Social Science: A second look*. Berkeley: University of California Press.

Dumont, L. (1985) "A modified view of our origins: The Christian beginnings of modern individualism". In M. Carrithers, S. Collins and S. Lukes (eds), *The Category of the Person: Anthropology, philosophy, history*. Cambridge: Cambridge University Press.

Dunn, J. (1984) "Early social interaction and the development of emotional understanding". In H. Tajfel (ed.), *The Social Dimension: European developments in social psychology*, vol. 1. Cambridge: Cambridge University Press.

Dworkin, A. (1981) *Pornography: Men possessing women*. London: Women's Press.

Eagly, A.H. and Kite, M. (1987) "Are stereotypes of nationalities applied to both women and men?" *Journal of Personality and Social Psychology*, 53, 451–62.

Edwards, D. (1991) "Categories are for talking: On the cognitive and discursive bases of categorization". *Theory & Psychology*, 1, 515–42.

Eisenstein, Z.R. (1988) *The Female Body and the Law*. Berkeley: University of California Press.

Ellison, R. (1952) *Invisible Man*. New York: Random House.

Erikson, E.H. (1959) *Identity and the Life Cycle*. New York: International Universities Press.

Errington, F. and Gewertz, D. (1987) *Cultural Alternatives and a Feminist Anthropology: An analysis of culturally constructed gender interests in Papua New Guinea*. Cambridge: Cambridge University Press.

Ervin-Tripp, S. (1969) "Sociolinguistics". In L. Berkowitz (ed.), *Advances in Experimental Social Psychology*, vol. 4. New York: Academic Press.

Estes, W.K. (1991) "What is cognitive science?" *Psychological Science*, 2, 282.

Fabian, J. (1983) *Time and the Other: How anthropology makes its object*. New York: Columbia University Press.

Fajans, J. (1985) "The person in social context: The social character of Baining 'Psychology'". In G.M. White and J. Kirkpatrick (eds), *Person, Self and Experience*. Berkeley: University of California Press.

Faludi, S. (1991) *Backlash: The undeclared war against American women*. New York: Crown.

Findlay, J.N. (1958) *Hegel: A re-examination*. New York: Oxford University Press.

Fiorenza, E.S. (1989) *In Memory of Her: a feminist theological reconstruction of Christian origins*. New York: Crossroad.

Firestone, S. (1971) The Dialectic of Sex. London: Paladin.

Flax, J. (1990) *Thinking Fragments: Psychoanalysis, feminism, and postmodernism in the contemporary west*. Berkeley: University of California Press.

Foucault, M. (1979) *Discipline and Punish: The birth of the prison*. New York: Random House.

Foucault, M. (1980) *The History of Sexuality, Vol. I: An introduction*. New York: Random House.

Freud, S. (1920/1959) *Beyond the Pleasure Principle*. New York: Bantam.

Freud, S. (1921/1960) *Group Psychology and the Analysis of the Ego*. New York: Bantam.

Freud, S. (1939) *Moses and Monotheism*. New York: Vintage.

Friedan, B. (1963) *The Feminine Mystique*. New York: Norton.

Funder, D.C. (1987) "Errors and mistakes: Evaluating the accuracy of social judgment". *Psychological Bulletin*, 101, 75–90.

Gardner, H. (1985) *The Mind's New Science: A history of the cognitive revolution*. New York: Basic Books.

Garfinkel, H. (1967) *Studies in Ethnomethodology*. Englewood Cliffs, NJ: Prentice Hall.

Gatens, M. (1991) *Feminism and Philosophy: Perspectives on difference and equality*. Cambridge: Polity Press.

Geertz, C. (1973) *The Interpretation of Cultures*. New York: Basic Books.

Geertz, C. (1979) "From the native's point of view: On the nature of anthropological understanding". In P. Rabinow and W.M. Sullivan (eds), *Interpretive Social Science*. Berkeley: University of California Press.

Gergen, K.J. (1987) "The language of psychological understanding". In H.J. Stam, R.B. Rogers and K.J. Gergen (eds), *The Analysis of Psychological Theory: Metapsychological perspectives*. New York: Hemisphere.

Gergen, K.J. (1989) "Warranting voice and the elaboration of the self". In J. Shotter and K.J. Gergen (eds), *Texts of Identity*. London: Sage.

Gergen, K.J. (1991) *The Saturated Self: Dilemmas of identity in contemporary life*. New York: Basic Books.

Gergen, K.J. and Gergen, M.M. (1988) "Narrative and the self as relationship". In L. Berkowitz (ed.), *Advances in Experimental Social Psychology*, vol. 21. San Diego, CA: Academic Press.

Gergen, K.J. and Semin, G.R. (1990) "Everyday understanding in science and daily life". In G.R. Semin and K.J. Gergen (eds), *Everyday Understanding: Social and scientific implications*. London: Sage.

Gilbert, G.N. and Mulkay, M.J. (1984) *Opening Pandora's Box: A sociological analysis of scientists' discourse*. Cambridge: Cambridge University Press.

Giles, H. and Coupland, N. (1991) *Language: Context and consequences*. Pacific Grove, CA: Brooks/Cole.

Gilligan, C. (1982) *In a Different Voice: Psychological theory and women's development*. Cambridge, MA: Harvard University Press.

Goffman, E. (1959) *The Presentation of Self in Everyday Life*. New York: Doubleday/Anchor.

Goodnow, J.J. (1990) "The socialization of cognition: What is involved?" In J.W. Stigler, R.A. Shweder and G. Herdt (eds), *Cultural Psychology: Essays on comparative human development*. Cambridge: Cambridge University Press.

Greenberg, J.R. and Mitchell, S.A. (1983) *Object Relations in Psychoanalytic Theory*. Cambridge, MA: Harvard University Press.

Greenwald, A.G. (1980) "The totalitarian ego: Fabrication and revision of personal history". *American Psychologist*, 35, 603–18.

Habermas, J. (1984) *The Theory of Communicative Action, Vol. I: Reason and the rationalization of society*. Boston, MA: Beacon Press.

Halbwachs, M. (1980) *The Collective Memory*. New York: Harper & Row.

Harding, S. (1986) *The Science Question in Feminism*. Ithaca, NY: Cornell University Press.

Harré, R. (1984) *Personal Being: A theory for individual psychology*. Cambridge, MA: Harvard University Press.

Harré, R. (ed.) (1986) *The Social Construction of Emotions*. Oxford: Basil Blackwell.

Harvey, J.H., Weber, A.L. and Orbuch, T.L. (1990) *Inter-personal Accounts: A social psychological perspective*. Cambridge, MA: Basil Blackwell.

Heelas, P. and Lock, A. (eds) (1981) *Indigenous Psychologies: The anthropology of the self*. London: Academic Press.

Hegel, G.W.F. (1807/1910) *The Phenomenology of Mind*. London: Allen and Unwin.

Hewstone, M. (1989) *Causal Attribution: From cognitive processes to collective beliefs*. Oxford: Basil Blackwell.

Hobbes, T. (1651) *Leviathan*. Cambridge: Cambridge University Press.

Hofstede, G. (1980) *Culture's Consequences: International differences in work-related values*. Beverly Hills, CA: Sage.

Horkheimer, M. and Adorno, T.W. (1944/1969) *Dialectic of Enlightenment*. New York: Seabury Press.

Howard, G.S. (1991) "Culture tales: A narrative approach to thinking, cross-cultural psychology, and psychotherapy". *American Psychologist*, 46, 187–97.

Irigaray, L. (1974/1985) *Speculum of the Other Woman*. Ithaca, NY: Cornell University Press.

Irigaray, L. (1977/1985) *This Sex Which Is Not One*. Ithaca, NY: Cornell University Press.

Jacoby, R. (1975) *Social Amnesia: A critique of conformist psychology from Adler to Laing*. Boston, MA: Beacon Press.

Johnson, M. (1987) *The Body in the Mind: The bodily basis of meaning, imagination, and reason*. Chicago: University of Chicago Press.

Jordan, J.V. (1989) "Relational development: Therapeutic implications of empathy and shame". *Work in progress, No. 39*. Wellesley, MA: Stone Center Working Papers Series.

Kagitcibasi, C. (1987) "Individual and group loyalties: Are they compatible?" In C. Kagitcibasi (ed.), *Growth and Progress in Cross-Cultural Psychology*. Lisse, The Netherlands: Swets & Zeitlinger.

Kelley, H.H. (1973). "The processes of causal attribution". *American Psychologist*, 28, 107–28.

Kessler, S.J. and McKenna, W. (1978) *Gender: An ethnomethodological approach*. New York: Wiley.

Kitzinger, C. (1987) *The Social Construction of Lesbianism*. London: Sage.

Kohlberg, L. (1969). "Stage and sequence: The cognitive–developmental approach to socialization". In D.A. Goslin (ed.), *Handbook of Socialization Theory and Research*. Chicago: Rand McNally.

Kojima, H. (1984). "A significant stride toward the comparative study of control". *American Psychologist*, 39, 972–3.

Kozulin, A. (1990) *Vygotsky's Psychology: A biography of ideas*. New York: Harvester Wheatsheaf.

Kurzweil, E. (1980) *The Age of Structuralism: Lévi-Strauss to Foucault*. New York: Columbia University Press.

Labov, W. (1966) *The Social Stratification of English in New York City*. Washington, DC: Center for Applied Linguistics.

Lacan, J. (1973/1981) *The Four Fundamental Concepts of Psycho-Analysis*. New York: W.W. Norton.

Lakoff, G. (1987) *Women, Fire and Dangerous Things: What categories reveal about the mind.* Chicago: University of Chicago Press.

Lakoff, G. and Johnson, M. (1980) *Metaphors We Live By.* Chicago: University of Chicago Press.

Larrick, R.P., Morgan, J.N. and Nisbett, R.E. (1990) "Teaching the use of cost–benefit reasoning in everyday life". *Psychological Science*, 1, 362–70.

Lave, J. (1988) *Cognition in Practice: Mind, mathematics and culture in everyday life.* Cambridge: Cambridge University Press.

Le Bon, G. (1895/1960) *The Crowd.* Harmondsworth: Penguin.

Lemaire, A. (1977) *Jacques Lacan.* London: Routledge & Kegan Paul.

Lewin, K. (1947a) "Frontiers in group dynamics: Concept, method and reality in social science; social equilibria and social change". *Human Relations*, 1, 5–41.

Lewin, K. (1947b) "Frontiers in group dynamics, II: Channels of group life; social planning and action research". *Human Relations*, 1, 143–53.

Lindsay, R.K. (1991) "Symbol-processing theories and the SOAR architecture". *Psychological Science*, 2, 294–302.

Lopes, L.L. (1991) "The rhetoric of irrationality". *Theory & Psychology*, 1, 65–82.

Lukes, S. (1985) "Conclusion". In M. Carrithers, S. Collins and S. Lukes (eds), *The Category of the Person: Anthropology, philosophy, history.* Cambridge: Cambridge University Press.

Lukes, S. (ed.) (1986) *Power.* New York: New York University Press.

Lutz, C. (1985) "Ethnopsychology compared to what? Explaining behavior and consciousness among the Ifaluk". In G.M. White and J. Kirkpatrick (eds), *Person, Self and Experience.* Berkeley: University of California Press.

Lutz, C. (1988) *Unnatural Emotions: Everyday sentiments on a Micronesian atoll and their challenge to western theory.* Chicago: University of Chicago Press.

Lyotard, J.-F. (1979/1984) *The Postmodern Condition: A report on knowledge.* Minneapolis: University of Minnesota Press.

Maccoby, E.E. (1990) "Gender and relationships: A developmental account". *American Psychologist*, 45, 513–20.

McCarthy, T. (1978) *The Critical Theory of Jürgen Habermas.* Cambridge, MA: MIT Press.

McGrane, B. (1989) *Beyond Anthropology: Society and the other.* New York: Columbia University Press.

MacIntyre, A. (1984) *After Virtue.* Notre Dame, IN: University of Notre Dame Press.

MacIntyre, A. (1988) *Whose Justice? Which Rationality?* Notre Dame, IN: University of Notre Dame Press.

MacKinnon, C.A. (1989) *Toward a Feminist Theory of the State.* Cambridge, MA: Harvard University Press.

Macpherson, C.B. (1962) *The Political Theory of Possessive Individualism.* London: Oxford University Press.

Mahler, M., Pine, F. and Bergman, A. (1975) *The Psychological Birth of the Human Infant: Symbiosis and individuation.* New York: Basic Books.

Marcus, G.E. and Fischer, M.J. (1986) *Anthropology as Cultural Critique: An experimental moment in the human sciences.* Chicago: University of Chicago Press.

Markus, H. and Kunda, Z. (1986) "Stability and malleability of the self-concept". *Journal of Personality and Social Psychology*, 51, 858–66.

Markus, H. and Nurius, P. (1986) "Possible selves". *American Psychologist*, 41, 954–69.

Martin, R.M. (1968) "The stimulus barrier and the autonomy of the ego". *Psychological Review*, 75, 478–93.

Maslow, A.H. (1959) "Cognition of being in the peak experience". *Journal of Genetic Psychology*, 94, 43–66.

Maslow, A.H. (1971) *The Farther Reaches of Human Nature*. Harmondsworth: Penguin.

Massaro, D.W. (1991) "Psychology as a cognitive science". *Psychological Science*, 2, 302–7.

Mauss, M. (1938/1985) "A category of the human mind: The notion of person; the notion of self". In M. Carrithers, S. Collins and S. Lukes (eds), *The Category of the Person: Anthropology, philosophy, history*. Cambridge: Cambridge University Press.

Mead, G.H. (1934) *The Social Psychology of George Herbert Mead*. Chicago: University of Chicago Press.

Mednick, M.T. (1989) "On the politics of psychological constructs: Stop the bandwagon, I want to get off". *American Psychologist*, 44, 1118–23.

Merchant, C. (1980) *The Death of Nature: Women, ecology and the scientific revolution*. San Francisco: Harper & Row.

Middleton, D. and Edwards, D. (eds) (1990a) *Collective Remembering*. London: Sage.

Middleton, D. and Edwards, D. (1990b) "Conversational remembering: A social psychological approach". In D. Middleton and D. Edwards (eds), *Collective Remembering*. London: Sage.

Miles, M.R. (1989) *Carnal Knowing: Female nakedness and religious meaning in the Christian west*. New York: Vintage.

Miller, D.T., Taylor, B. and Buck, M.L. (1991) "Gender gaps: Who needs to be explained?" *Journal of Personality and Social Psychology*, 61, 5–12.

Miller, G.A. (1969) "Psychology as a means of promoting human welfare". *American Psychologist*, 24, 1063–75.

Miller, J.B. (1984) "The development of women's sense of self". *Work in progress*, No. 12. Wellesley, MA: Stone Center Working Papers Series.

Miller, J.B. (1987) *Toward a New Psychology of Women*. Boston, MA: Beacon Press.

Miller, J.G. (1984). "Culture and the development of everyday social explanation". *Journal of Personality and Social Psychology*, 46, 961–78.

Millett, K. (1972) *Sexual Politics*. London: Abacus.

Money, J. (1987) "Sin, sickness or status? Homosexual gender identity and psychoneuroendocrinology". *American Psychologist*, 42, 384–99.

Monk, R. (1990) *Ludwig Wittgenstein: The duty of genius*. New York: Free Press.

Morawski, J.G. and Steele, R.S. (1991). "The one or the other? Textual analysis of masculine power and feminist empowerment". *Theory and Psychology*, 1, 107–31.

Morris, C. (1972) *The Discovery of the Individual 1050–1200*. London: Camelot Press.

Morrison, T. (1992) *Playing in the Dark: Whiteness and the literary imagination.* Cambridge, MA: Harvard University Press.

Morson, G.S. and Emerson, C. (1990) *Mikhail Bakhtin: Creation of a prosaics.* Stanford, CA: Stanford University Press.

Moscovici, S. (1976) *La Psychanalyse, son image et son public.* Paris: Presses Universitaires de France.

Moscovici, S. (1981) "On social representations". In J. Forgas (ed.), *Social Cognition: Perspectives on everyday understanding.* London: Academic Press.

Moscovici, S. (1984) "The phenomenon of social representations". In R. Farr and S. Moscovici (eds), *Social Representations.* Cambridge: Cambridge University Press.

Moscovici, S. (1985) "Social influence and conformity". In G. Lindzey and E. Aronson (eds), *Handbook of Social Psychology,* 3rd edn. New York: Random House.

Mulkay, M.J. (1979) *Science and the Sociology of Knowledge.* London: Allen & Unwin.

Noddings, N. (1984) *Caring: A feminine approach to ethics and moral education.* Berkeley: University of California Press.

O'Brien, M. (1980) *The Politics of Reproduction.* London: Routledge & Kegan Paul.

Ochs, E. (1988) *Culture and Language Development: Language acquisition and language socialization in a Samoan village.* Cambridge: Cambridge University Press.

Ochs, E. and Schieffelin, B.B. (1984) "Language acquisition and socialization". In R.A. Shweder and R.A. LeVine (eds), *Culture Theory: Essays on mind, self and emotion.* Cambridge: Cambridge University Press.

Ortiz, A. (1991) "Through Tewa eyes: Origins". *National Geographic,* 180, 6–13.

Osherson, D.N., Kosslyn, S.M. and Hollerback, J.M. (eds) (1990) *An Invitation to Cognitive Science. Vol. 2: Visual cognition and action.* Cambridge, MA: MIT Press.

Osherson, D.N. and Lasnik, H. (eds) (1990) *An Invitation to Cognitive Science. Vol. 1: Language.* Cambridge, MA: MIT Press.

Osherson, D.N. and Smith, E.E. (eds) (1990) *An Invitation to Cognitive Science. Vol. 3: Thinking.* Cambridge, MA: MIT Press.

Pagels, E. (1981) *The Gnostic Gospels.* New York: Vintage.

Perls, F., Hefferline, R.F. and Goodman, P. (1951) *Gestalt Therapy: Excitement and growth in the human personality.* New York: Dell.

Perret-Clermont, A.-N., Perret, J.-F. and Bell, N. (1991) "The social construction of meaning and cognitive activity in elementary school children". In L.B. Resnick, J.M. Levine and S.D. Teasley (eds), *Perspectives on Socially Shared Cognition.* Washington, DC: American Psychological Association.

Piaget, J. (1929) *The Child's Conception of the World.* London: Routledge & Kegan Paul.

Potter, J., Stringer, P. and Wetherell, M. (1984) *Social Texts and Contexts: Literature and psychology.* London: Routledge & Kegan Paul.

Potter, J. and Wetherell, M. (1987) *Discourse and Social Psychology: Beyond attitudes and behavior.* London: Sage.

Putnam, H. (1990) *Realism with a Human Face.* Cambridge, MA: Harvard University Press.

Rawls, J. (1971) *A Theory of Justice.* Cambridge, MA: Harvard University Press.

Resnick, L. B. (1991) "Shared cognition: Thinking as social practice". In L.B. Resnick, J.M. Levine and S.D. Teasley (eds), *Perspectives on Socially Shared Cognition*. Washington, DC: American Psychological Association.

Resnick, L.B., Levine, J.M. and Teasley, S.D. (eds) (1991) *Perspectives on Socially Shared Cognition*. Washington, DC: American Psychological Association.

Riley, D. (1988) *"Am I that Name?" Feminism and the category of "women" in history*. Minneapolis: University of Minnesota Press.

Rogoff, B. and Lave, J. (eds) (1984) *Everyday Cognition: Its development in social context*. Cambridge, MA: Harvard University Press.

Rorty, R. (1979) *Philosophy and the Mirror of Nature*. Princeton, NJ: Princeton University Press.

Rorty, R. (1989) *Contingency, Irony & Solidarity*. Cambridge: Cambridge University Press.

Rosaldo, R. (1989) *Culture and Truth: The remaking of social analysis*. Boston, MA: Beacon Press.

Ross, L. (1977) "The intuitive psychologist and his 'shortcomings': Distortions in the attribution process". In L. Berkowitz (ed.), *Advances in Experimental Social Psychology*, vol. 10. New York: Academic Press.

Rubin, J. (1962) "Bilingualism in Paraguay". *Anthropolitical Linguistics*, 4, 52–8.

Russell, J.A. (1991) "Culture and the categorization of emotions". *Psychological Review*, 110, 426–50.

Sahlins, M. (1976) *Culture and Practical Reason*. Chicago: University of Chicago Press.

Said, E. (1979) *Orientalism*. New York: Random House.

Sampson, E.E. (1977) "Psychology and the American ideal". *Journal of Personality and Social Psychology*, 35, 767–82.

Sampson, E.E. (1983) *Justice and the Critique of Pure Psychology*. New York: Plenum.

Sampson, E.E. (1985) "The decentralization of identity: Toward a revised concept of personal and social order". *American Psychologist*, 40, 1203–11.

Sampson, E.E. (1988) "The debate on individualism: Indigenous psychologies of the individual and their role in personal and societal functioning". *American Psychologist*, 43, 15–22.

Sampson, E.E. (1989) "The challenge of social change for psychology: Globalization and psychology's theory of the person". *American Psychologist*, 44, 914–21.

Sampson, E.E. (1991) "The democraticization of psychology". *Theory & Psychology*, 1, 275–98.

Sandel, M.J. (1982) *Liberalism and the Limits of Justice*. Cambridge: Cambridge University Press.

Sarbin, T.R. (1986) *Narrative Psychology: The Storied Nature of Human Conduct*. New York: Praeger.

Sartre, J.-P. (1946) *No Exit and Three Other Plays*. New York: Vintage.

Schank, R.C. and Abelson, R.P. (1977) *Scripts, Plans, Goals and Understanding*. Hillsdale, NJ: Erlbaum.

Schatzman, L. and Strauss, A. (1955) "Social class and modes of communication". *American Journal of Sociology*, 60, 329–38.

Schieffelin, B.B. (1990) *The Give and Take of Everyday Life: Language socialization of Kaluli children*. Cambridge: Cambridge University Press.

Schudson, M. (1990) "Ronald Reagan misremembered". In D. Middleton and D. Edwards (eds), *Collective Remembering*. London: Sage.

Schwartz, B. (1990) "The reconstruction of Abraham Lincoln". In D. Middleton and D. Edwards (eds), *Collective Remembering*. London: Sage.

Scott, J.W. (1988) *Gender and the Politics of History*. New York: Columbia University Press.

Sedgwick, E.K. (1985) *Between Men: English literature and male homosexual desire*. New York: Columbia University Press.

Sedgwick, E.K. (1990) *Epistemology of the Closet*. Berkeley: University of California Press.

Sherif, M. and Sherif, C.W. (1953) *Groups in Harmony and Tension*. New York: Harper.

Shotter, J. (1990) *Knowing of the Third Kind*. Utrecht, The Netherlands: University of Utrecht.

Shotter, J. (1991) "Rhetoric and the social construction of cognitivism". *Theory & Psychology*, 1, 495–513.

Shweder, R.A. (1984) "Anthropology's romantic rebellion against the enlightenment, or there's more to thinking than reason and evidence". In R.A. Shweder and R.A. LeVine (eds), *Culture Theory: Essays on mind, self and emotion*. Cambridge: Cambridge University Press.

Shweder, R.A. (1990) "Cultural psychology – What is it?" In J.W. Stigler, R.A. Shweder and G. Herdt (eds), *Cultural Psychology: Essays on comparative human development*. Cambridge: Cambridge University Press.

Shweder, R.A. and Bourne, E.J. (1984) "Does the concept of the person vary cross-culturally?" In R.A. Shweder and R.A. LeVine (eds), *Culture Theory: Essays on mind, self and emotion*. Cambridge: Cambridge University Press.

Shweder, R.A. and LeVine, R.A. (eds) (1984) *Culture Theory: Essays on mind, self and emotion*. Cambridge: Cambridge University Press.

Siegal, M. (1991) "A clash of conversational worlds: Interpreting cognitive development". In L.B. Resnick, J.M. Levine and S.D. Teasley (eds), *Perspectives on Socially Shared Cognition*. Washington, DC: American Psychological Association.

Skinner, B.F. (1989) "The origins of cognitive thought". *American Psychologist*, 44, 13–18.

Solomon, R.C. (1984) "Getting angry: The Jamesian theory of emotion in anthropology". In R.A. Shweder and R.A. LeVine (eds), *Culture Theory: Essays on mind, self and emotion*. Cambridge: Cambridge University Press.

Stam, H. (1987) "The psychology of control: A textual critique". In H.J. Stam, T.B. Rogers and K.J. Gergen (eds), *The Analysis of Psychological Theory: Metapsychological perspectives*. New York: Hemisphere.

Stigler, J.W., Shweder, R.A. and Herdt, G. (eds) (1990) *Cultural Psychology: Essays on comparative human development*. Cambridge: Cambridge University Press.

Sullivan, H.S. (1953) *The Interpersonal Theory of Psychiatry*. New York: W.W. Norton.

Tajfel, H. (1978) *Differentiation between Social Groups: Studies in the social psychology of intergroup relations*. London: Academic Press.

Tajfel, H. (1982) "Social psychology of intergroup relations". *Annual Review of Psychology*, 33, 1–39.

Taylor, S.E. (1989) *Positive Illusions*. New York: Basic Books.

Todorov, T. (1984) *Mikhail Bakhtin: The dialogical principle*. Minneapolis: University of Minnesota Press.

Triandis, H.C., Bontempo, R. and Villareal, M.J. (1988) "Individualism and collectivism: Cross-cultural perspectives on self–ingroup relationships". *Journal of Personality and Social Psychology*, 54, 323–38.

Turkle, S. (1978) *Psychoanalytic Politics: Freud's French revolution*. Cambridge, MA: MIT Press.

Turner, J.C. and Giles, H. (eds) (1981) *Intergroup Behavior*. Oxford: Basil Blackwell.

Tversky, A. and Kahneman, D. (1974) "Judgment under uncertainty: Heuristics and biases". *Science*, 185, 1124–31.

Van Gelder, L. (1989) "It's not nice to mess with mother nature: An introduction to ecofeminism 101, the most exciting new 'ism' in eons". *Ms.*, January/February 1989, 60–3.

Voloshinov, V.N. (1927/1987) *Freudianism: A critical sketch*. Bloomington: Indiana University Press.

Voloshinov, V.N. (1929/1986) *Marxism and the Philosophy of Language*. Cambridge, MA: Harvard University Press.

Vygotsky, L.S. (1978) *Mind in Society: The development of higher psychological processes*. Cambridge, MA: Harvard University Press.

Waterman, A.S. (1981) "Individualism and interdependence". *American Psychologist*, 36, 762–73.

Watson, J.B. (1913) "Psychology as a Behaviorist views it". *Psychological Review*, 20, 158–77.

Watts, S. (1992) "Academe's leftists are something of a fraud". *The Chronicle of Higher Education*, 29 April 1992, p. A40.

Weiss, J., Sampson, H. and the Mount Zion Psychotherapy Research Group (1986) *The Psychoanalytic Process: Theory, clinical observations and empirical research*. New York: Guilford Press.

Wertsch, J.V. (1991) *Voices of the Mind: A sociocultural approach to mediated action*. Cambridge, MA: Harvard University Press.

Westen, D. (1991) "Social cognition and object relations". *Psychological Bulletin*, 109, 429–55.

Wetherell, M. and Potter, J. (1989) "Narrative characters and accounting for violence". In J. Shotter and K.J. Gergen (eds), *Texts of Identity*. London: Sage.

Wheeler, L., Reis, H.T. and Bond, M.H. (1989) "Collectivism–individualism in everyday social life: The Middle Kingdom and the melting pot". *Journal of Personality and Social Psychology*, 57, 79–86.

White, G.M. and Kirkpatrick, J. (eds) (1985) *Person, Self and Experience: Exploring Pacific ethnopsychologies*. Berkeley: University of California Press.

Whitehead, A.N. (1938) *Modes of Thought*. New York: Free Press.

Whitford, M. (ed.) (1991) *The Irigaray Reader*. Oxford: Basil Blackwell.

Winkler, K.J. (1991) "Scholars examine issues of rights in America". *The Chronicle of Higher Education*, 20 November 1991, pp. A9, A13.

Wittgenstein, L. (1953) *Philosophical Investigations*. Oxford: Basil Blackwell.
Wittgenstein, L. (1958) *The Blue and Brown Books*. New York: Harper & Row.
Woolf, V. (1929/1989) *A Room of One's Own*. San Diego, CA: Harvest/HBJ.
Woolf, V. (1938) *Three Guineas*. San Diego, CA: Harvest/HBJ.
Woolgar, S. (ed.) (1988) *Knowledge and Reflexivity: New frontiers in the sociology of knowledge*. London: Sage.
Young, I.M. (1990) *Justice and the Politics of Difference*. Princeton, NJ: Princeton University Press.

Index

Lightning Source UK Ltd.
Milton Keynes UK
01 June 2010

154946UK00002B/309/P